THE WELL-TEMPERED CELLO

THE WELL-TEMPERED CELLO

LIFE WITH BACH'S CELLO SUITES

MIRANDA WILSON

ISBN: 978-1-62992-046-7

Published by Fairhaven Press.

Front and back cover design by Mark Reid.

Printed in the US, UK, EU and Australia.

Fairhaven Press is an independent publishing company. We thank you for supporting us by purchasing or considering our titles.

www.fairhavenpress.com

For Sean Butterfield

ACKNOWLEDGMENTS

This book could not have been written without the help of people too numerous to mention individually. Top billing goes to the College of Letters, Arts, and Social Sciences and the Office of Research and Economic Development at the University of Idaho, who jointly funded the purchase of my five-string cello. I am indebted to the University of Idaho administration for granting me a semester of sabbatical leave to research and write. The faculty and staff of the University of Idaho Library were endlessly patient with my constant requests for assistance, and managed – through what wizardry I can only imagine – to acquire all the materials I needed, even at the height of the COVID-19 pandemic. The faculty and students of the Lionel Hampton School of Music kept me inspired throughout this journey, especially Jason Johnston, Leonard Garrison, and my Idaho Bach Festival co-directors Christopher and Lynette Pfund.

Heartfelt thanks go to Mike Hollis of Fairhaven Press for believing in my work, and to Gillian Bibby, Brian Hodges, Michael Kyte, Gill Tennant, Lyn Warwick, and Roger Wilson for reading and commenting on drafts of the manuscript.

Lastly, I would like to thank Sean and Eliana for their love and encouragement. Thank you, thank you, thank you.

AUTHOR BIOGRAPHY

Miranda Wilson is an internationally performing cellist and author. She is Professor of Cello at the University of Idaho and Co-Artistic Director of the Idaho Bach Festival.

CONTENTS

PRAELUDIUM

Bach's Cello Suites come into my life at the end of a storm. For the past week, a vicious southerly wind from Antarctica has swept up both islands, bending the pohutukawa trees into cringing submission, ripping sheets of corrugated iron from the roofs, and howling through the narrow alleys between buildings. Tourists naïve enough to imagine they can use umbrellas here lose them immediately as the wind flips them inside out, then yanks them away altogether. Salt spray from the sea blasts the parked cars around the waterfront. Then this morning, as suddenly as it came, the southerly is gone. The harbor is opaque.

It's one of those Wellington days after a storm where mist rises to the tops of the forests on the hills, where the smell of damp earth and damp ferns makes you feel alert with possibility. My mother and I are in the car, teetering up my cello teacher's narrow, moss-covered driveway on our way to my weekly lesson. The cello lies diagonally across the backseat in its canvas bag, my music satchel stuffed between it and the door to hold it steady up hills and around corners.

My teacher, Judy Hyatt, is a cellist in the New Zealand Symphony Orchestra, and she lives in a great ghostly Victorian house in the oldest part of Khandallah. There are fourteen-foot corniced ceilings and dark book-lined corridors carpeted with Persian rugs. The brass handles on the heavy carved doors seem slightly too low. Behind a door in the hallway, a circular staircase leads up to a turret in the roof. How I long to live in a house with a turret! If I had a turret, I would sit there all day in a long green gown like a princess, writing poems and eating strawberries. This is the kind of house where any of the wardrobes might transport you to Narnia. A house where New Zealand's greatest writer, Katherine Mansfield, might appear in the drawing-room in a white lace dress, light an illicit cigarette, and utter something brilliant and scathing about colonial hypocrisy.

I am a skinny nine-year-old, all eyes and elbows and teeth. I have grown out of my bright blue corduroy pinafore, which hangs too-short over white tights and white sneakers fastened with pink velcro straps. Adults keep telling me that I'm going through a phase, using the kind of voice that implies they hope I'll soon grow out of it. Judy never talks to me that way. Dear, kind Judy, twinkling and jovial as Mrs. Tiggy-Winkle, treats me as though I'm much older than nine. She asks me questions and takes my opinions seriously.

I twist the old-style doorbell, and Judy is there in a trice to usher my mother and me into her music studio. The room is full of antique furniture, because Judy loves old things, and because I love her, so do I. A hundred-year-old upright piano lives against the far wall, gilt candle-holders on either side of its music-rack. We sit to play our cellos on heavy round-backed mahogany dining chairs. There's a carved wooden cabinet where Judy and her cellist husband John keep their scores, and a writing-desk with a lid you can flip up to reveal compartments for fountain-pens and blotters. Three or four cellos stand up in their cases like mummies in sarcophaguses. A slightly spotted mirror leans against the wall so you can check your posture and your bow-hold, but Judy has angled it so you can't see your head. She explained to me once that she always gets a shock when she looks in the mirror and sees a gray-haired woman instead of the seventeen-year-old she feels like inside. Though she is only in her late fifties at this time, to me she is ancient. I want to be exactly like her when I'm old.

"Today," Judy says in a reverential tone, "I think we might be ready to start on some Bach."

I already know who Bach is, because my mother is a pianist and my father an opera singer, and we have compact discs of Bach's music all over the living room. Unlike our neighbors, we own neither a video cassette recorder, nor a computer, nor a microwave oven, but we do have a compact disc player, and we're the first people in our street to have bought one. My parents' friends come to the house and gaze with awe and respect as we carefully place the shiny silver discs in the tray and push the open-close button. When the music starts, we watch their faces, enjoying the expressions of wonder when the music starts. "Oh! The *sound!*"

So far, my cello lessons have included scales, arpeggios, and technical etudes by Justus Johann Friedrich Dotzauer, Alfredo Piatti, and Friedrich

Grützmacher, since Judy is conscientious about fundamentals. For repertoire, we've worked on Romantic salon pieces like the *Tarantella* by William Henry Squire, the study concertos of Georg Goltermann, and *La Cinquantaine* by Gabriel Marie. Judy tells me that Katherine Mansfield herself might have played these classics of the literature back when she was little bookish Kass Beauchamp. "She was as obsessed with the cello as she was with writing stories," says Judy. Long ago in some long-forgotten biopic, Judy was Katherine Mansfield's cello-playing body double.

We haven't yet done anything by the great composers, but I know that great composers exist because my parents take me to concerts and operas. I can already tell the difference between Mozart and Haydn, and what I think of as the Shoe composers, Shoe-mann and Shoe-bert. My dad sings in Bach oratorios several times a year, and my mum plays Bach's Partita in B-flat over and over on her piano. Sometimes they do recitals together, mostly of songs in German by one of the Shoes.

"We'll start with Bach's First Cello Suite, the one in G major," says Judy, "but let's not start at the very beginning with the Prelude, because it's a bit hard, dear. We'll start in the middle with the two Menuets, and after that the Gigue. And when you've got those under your fingers, we'll have a go at the Courante. The Prelude, Allemande, and Sarabande are a bit harder, but we'll get to them eventually." Her eighteenth-century Italian cello – a cello as old as Bach! – is already out of its case, and she plucks the strings to check their tuning as I go through the familiar rituals of taking out my bow, applying rosin, and finally lifting the canvas bag from my own half-size cello. Sitting by the piano, mother busies herself with a lined school notebook, writing down everything Judy says.

I'm not yet very adept at sight-reading, so Judy demonstrates a few bars of Menuet I on her own cello. Suddenly I understand that this is no pedagogical work, no pretty salon piece for dutiful children. The opening arpeggio sings and dances out of Judy's cello, and something awakens in my nine-year-old mind that changes music for me forever.

My squeaky little cello is no match for Judy's glorious tone, but over the course of the hour I manage to stumble through the Menuets, stopping many times to write fingerings and bowings in the score. Judy explains that the Menuets are to be played *da capo*, that once you've played them both you have to repeat Menuet I. "There's a happy one and a sad one," she tells me. "The first one's in G major, and the second in G minor. See how the melodic line goes up at the beginning of Menuet I and down at the beginning of Menuet II? There's a composer who likes to make contrasts! It's as if Menuet II is a thundercloud, and the return of Menuet I is like the sun coming out. Do you see?"

Yes, I see. And I want to know everything I can find out about this Bach, a composer who could have dreamed up such a piece for the cello alone, with no need for cute titles or plinking piano chords. A composer who wrote music for grown-ups.

Outside, the sun hasn't yet come out, but looks as if it might be thinking about it. As my mother steers the car down the steep slopes and sharp corners of the Ngaio Gorge Road, I say "Mummy?"

"Yes, darling?"

"I think my three favorite things in the world might be eating, sleeping, and playing the cello."

My mother looks very, very pleased.

*

Twenty-one years later, I'm sitting stunned on the dingy tiled floor of my office at the University of Idaho, music scores all around me, my right hand clapped to my temple. I'm actually seeing stars, like in the cartoons. Outside my window, the leafy neo-Gothic campus is abuzz with the chatter of students moving into dormitories, signing up for clubs, and planning parties. Just a few feet from them, I'm crouched in tears after a hardback volume of Beethoven's complete string quartets has toppled from the highest level of my bookshelf, hitting me on the head and causing me to fall over. I know I should have borrowed a stepladder from the custodian before starting to unpack my scores and books, but because I'm tall it never occurs to me that I might need help reaching high shelves.

No one outside the window has seen the accident, but I'm not just crying because of the blows to my head and my pride. It's because I think I might be beginning, albeit a little on the early side, some kind of midlife crisis. In hitting my head, the Beethoven score has also hit my mind with an inescapable thought that I might go to my grave without playing everything within its covers.

Dante Alighieri was only in his forties when he wrote "In the middle of life's journey, I found myself again in a dark wood, because the straightforward pathway was lost." He knew, having lived half of his biblically allotted three score years and ten, that he might have seen more yesterdays than tomorrows. It seems absurd to think your time's running out when you're only thirty, but isn't everyone's? I suddenly realize that because of spending the first half of my twenties in the single-minded pursuit of advanced degrees and the second half being in a string quartet, I've been locked in a practice room for the entire decade that people usually spend finding themselves. I have experienced none of the rites of passage that people tolerate in twentysomethings, but frown upon in those old enough to know better: I have never hitchhiked around Europe, worked on an organic farm, sung karaoke, lived in a commune, backpacked in Thailand, dyed my hair an eccentric color, or chained myself to a tree in the name of environmental activism. Thanks to the life-eating profession of classical music, it's now too late to try on the lives of the people I might have become and didn't. It's time to face up to the life I have now as a cello-playing adult.

Except for the problem that I haven't even done cello properly, because I haven't played all the Beethoven quartets and now I probably never will.

Several other volumes besides the Beethoven quartets have fallen too, including the orchestral scores of the cello concertos by Dvořák, Schumann, and Shostakovich. Despite years of practicing these pieces, I've never performed them with a major symphony, or any symphony at all, and now I'm never likely to. Wait, hadn't I thought I would grow up to be the next Jacqueline du Pré? When I was a cello-mad teenager, I assumed my hours of practice would automatically confer greatness and fame upon me. I thought that some mysterious magnetic process would attract agents, managers, conductors, and recording contracts with very little extra effort from me, since talent ought to be enough, oughtn't it?

Now I'm furious. Not one of my teachers ever disabused me of these absurd imaginary notions. Why did they encourage me, egg me on, tell me to aim high and dream big and go for it? Why did no one tell me how idiotically, delusionally wrong I was? Why didn't anyone say "Look, this profession is ridiculous and almost no one succeeds in it. Don't imagine you're going to be Yo Yo Ma. Even Yo Yo Ma doesn't get to be Yo Yo Ma. If you persist in this, you will work yourself half to death, you'll never make much money, you won't get to choose where you live, and most of the time you won't even get to choose the music you play. Why not qualify as something sensible like a doctor or lawyer so that you can have a good income, live where you want, and buy lots of lovely things?" Whether I'd have listened is anyone's guess, but it would have been nice if someone had so much as mentioned some of the realities of life as a classical musician.

For a while, it felt as if the string quartet was succeeding. We had concerts, tours, outreach, and a respectable number of competition prizes. We had a lot of financial support from the New Zealand government, and huge professional boosts from our mentors in the United States. We put in what felt like superhuman effort, rehearsing ten hours a day seven days a week, with no days off. We performed all over the world, competed in contests, taught masterclasses, recorded discs, cold-called potential sponsors, wrote press releases, applied for grants. For several years, I was proud to devote my life to performing in a medium that seemed to bring out the best in composers. We worked our way through Haydn, Mozart, Beethoven, Schubert, Mendelssohn, Schumann, Brahms, Bartók, and Shostakovich, and I loved it all, especially Beethoven. I had the career I had always dreamed of.

What had made it so impossible to continue down this path? Mostly, the realization that I could not be in a quartet and simultaneously have a happy life. For years I had made sacrifice after sacrifice and pretended not to have any normal human needs, but once I started to think about having a happy life, I couldn't stop. I longed to have a baby, and a specialist had told me that I would have trouble both getting and staying pregnant. How could I manage a high-risk pregnancy when I spent seven months of the year in planes and hotel rooms in countries where I had no health insurance, knew no doctors, and often didn't speak the language? Even if such an ordeal were manageable, who would look after the baby once it was born? It clearly couldn't be me, since the quartet rehearsed ten hours a day, seven days a week. Would my fiancé, Sean, give up his career to be a stay-at-home dad? Was it fair to ask him to do this when I would never in a million years consider giving up my own career? Most of all, who would pay for a husband and baby when I barely made enough money to cover my own living expenses?

It took me three months to find the words to tell the quartet I was leaving. I had no teaching job to go to, but I planned to apply for anything and everything. Most universities had hiring freezes at that point in the Great Recession, so when I got into the finals for two cello professorships it seemed like a sign. With love, and not without pain, I finally told my colleagues I was finished. A week later, they decided they would not continue without me.

String quartet players often compare the group dynamic to a marriage with none of the advantages and all of the disadvantages. In the weeks and months after disbanding, I mourned the quartet more than I'd ever mourned a failed romance. I'm still mourning it now, sitting on this dusty floor at my new university in northern Idaho, where I've come in pursuit of a happy life.

So when am I going to start being happy? I've worked hard to get my job, but I know part of it is pure luck. I've heard a report from a former classmate in London that our old professor has been using my example as a stick to beat his students. "Mirandochka has made it," he tells them in his thick Russian accent. "What are *you* doing to build your career?" He never tells me directly that he thinks I've made it, but knowing he's said it warms my heart a little.

I'm lucky in other ways, too. I'm in love and newly married, and this very morning Sean and I signed mortgage documents on a little cottage set picturesquely among pine trees. We've adopted a dog. There's a stack of books about getting pregnant on our kitchen table. Compared with so many of my friends who have doctorates and no jobs, I've hit the jackpot. I should be floating in bliss, and yet here I am, weeping over a book full of unplayed notes.

Weeping because gradually, subtly, one by one, doors have started to close on me.

On the eve of my thirtieth birthday, I performed in the final of an international chamber music competition. It was good timing, because had it been scheduled one day later I'd have been too old to compete. There are a few competitions open to older applicants, but not many.

Then there's the cello problem. When we still had the quartet, a generous patron loaned me an instrument whose golden tone and quick response made playing it a heavenly experience. Its value was in the region of six figures. The patron took it back after the quartet disbanded, because he wanted to loan his instruments to young quartet players and I no longer qualify as either. The only cello I actually own is a student instrument that can't handle the level of sound I want to pull out of it. Just when I've gotten used to reveling in what a great cello can do, I now have to plan my playing around what this old clunker can't. If I forget that I can't bow the strings too heavily, they reward me with ugly, scratching noises.

When I call instrument banks and sponsors to ask about borrowing a cello, they demur. "My instrument collection is for young up-and-comers," one explains. "You have a job now." It's not worth protesting that journalists had described our quartet as young up-and-comers mere months ago. The message is clear: I am too old and too employed for any benefactor to want to buy me a cello. No one seems to care that my professorial salary, even though it's more money than I've ever dreamed of making, won't stretch to a good cello. Between us, Sean and I have thousands of dollars of credit card debt, and even if we didn't, a bank manager would be a fool to loan me the kind of money I'd need.

I sniff and wipe my face disgustingly on the sleeve of my t-shirt. That's when I notice the last of the fallen scores. It's the book of facsimiles of the four eighteenth-century manuscript copies of Bach's Six Cello Suites.

A voice in my head, my own voice, says "You've still got Bach."

It's been years since I played Bach's Cello Suites. I learned the first two in childhood and adolescence, the Third and Fourth as an undergraduate, and the Fifth for a competition. Aside from some practice-room noodling, I've never played the Sixth. Actually, it's been years since I played anything at all by Bach, because for a long time I only had time for the string quartet repertoire and Bach's lifetime predates the genre.

Bach's lifetime. It's funny, I think to myself, the way I've always pictured Bach as a satisfied old man in the wig with the lace ruff and shiny buttons. The famous oil painting by Elias Gottlob Haussmann dates from 1746, near the end of Bach's life. By that time he was an establishment figure as the learned Cantor of Leipzig. It occurs to me now that half a lifetime had passed between 1720, the probable year he composed the Cello Suites, and the year he sat for his portrait. Cello-Bach, the younger, thinner, pre-wig version, was in the middle of his own life's journey when he wrote the Suites in the tiny hamlet of Cöthen in eastern Germany. Cow-Cöthen, they called it. While his job as court Capellmeister was pleasant, it compelled him to live in the middle of nowhere. And there was no use there for two of his most luminous gifts, playing the organ and composing Lutheran sacred music. The Cöthen court didn't need Bach's elaborate, near-operatic church cantatas for their Calvinist services, so his job was to provide secular entertainment. This wasn't necessarily bad, because the thing about Bach was that he was a great virtuoso at more or less everything. While he was there, he composed not just the Cello Suites, but many other top instrumental works. Cow-Cöthen wasn't perfect, but it was still a pretty good gig.

Bach lived in Cow-Cöthen, and I live in Mos-Cow, Idaho. I've already noticed that when the wind is blowing from the west, I can both hear and smell the cows in the Agriculture Department on the other side of campus. "No cows in Moscow!" the locals gleefully correct visitors who don't know that it's pronounced Moss-Co. And yet, alongside the lentils and soybeans that grow on the strange undulating hills of the Palouse, there are lots and lots of cows. This is the first place I've lived that wasn't a city.

For the first time in my life, I start feeling a kinship with Cello-Bach. We're of a similar age, both living in isolated small towns because of our profession. Neither of us is getting to do the things we're best at. I'm even conceited enough to imagine that if we lived in the same time and place, we would be friends. We would have coffee. I love coffee, and Bach must have too, since he once wrote an entire cantata about it.

The voice in my head is gathering speed. "You could do a Bach project. You could do a marathon concert of Bach's Six Cello Suites and have it live-streamed on the internet."

No, I can't do this. The Sixth Cello Suite is a real monster, practically impossible unless you have a five-string cello, and I barely have a regular four-string one. I'd make a fool of myself trying.

"No, you wouldn't," the voice persists. "You could make a CD too. You need a big creative goal for your thirties. The thirties are supposed to be about creativity, you know."

"Nonsense," I tell the voice, "I'm not going to make a CD. Who wants yet another recording of one of the best-known pieces, most-recorded pieces in the repertoire? Who cares about anything I might do alone, away from the quartet?"

The voice acts as if it hasn't heard this. "Let's set a time limit," it says. "You have to do it by the time you're thirty-five."

No, that's ridiculous. Thirty-five will be the year I'm up for tenure, and by then I need to have published a book and loads of articles. Plus, I want to have a baby, and I have no idea how much work I'll be able to accomplish when I'm exhausted and sleep-deprived.

"All right then, forty. That'll give you time to write some books and make some babies. And hopefully to get yourself a new cello. And another one with five strings. Aim high! Dream big!"

Shut up, voice.

The problem with compelling ideas is that once you've had them, you can't get rid of them. The idea of a Bach marathon stirs up my restlessness, my fear of professional irrelevance, and, if I am to be strictly truthful, my love of showing off. I resolve right away that I'm going to do it. I will relearn the five Suites I already know, master the Sixth, and perform them individually on other recital programs in the next few years so that I'm comfortable with them all. Each Suite advances in difficulty, and while the first three have their tricky moments, the last three are extremely challenging. To say I'm scared is an understatement.

And yet I feel a huge *yes* welling up inside me. I scramble to my feet with the Bach facsimiles, the dropped quartet scores forgotten on the floor. I take out my cello, prop the score open at the first page of the First Cello Suite in the hand of Anna Magdalena Bach, and play and play and play.

Part One

IN THE PRINCE'S BALLROOM

Suite No. 1 in G Major, BWV 1007

I. PRELUDE

The bow moves across the strings of the cello in an arc as the melody travels upwards from G to D towards B. A rippling motion takes the line back down again, and the pattern is set in motion. It comes back again and again, changing a note here and there as the harmony makes its seamless progress from chord to chord and key to key. The effect is meditative, even mesmerizing.

Bach wrote the Prelude of the First Cello Suite using a technique called *ondulé,* "undulating." It's a beautiful word, and perfectly describes the wave-like motions of the cellist's right arm. The undulation is necessary for us to have music that is harmonically complete. It's not possible to play more than two simultaneous pitches on the cello, so chordal patterns appear in arpeggiated form. This is crucial to Bach's musical language throughout the Six Cello Suites, and shows his intimate, idiomatic understanding of what the cello and cellists are capable of.

Nothing like Bach's Six Cello Suites had ever been written before, or at least not for the cello. In 1720, it was a relatively new instrument, and mostly used for bassline accompaniments in ensemble music, not for solos. Where on earth did Bach get the idea to write six long, difficult pieces for unaccompanied cello? Was he attempting to bring the cello onto an equal footing with the viola da gamba, a much older instrument of roughly the same size and range? Or, since the Cello Suites were to be a companion volume for the Six Sonatas and Partitas for solo violin, had he decided a cello was just a big violin? We don't know the answers to these questions, because Bach was not in the habit of explaining himself. He kept no diary, wrote no method-book, and didn't even write that many letters. "Bach does not sing about himself," writes the great cellist and Bach interpreter Anner Bylsma. "His music speaks about mankind, about fate."[1]

The Cello Suites are thought to date from the period of Bach's employment in the small town of Cöthen, Germany, where he was court Capellmeister to the learned and cultivated Prince Leopold of Anhalt-Cöthen. Between 1717 and 1723, Bach's prolific output included the six Brandenburg Concertos, the orchestral suites, the solo violin and cello music, and the first book of *The Well-Tempered Clavier*, a collection of Preludes and Fugues for keyboard in all 24 major and minor keys.

The latter provides a clue to Bach's motivation in writing six long and difficult pieces for solo cello. On the front page of his manuscript of *The Well-Tempered Clavier*, he wrote the following inscription: "For the use and profit of the musical youth desirous of learning, as well as for the pastime of those already skilled in this study."[2] Cellists are wise to approach Bach's Six Cello Suites with this attitude. The Suites might not be a method book in the traditional sense, but they do increase exponentially in difficulty as we progress from one to the next. If the first three Cello Suites are in relatively cello-friendly keys, the Fourth Cello Suite requires us to play in E-flat, which for tuning reasons is far more complicated. In the Fifth Cello Suite, Bach demands that we tune the cello's A-string down to a G, throwing our fingering patterns and the meaning of the printed pitch into disarray. In the Sixth Cello Suite, Bach asks us to pick up a different instrument altogether, a five-string cello. Most cellists have never even seen a five-string cello, much less owned one, so if we want to play the Sixth Cello Suite we have to cultivate a level of technique that transcends its immense difficulty. It's a world away from where we started in the First Cello Suite. In this sense, just like *The Well-Tempered Clavier* for pianists and harpsichordists, Bach's Six Cello Suites represent the cellist's *Gradus ad Parnassum*, a journey to the summit of cello technique.

Many listeners notice that the Prelude of the First Cello Suite sounds a lot like the Prelude in C major from Book One of *The Well-Tempered Clavier*. It's an astute observation, since both pieces are composed of arpeggiated chord progressions. The musical term for this brand of back-and-forth pattern is *bariolage*, another wonderful French word. With the literal meaning of "an assemblage of colors," it hints at rainbows and kaleidoscopes of musical shading. Bach's patterns repeat themselves hypnotically, changing a note here and there as the harmonies merge and morph into different keys and back again, taking us through a vast sound-world of color and emotion. Both Preludes feature a single melodic line, and both nevertheless give an impression of multiple harmonic voices in their texture.

Playing Bach's Six Cello Suites is a cellist's lifelong project, a measure of our progress in cello playing and in life. My first experience of the Prelude of the First Cello Suite was that I simply couldn't play it. Teachers often assign the First Cello Suite to children because it's the "easiest." The scare quotes are here because it isn't easy at all. You need great control of the bow to play the rising and falling eighth-note patterns of the Prelude evenly, and aged nine I didn't have it. Aged thirty, the techniques involved are no big deal, but through some strange sense of muscle memory I start tensing and overworking my arm the way I did as a child. Twenty-one years have passed, during which time every cell in my body has replaced itself, but I still have to fight the temptation to work too hard. One of my teachers liked to say that "Good technique is the easiest way," and it's true. It's just that relaxed, efficient cello technique is not necessarily intuitive or self-explanatory. It took me many years to figure out how to play the cello "naturally."

It didn't help that I first learned the First Cello Suite from old-fashioned, highly edited scores full of bowing and fingering suggestions thought to be "good for learners." Until I went to university, I mostly used Janos Starker's edition, and for a time it was useful. I realized as an undergraduate, however, that it contained many pitches and markings that differed greatly from those in scholarly editions. My first resolution on my journey back through the Bach Cello Suites is to leave the dozens of editions on the shelf where they belong, and go straight to the early source material.

This is where things get problematic, because Bach's autograph manuscript is lost and unlikely to turn up. The closest we have to primary source material are five eighteenth-century manuscript copies known to cellists as Sources A, B, C, D, and H. Most cellists, and most editions, rely on Source A, the copy Bach's second wife Anna Magdalena made some time between 1727 and 1731.[3] Anna Magdalena copied hundreds of her husband's compositions, but though her penmanship is ornate and beautiful, she worked distractedly and in a hurry. There was plenty to distract her, including no fewer than thirteen pregnancies and a household full of children no doubt demanding attention and snacks.

Editors often use Source B, the copy by Johann Peter Kellner, for clarification of the many ambiguities in Anna Magdalena Bach's copy. Dating from around 1726, it's the earliest of the four copies, and according to some scholars the most accurate.[4] Kellner, however, was far from mistake-free, and is also missing a large chunk of the Fifth Cello Suite.

Then there are Sources C and D, both of which date from later in the eighteenth century. Source C is the work of one Johann Nikolaus Schober, who may have been an acquaintance of Bach's son Carl Philipp Emanuel, and a second, anonymous copyist. Source D is by a single anonymous copyist. Last of all is Source H, the only manuscript we have in Bach's handwriting. It contains only one of the Cello Suites, the Fifth, in a revised version for the lute. It's in a different key and has some added bass notes that work well on the lute, but otherwise is not drastically different.

Several editors have attempted to cobble together versions of Bach's Cello Suites using the five manuscript sources, but the task isn't easy. Sources A, B, C, and D are markedly different from one another in terms of notes, articulations, ornaments, and bowing patterns. To add to the confusion, there may have been more than one original manuscript or copy. Since Sources C and D are so different from Sources A and B, we can conclude that Bach might have made revisions to his manuscript in the interim, or created a revised copy.

Amazingly – to modern Bach fans, anyway – the Six Cello Suites weren't published until 1824, more than a century after Bach composed them. The editor, thought to be the French cellist Louis Norblin, claimed in the introduction to have based his work on a "precious manuscript."[5] Which one was it? His edition has certain similarities to Sources C and D, but may in fact be based on another copy that is now lost.

Working my way through the early sources feels rather like a fairy-tale hero hacking through forests of thorns. Where and what is the truth? Is there any such thing as the truth, anyway? What is the meaning of a musical composition? What is the meaning of a manuscript? What is meaning? Getting out of my comfort zone and away from printed editions is both terrifying and liberating, like getting into a time machine to the eighteenth century. My first teacher, Judy Hyatt, had a facsimile of the Anna Magdalena Bach manuscript on the writing-desk in her studio. She'd had to order it from

Europe at immense expense, and it was a prized possession. Later, when I went to university and wanted to get a look at the Sources, I had to walk to the library and face down a terrifying librarian who wouldn't even let me take the volume out of the building. These days, thanks to technology, we can download all the Sources in seconds and for free at the International Music Scores Library Project.

Bach's Six Cello Suites are so embedded in my memory from years of studying and performing them that I find I can read the manuscripts without too much trouble, even if parts of the Sixth Cello Suite are notated in the alto clef. This said, their discrepancies and ambiguities raise more questions than answers. I find that I need practical and contextual help, and the first place I look for it is Anner Bylsma's *Bach, the Fencing Master*, his idiosyncratic and intimate reading of Anna Magdalena Bach's manuscript. The second place is the documentary film *392*, a companion to Pieter Wispelwey's 2012 audio recording of Bach's Cello Suites. Wispelwey's attendants on his own journey through Bach are the distinguished Bach scholars John Butt and Laurence Dreyfus, who follow him around telling him interesting facts about Bach and saying flattering things about his cello playing. I watch the film again and again, thinking "This is *exactly* what I need."

Unlike Wispelwey, I don't have two marvelous instruments to play on, or two genial Oxbridge musicologists to help me with my project. The thought of having to do my own research and chase down my own cellos is daunting, to say the least. What happens over the coming years involves all manner of unforeseen distractions, diversions, and rabbit-holes as I try to get to know Bach's Cello Suites on their own terms.

II. ALLEMANDE

The small German town of Cöthen, where Bach wrote the Six Cello Suites, makes for an agreeable day-trip destination. Though the spelling has changed to Köthen, much of the town is unchanged since the lifetime of its most famous resident. Bach-loving tourists can admire his statue in the Bachplatz on Schulstrasse, then take a leisurely stroll down to the Schloss, Prince Leopold's ancestral seat and Bach's workplace. There you'll find the Historical Museum and Bach Memorial. Nearby, on the other side of the castle grounds, is the Naumann Museum, which houses the extensive bird and egg collections of Johann Naumann, founder of modern ornithology. Just about every corner has a *Bäckerei* selling dense, seed-covered rolls for breakfast and splendid cakes for afternoon tea. When you've had enough of Köthen's charms, you can head back to the *Bahnhof* and, after a few minutes of puzzlement over the ticket-machine while kind German strangers help you push buttons and feed in your fifteen euros, jump on the high-speed train and reach Leipzig in less than an hour.

Life in Köthen looks rather nice now, but Bach's Cöthen must have felt considerably more like the middle of nowhere. "Cow-Cöthen," as its detractors nicknamed it, was located in a very, very rural setting, and travel to Leipzig – or any other significant cultural center – took several days. No wonder culture-loving Prince Leopold insisted on maintaining such a good group of musicians. There wasn't much else to do in Cöthen if you weren't fond of cows.

Musicians, then and now, are a nomadic lot. We move to where the work is, even if the location isn't what we'd have chosen for ourselves. The microcosm of a royal court orchestra or university music department can be absorbing enough at times to make you forget your geographical isolation. Other times, you can feel very lonely indeed. It's unlikely Bach would otherwise have chosen to live in Cow-Cöthen, any more than I'd have chosen Mos-Cow. Like the other new young professors here, it's the first time I've lived anywhere rural, and I'm experiencing something approaching culture shock. Shops here close on Sundays, and there aren't any trains or interstate freeways to help you escape. The closest urban area, ninety minutes away, is the grandly decaying Victorian city of Spokane in Washington State. If I want to get my bow re-haired, I have to make the three-hour round trip along twisting country roads, wait a few days, then do it again to collect the finished bow. This effectively wastes two half-days of my work week. Everything from travel to shopping to gigs takes a lot more planning now than it used to when I lived in cities.

Bach arrived in Cöthen in 1717 with his first wife, Maria Barbara, and their small children. Family is a blessing at the best of times, but especially when work compels you to live in an isolated area. Senior colleagues here in Moscow, the lifers, comment that it's good that I've come to my job as a newly married woman. Single professors don't tend to last long here, because the loneliness gets to them. More exciting places, such as the state capital Boise or the cosmopolitan city of Seattle, are five-hour drives away in opposite directions. It's hard to settle in and make a life here.

I haven't quite figured out what to make of my new home, but at least it has the redeeming feature of being beautiful. When I first saw it in the spring, the strange rolling curves of the Palouse hills glowed highlighter-green with the shoots of new lentil crops. Now, in late summer, the fields are bleached gold and ready for harvest. I don't know it yet, but in the autumn the trees will blaze red and pink until the snows come at Thanksgiving. White pines and ponderosa pines tower over the town and line the sides of dark Moscow Mountain in the distance.

The lack of distraction can prove marvelously invigorating to creativity, and Bach may have found that his isolation made it easier to get work done. Inventing a whole new genre of cello music was a big project, and one that he planned in a highly structured manner. All six of the Cello Suites begin with a Prelude, a word whose Latin roots give it the literal meaning "before playing." As the elaborate introduction to the keys, colors, and characters of the Suite as a whole, a Bachian Prelude also belongs to a much older German tradition of *präludieren*, or "preluding." Most of the time, this meant improvising in virtuoso fashion on a church organ before the more serious liturgical music began. Bach's Six Cello Suites were not intended for church services, but I like to keep the image of the pious organist in my mind when I play the Preludes.

After this compelling introduction, Bach writes five dance movements with French titles. In order, these are the Allemande, Courante, Sarabande, a pair of *galanterie* movements such as Menuets, Bourrées, or Gavottes, and finally the Gigue. Just as the cello Preludes weren't meant for a church setting, these dances aren't for dancers. Rather, they're stylized instrumental pieces designed for a concert setting, not the ballroom. Because there are no dancers present, performers need to find a way to suggest the graces and gallantries of the courtly ballet. For me, this means learning more about the culture and context of Baroque dancing so that I can conjure up imaginary dancers around me on the concert stage.

It may seem curious that a German composer like Bach should give his pieces and movements French titles, but this wouldn't have seemed strange to the Francophile Prince Leopold. As city-states recovered their stability after the Thirty Years' War, statesmen like Bach's employer were eager to celebrate peacetime by patronizing the arts. It made sense to look westward for inspiration, since France was the epicenter of fashion and culture. Then as now, the French were just more sophisticated than anyone else. In modern times, the self-help section of any American bookstore contains a clutch of books affirming this. French women, the authors claim, are effortlessly thinner, healthier, and better-dressed than American women, even if they eat pastry for breakfast and take no exercise other than mincing to the Métro station in stiletto heels. French children, by the same token, never throw tantrums like their spoiled American counterparts, and are always to be found joyfully eating vegetables and cooperating with their parents. It's always been like this.

French culture was particularly rich and enviable in the seventeenth and early eighteenth centuries because of the influence of Louis XIV. The Sun King, as his acolytes flatteringly nicknamed him, presided for seventy-two years over a court that was as notable for its music and dancing as for its political power. The king himself was a magnificent dancer who devoted many hours each day to practicing under the supervision of his personal dancing master, Pierre Beauchamps. Thanks to Louis, skill at dancing became just as much a hallmark of an aristocrat's bearing as riding or fencing. In this artistically agreeable environment, the court's top dancers came up with the foot positions, arm movements, and dance steps that are still used in modern ballet. Dancing had to have music, of course, and one of Louis's top employees was an ambitious composer and dancer named Jean-Baptiste Lully. Lully's influence on Bach cannot be underestimated, especially when it comes to the dance movements of the Cello Suites.

Ambitious German noblemen like Bach's employer engaged French dancing masters whenever they could get them. At that time, a dancing master typically played the violin to accompany his pupils, for the eminently logical reason that you can dance and play the violin at the same time. For a while, the connection between violins and dancing masters gave the instruments of the violin family lower-class associations, since dancing masters were professionals and therefore inherently lower-class. Because of this, some aristocratic fanatics of the viola da gamba objected to the cello's superseding the viola da gamba in "serious" music. Cellos might be less portable than violins, but they still had a hint of the dancing studio about them.

It's significant that Bach chose to write the Suites for the cello and not for the viola da gamba. He wrote music for both instruments over the course of his career, but I can't help wondering if his choice of the cello here might emblematize social change. Luckily for the cellists of the next three hundred years, Prince Leopold was not among the cello-hating noblemen; though he played the viola da gamba well enough to perform alongside his Capellmeister, he employed both a cellist and a viola da gambist in the court ensemble. The cellist, Christian Bernhard Linigke, seems a likely candidate for first performer of Bach's Cello Suites, though several scholars have also suggested Bach's friend Christian Ferdinand Abel, the viola da gambist, for this honor. Like so much about Bach's Cello Suites, no one knows the details of the first performance or the dedication, if there was one.

As a court employee, Bach would have had the chance to observe aristocratic dancing, and therefore knew what the moves to the accompanying musical forms looked like. By his time, the Allemande had fallen from favor in the ballroom, and now was mostly a purely musical form. Somewhat confusingly, its title is a French word meaning "German," but that's because it was the sole German contribution to French courtly dance. In its beginnings, the danced Allemande was a processional, and some decades later ended up as more of a folk dance. In the sixteenth century, according to an expert of the French Baroque with the wonderful name of Betty Bang Mather, an Allemande was performed by a line of couples who danced down the length of a room, turned, and danced back again by means of an elegant, springing hop.[6] In an interesting detail, considering that polite society kept single men and women separated for the good of their characters, the Allemande was the one dance that permitted them to touch hands in a twining finger-hold. Anywhere outside the ballroom, this gesture might have been improper.

Learning the Allemande of the First Cello Suite aged nine, I lacked this frame of reference. I was chiefly concerned with negotiating the speed and distribution of my bowstrokes, and trying to stay in tune on my left-hand position shifts around the fingerboard of the cello. After Preludes, Allemandes are usually the longest and most difficult movements in Bach's Cello Suites, and this one is particularly so. Leafing through the old edition I was using then, I see exhortations like "Dance!" and "Sing!" in my teacher Judy's sloping handwriting. At the time, I could only imagine eighteenth-century dancers as stuffy old bewigged people in a picture-frame. They didn't quite seem human. Now, I'm trying to imagine them as living, breathing human beings for whom the ball and the ballet were the chief places women and men could interact.

Social dancing was, after all, one of the very few ways in which upper-class women got to spend relatively unsupervised time with men. Chaperones were watching, of course, but the noise and bustle of the dance floor meant that conversations between dancers were less audible to others. That Jane Austen's female characters are constantly badgering their neighbors to host a ball is not exclusively due to their love of dressing up, nor of bopping about athletically in a Scotch reel or a cotillion. They're looking for the dangerous thrill of contact with men, albeit in a socially sanctioned setting. Elizabeth Bennet's ballroom conversations with Mr. Darcy sound like a verbal-sword fight charged with an unmistakably intense attraction.

Lizzy starts: "'I have always seen a great similarity in the turn of our minds. We are each of an unsocial, taciturn disposition, unwilling to speak, unless we expect to say something that will amaze the whole room, and be handed down to posterity with all the éclat of a proverb.'

'This is no very striking resemblance of your own character, I am sure,' said he. 'How near it may be to *mine*, I cannot pretend to say. *You* think it a faithful portrait undoubtedly.'

'I must not decide on my own performance.'"

Women of Miss Elizabeth Bennet's station weren't allowed to do anything so unladylike as sword-fighting, so this was as close as she could get to throwing down the gauntlet.

Part of what makes ballroom interactions so edgy is the ever-present possibility – for women, anyway – of downfall. Jane Austen's novels contain plenty of fallen women, but they're secondary characters and mostly used for cautionary purposes. In Tolstoy's *Anna Karenina*, the fallen woman gets a whole book named after her. The ballroom scene is where the scandal begins, as we witness Anna and Vronsky falling disastrously in love while dancing a mazurka. We observe them through the dismayed gaze of poor heartbroken Kitty Shcherbatskaya, who knows she hasn't a chance against fascinating, black-clad Anna. In Simon Langton's 1985 film of the novel starring Jacqueline Bisset and Christopher Reeve, this scene ends with a lingering close-up of Anna's and Vronsky's hands – his white-gloved, hers bare – as their fingers intertwine in an electrifyingly suggestive manner.

I think of this now as I reimagine an interpretation of the Allemande of the First Cello Suite. If this is the only dance in which men and women get to hold hands, I want to make it count. Like all the dance movements in Bach's Cello Suites, the Allemande has an unequal binary structure consisting of two repeated sections. Harmonically, the purpose of the first section is to migrate from the home key of G major to the secondary key of D major. The second section has to get back to G again, and does so by means of sequentially repeating progressions of chords. Since it's always harder to go back home again than it is to leave in the first place, the second "halves" of the dance movements are almost always longer than the first. As Bach negotiates the drama of getting back to G, he gives a striking impression that more than one voice is present in the texture – even when the cellist is playing single notes. It's a linear way of creating harmonic conversation, perhaps even a substitute for the missing bassline. Playing my way through the second half of the Allemande, I realize that even if you take a cellist away from the bassline, you can't take the bassline away from a cellist. The title page in Anna Magdalena Bach's copy of the Cello Suites might read *6 Suites a Violoncello Solo senza Basso*, but that doesn't mean there's no bassline present, just that there isn't a second player providing accompaniment. The cellist has to be his or her own accompaniment. The higher versus lower pitches in the second half of the Allemande fall into patterns where the higher notes form a melodic voice, whereas the lower notes seem to punctuate it. As I rethink my conception of this movement, I decide to play the melodic pitches in *cantabile* style, but make the lower ones dance with a bowstroke approximating the springing steps of the ballroom.

Bach's Cello Suites might ask for just one player, but the cellist has to act more than one role in the musical drama. It's a dialogue, not a monologue, and we must be melodist and harmonist, singer and dancer alike.

III. COURANTE

The word Courante comes from the French *courir*, to run. This knowledge led my younger self to suppose that Courantes therefore went at break-neck speed. It's only now that I learn I've been wrong all along. *Courir* also means "to flow," and is related to *cour*, the court. A Courante, according to Meredith Little and Natalie Jenne, is the slowest of the triple-meter courtly dances.[7] Grand, grave, and noble, it was a favorite at the court of Louis XIV. Of Bach's six cello Courantes, only one – that of the Fifth Cello Suite – is a true French Courante. The others are technically Italian Correntes.[8]

Courante and Corrente might sound like cognates, but apart from triple meter, the two forms differ significantly. Unlike the Courante, a Corrente does go fast, and has associations with flashy solos for violin and keyboard instruments. This accounts for much of the swaggering charm in the Courante of the First Cello Suite.

This misnamed Corrente is a miracle of quickness and grace, and joyously fun to play. Its rapid phrases seem jumpy and fragmented, with multiple large leaps from high to low pitches and back. This is how Bach creates the suggestion of fully-harmonized music even within a single melodic line. He takes a little melodic snippet of a phrase, then interrupts it with two affirming bass notes. This sparks an image in my mind of a sycophantic courtier nodding and agreeing after his monarch's every utterance. "That's true!" "Quite right!" Playing through the Courante now, I make as much contrast as I can in my bow articulations to bring out the two characters – a graceful *legato* for the upper voice, and a lighter, brushier stroke for the punctuating utterances of the bass voice.

When I first learn the Courante, aged eleven, all this relentless jumping around is a nightmare. I'm preparing it for the dreaded ordeal that music teachers of the British Commonwealth inflict annually on children, the Associated Board of the Royal Schools of Music examination. I have to prepare the usual collection of scales and arpeggios, sight-reading, and ear training, plus three pieces to be performed from memory. After some discussion, Judy and my mother pick *Intermezzo* by Enrique Granados, *Elégie* by Gabriel Fauré, and the Courante of Bach's First Cello Suite from the repertoire list. The first two I can pull off with a bit of melodramatic bravado, but the Courante is much harder. I have to get my fingers around its incessant shifts of position at a brisk tempo, and simultaneously execute clean crossings between the strings with my bow. Sometimes I bump into the D-string when I'm supposed to be playing the G, and vice versa. Other times I play wildly out of tune when I move my hand up or down the fingerboard in search of notes. When she sees how frustrated I am, kind Judy tries to encourage me. "Try not to get backed up into the tip of the bow, dear," she advises. "Save bow on the down-bow strokes, and come back light and fast on the up-bows. Let the frog of the bow do the work of getting you to the other strings. Balance it, dear, as if it's a see-saw." But I can't seem to do any of this, and end up stuck at the tip of the bow where the sound is weakest and the arm furthest from the body. Judy looks perplexed. "Perhaps it was a *little* too soon to start this?"

The day of the exam comes. My mother has coaxed special permission from my school principal to take me out of class for an hour and a half. When I look down at my knees in the car, they're covered with gooseflesh. My mother believes that stage fright is a nonsensical social construct, so I never admit to her that I'm nervous. Still, as the car inches closer and closer through the Jervois Quay traffic towards Turnbull House, the exam venue, all I can think is *I don't want to I don't want to I don't want to*. My hands are freezing, but there's no use complaining about that either. In addition to her belief that anxiety is a learned behavior, my mother has no patience with people who moan about being cold. ("No, you can't have the heater on. Put on another cardigan.") And so it's with mute terror and an inability to get warm that I sit down in the exam room, my mother behind me at the grand piano. The scales go decently, but my bow gets shaky in the Fauré and I miss a big position shift in the Granados. By the time I get to the Courante I at least have some feeling back in my fingers, but on the whole I think the exam has gone irredeemably badly. The kindly British examiner attempts to engage me in conversation, and I'm too paralyzed with shyness to reply in answers of more than a syllable.

"Why wouldn't you talk to him?" my mother asks as we're driving back to my school. "He was so complimentary. He even said he hoped you'd continue with cello at university one day."

"He was only trying to make me feel better," I say sulkily.

The certificate arrives in the mail a few weeks later with the mark of Distinction. I stare at it in amazement before handing it to my parents, who make a huge fuss and take my brother and me out for ice creams to celebrate. In my head, a little voice says *maybe I can actually do this thing.*

*

Twenty years later, the Courante is one of the easier movements in the First Suite. Easier, at any rate, than the Prelude and Allemande. There are no multi-note chords and just one double-stop right at the end. I remember every bit of the struggle I had with it as a child, but now that I've gained some control over my arms and my equipment, I can enjoy its sociable charm. It gives me the most glorious feeling of showing off, like fluking strike after strike at the bowling alley. Towards the end, a repeating melodic idea changes just one note on every iteration, giving the impression of zooming up a scale toward the movement's conclusion. It reminds me of a peacock abruptly fanning out his iridescent plumage. *Look at me!*

*

An aristocrat of the Baroque era who wished to impress his peers had to know the steps of the Courante, and dance them in an outfit of which a peacock would approve. The choreography of the dance changed over several centuries, but the sense of exhibitionism didn't. A sixteenth-century cleric named Thoinot Arbeau was one of the first people to write about this in detail. In his book, *Orchésographie*, Arbeau presents the Courante as a bawdy farce. "In my youth," he observes with obvious nostalgia, "the Courante was a kind of game or mime. Three young men chose three girls. And each in turn led his young lady to the end of the room and left her there, returning to his companions. When the second and third had returned, the first clowned about pulling amorous faces, while making a show of pulling up his stockings and tucking in his shirt. Then he'd go back to his young lady, who, seeing him, would turn her back on him until he started to go back without her. Then she pretended to be in despair. The two others did the same. Finally, all three went back together to their young ladies and asked their forgiveness with their hands clasped. Then young ladies went into their arms and danced the said Courante, pell-mell."[9]

By the time of Louis XIV, the choreography of the Courante had gained some composure, having evolved over two centuries into the most elegant of the courtly dances. According to the great choreographer Pierre Rameau, King Louis insisted on practicing it every day with his dancing master Beauchamps. "By its grave and distinguished features," Rameau recalled in 1725, "it inspires an air of nobility... After the Branles, which were the dances that began the court balls, His Majesty then danced the Courante. Truly, he danced it better than anyone in his court, and he gave it an infinite grace."[10]

Rameau's bestselling self-help book *The Dancing Master* was extremely useful for a would-be courtier anxious to avoid ballroom blunders. Since it was nearly contemporaneous with Bach's time in Cöthen, we can assume that Rameau's advice was relevant to the French-influenced court of Prince Leopold. Superbly informative and astonishingly thorough, Rameau goes over every dance form in step-by-step instructions, and devotes no less than a third of his pages to the related art of etiquette. Between directives on the foot positions for the courtly ballet, Rameau discreetly explains the proper methods and occasions for taking off one's hat, holding it at one's side, and bowing with it in one's hand. Engraved illustrations depict a succession of unsmiling, bewigged men performing these procedures. Care had to be taken over how one put the hat back on when all the bowing and scraping was complete, since to do so incorrectly was a horrifying *faux pas*. "To wear the hat backwards gives one a foolish and idiotic appearance," Rameau warns darkly, "just as to wear it pressed down too much in front gives one a cunning, angry, or dreamy look; whereas, if the hat be worn as I have directed, you will appear well bred, modest, and agreeable."[11] Though his target audience is largely the ambitious gentlemen of the court, he doesn't neglect the ladies, expounding at some length upon the correct way to curtsey, flutter one's fan, walk in high heels, and hold voluminous skirts while dancing. Woe betide the lady who "squeezes" her skirts.

The antics of Rameau's rarified dancing studio may seem comical now, but they were closer to the social expectations of Bach's day than anything I've experienced. As I move forward in my re-exploration of the Cello Suites, I find myself yearning to know the things Bach knew, and not just the explicitly musical knowledge of how he tuned his instruments and organized the lines of his counterpoint. Manners and rituals that seem foreign or even absurd to our modern sensibilities were part of his world, and in my imagination his dance movements never stray far from the thrilling royal ballroom.

IV. SARABANDE

The earliest form of the danced Courante might have been ribald enough to raise a few artfully plucked Renaissance eyebrows, but next to the original Sarabande it was tame stuff. Leafing through a music encyclopedia in my early teens, I learn to my surprise and delight that the earliest danced Sarabande was so wildly obscene that in 1583, a group of shocked Catholic priests lobbied Philip II of Spain to ban it. The Sarabande, or Zarabanda, as it was first known, was a recent import from the New World. Danced to the voluptuous accompaniment of the Spanish five-course guitar, castanets, and tambourines, it featured moves that alarmed the locals. In his discouragingly-titled *Treatise Against Public Amusements* (1609), one Father Juan de Mariana railed against the Sarabande as "a dance and song so loose in its words and so ugly in its motions that it is enough to excite bad emotions in even very decent people."[12] The poet Giambattista Marino joined in the disapproval in *L'Adone* (1623): "The girls...exhibit indecency in a thousand positions and gestures. They let the hips sway and the breasts knock together. They close their eyes and dance the kiss and the last fulfillment of love."[13]

If you are eager to see some of these dreadful dance moves, if only to make sure that you possess sufficient moral rectitude to withstand bad emotions, you can't. No one ever wrote down the steps. By the time the danced Sarabande arrived in France, it had become a serious, orderly affair in a slowish tempo, with three beats to the measure and an accent on the second beat. By the time anyone thought to notate its steps and moves, it had become significantly less racy.

Like those of the French court, Bach's Sarabandes typically fall into the "one-*two*-three" rhythmic pattern. The accented second beat sometimes gets even further emphasis and elongation in the form of a dotted rhythm, as it does in the Sarabande of the First Cello Suite. In these cases, the interpreter should give the first beat a certain lightness of bowstroke and direct the phrase to its high point in the middle of the measure. In their study of dance styles in Bach's music, Meredith Little and Natalie Jenne describe the courtly danced Sarabande as a spectacle with many difficult techniques, passionate glances, and most importantly, an air of studied nonchalance.[14] I think of this as I play the Sarabande of Bach's First Cello Suite, imagining a dancer's feet in exquisitely beribboned slippers. Sliding noiselessly along the floor on the first beat, she goes up *en pointe* on the second in an effortless display of technique and control.

Cellists sometimes get so wrapped up in trying to sound beautiful in Bach that we neglect the idea of actual dancers in the dance movements. The cellist Nathaniel Rosen, in a long-ago Internet Cello Society interview, typifies this attitude. "They're not dance movements!" he exclaims. "They are works for unaccompanied cello which have, with the exception of the Preludes, titles of dance movements."

When the interviewer, Tim Janof, points out that "they do retain the dance form implied in the titles," Rosen gets annoyed.

"Yes, they have the titles of Renaissance dances that had not been danced for hundreds of years before Bach! People weren't dancing allemandes in Bach's time. They were just convenient musical forms whose French titles he borrowed."[15]

Rosen's point, while reasonable, is only partially accurate. It's true that some of the dances no longer featured in the ballrooms of 1720, but others were still current. In any case, the danced origins of his movement titles would still have been within Bach's frame of reference. If we're to know Bach, we need to understand some of the things he knew. The physical embodiment of dance forms can teach us a lot about many aspects of musical interpretation, not least tempo.

With this in mind, I decide to give Little and Jenne's ideas a chance. I'm as guilty as the next cellist of playing Sarabandes at a funereal pace, since all of us like to do that Dying Swan thing. That said, what would happen if a dancer tried to dance to such self-indulgent tempi? Good dancers can, of course, control their movements at any speed, but gravity is gravity and they can't be expected to suspend themselves in midair after a jump or hop. Little and Jenne advise performers to think of Sarabandes at a metronome marking of around 69 beats per minute, cautioning that even then "some dancers will not be able to sustain the difficult, slow gestures of choreographies at that tempo."[16]

I have a love-hate relationship with the idea of playing Bach with a metronome, and usually justify not using one because they hadn't been invented in Bach's time. However, after trawling YouTube for videos of historically-informed dancers dancing the Sarabande, it seems that a lot of them are going at Little and Jenne's recommended tempo. I turn the metronome on to gauge how far off I am, and realize with chagrin that I'm going at the glacial pace of 45 b.p.m. It appears my whole concept is faulty. I've always interpreted the Sarabande of Bach's First Cello Suite as a poetic, timeless meditation, and meditations tend to be slow. When I listen to the recording of my day's practice that I've made on my phone, I get the uncomfortable feeling that what I'm doing is alien to the idea of the dance. My "meditative" tempo doesn't work because it obscures the characteristic Sarabande meter of "one-*two*-three."

It's time to crank up the speed, but my first attempts are hugely frustrating. How can I possibly play in a nuanced way at such a clip? It takes time and patience to learn to live with the new tempo, and a rethink of what nuance even means. The idea of a controlled tempo might seem antithetical to true feeling, but then, there are a lot of rewards in the cello world for being *out* of control. We only need to look at the popularity of certain celebrity cellists for proof, with their thrashing gestures and histrionic facial expressions. How easily we confuse such antics with genuine emotion.

When I record myself again at the new, faster tempo, I notice for the first time that the harmony in the first two measures of the Sarabande exactly replicates that from the first four measures of the Prelude. How such cyclical unity escaped me before, I can't explain. All I know is that playing at the new tempo reveals a better sense of harmonic, rhythmic, and structural coherence. All the emotion I've always felt for the Sarabande is still in there, just with a lid on, like a pressurized canister that could explode at any moment, but doesn't. All I had to do was kill off the Dying Swan. I make a note to aim for swan-free interpretations of future Sarabandes.

V. MENUETS

The road map for each of Bach's Cello Suites is roughly the same. In all six, we find the Prelude, Allemande, Courante, Sarabande, and Gigue. Between the Sarabande and Gigue, however, are a pair of variable *galanterie* dances. For the First and Second Cello Suites, the dances are Menuets; for the Third and Fourth, Bourrées; and for the Fifth and Sixth, Gavottes. The dances are played *da capo*, meaning that after finishing the second, the cellist must return to the first dance and play it in its entirety without repeats. The reprise gives the cellist the chance to display virtuosity by means of a few improvised ornaments such as trills, turns, and grace notes. Bach, one of history's most prodigious improvisers, could probably do this brilliantly on the spot, but for most of us the spontaneity is premeditated.

Revisiting the Menuets of Bach's First Cello Suite always fills me with sentimental nostalgia, since they were the first solo Bach piece I learned. The first three notes – G, D, and B in ascending motion – give me a feeling of traveling across time and oceans to the studio in Judy and John's wonderful house. For a fleeting second I get to be that owlish little girl again, playing her first notes of the Cello Suites.

I learned the Menuets as a stand-alone piece because I couldn't yet tackle the other, more difficult movements. They're enchantingly lovely all by themselves, but in their context within the Suite, where they follow the serious Sarabande, their lightness seems especially touching. By opening with G, D, and B – as he did in the Prelude, Allemande, and Sarabande – Bach shows us that he conceived the First Cello Suite as an integrated whole. As unifying devices go, this one is pretty heart-lifting.

If Sarabandes tend towards complicated emotions, Menuets are rather simpler in style and design. They're always in triple meter and a moderate tempo, with an emphasis on the first beat of the measure. The Menuet was still a dance form in Bach's time, having been wildly popular in the ballet and ballroom of the French court a generation earlier. Bach himself wrote more than forty Menuets, and Jean-Baptiste Lully no fewer than ninety-two. Pierre Rameau, the choreographer, dedicates five entire chapters of *The Dancing Master* to the various graces and gestures of a good Menuet. Elegant steps took the dancers around the room in the form of a letter Z, and while this was going on, the ladies and gentlemen often joined hands, the lady's draped gracefully over the man's. "In making this *pas de menuet*," Rameau instructs, "you both hold your right shoulders clear, turn your heads slightly to your left and look at each other, and retain this manner throughout the dance."[17] These locked gazes and figure-flattering stances must have made for some thrilling ballroom courtships. Relearning the notes of the Menuet of the First Cello Suite, I occasionally add in a down-up-up bow-stroke to emphasize the first beat and give special lightness to the second and third. As I do so, I imagine the dancers bending their knees for the *demi-coupé*, then springing into motion, toes arching delicately inside satin dancing-slippers.

Alone among the movements of the First Cello Suite, the second Menuet is not in G major but in G minor. The character change from the first Menuet is striking, and not just because of the minor mode. The melodic lines of the first Menuet tend to go upwards in pitch, whereas those in the second are largely built from descending motion. One of the many things I didn't notice about the second Menuet in childhood is that it's built on a common Baroque bass line. In one of those self-accompanying gestures that Bach does so well, the low pitches G – F – E-flat – D are embedded within the notes of the single melodic line in the first section. By doing so, Bach is obliquely but deliberately introducing the passacaglia, a repeated descending bassline often used for improvising.

The art of improvisation doesn't typically feature in classical music pedagogy in the twenty-first century, but for Bach it was an essential component of musicianship. It wasn't until I played in an early music ensemble in graduate school that I got to try Baroque improvisation myself. One rehearsal day, the professor asked me to loop a passacaglia bassline over and over while the violinists and woodwind players tried their hand at improvising. None of us had ever studied jazz or any other improvisatory musical style, so this was not something we had in our skill set. A group of high achievers who didn't like being bad at things, we all felt suddenly vulnerable.

"Don't be frightened," our professor assured us. "In improvisation, there are no wrong notes, only unfortunate choices. Isn't that a liberating thought?"

"Yeah, right," I thought, feeling relieved that as a bassline player, I wouldn't have to improvise in front of the others. That is, until the professor, who was directing from the harpsichord, suddenly announced "Miranda has been playing away so patiently. Why don't you take your turn improvising, Miranda?"

On the spot, all that saved me from complete terror was remembering that the passacaglia bassline outlines a series of chords known as the Andalusian progression, so called because it's common in flamenco and other traditional forms in Spanish music. I started by guessing melodic notes based on whether they were part of the implied chord progression, with mixed success. Then it occurred to me that I could try to approximate the style of two pieces I knew well that featured passacaglia basslines: the second Menuet of Bach's First Cello Suite, and "Amor" from Claudio Monteverdi's madrigal *Lamento della ninfa*. I changed a few notes around and added some ornaments, but it was a fairly obvious rip-off of both compositions.

"Isn't that cheating?" teased one of my friends.

"No," said the professor. "How do you think Bach and Monteverdi figured out how harmony worked?"

I don't know if Bach knew Monteverdi's *Lamento della ninfa*, or anything by Monteverdi at all, but after coming across this arresting madrigal in my teens, I could never unhear it when I played the second Menuet of the First Cello Suite. Nor could I forget its passionate protagonist, a nymph lamenting her desertion by a lover. Narrating the drama are three male singers, who for some reason I always imagine as shepherds. The nymph pleads for the faithless lover to return, but we know from the relentless, constraining passacaglia that her pleas will be in vain. The ever-present bassline is the fifth character in the drama, a non-speaking role but somehow always in control.

And that's why I can't get enough of playing basslines. Finding the passacaglia subtly but unmistakably hidden like this in Bach's Cello Suites fills me with excitement. When there is only one player present on the stage, that person has to be every character in the play. In Bach, the cello is the leading lady, the supporting actors, and the foundation underlying the direction of the drama.

It's hard to come back from a dark passacaglia. In the Menuets of Bach's First Cello Suite, the first, major-key Menuet and its reprise function as bookends to the minor-key second Menuet. We can never unhear the darkness of the *minore* Menuet, but we can rejoice even more in the renewal of the major.

VI. GIGUE

Long after childhood and well into my professional life, I thought the Gigues of Bach's Cello Suites were more or less analogous to the British jig. In Shakespeare's *Much Ado About Nothing*, the sharp-tongued Beatrice advises naïve Hero "Wooing, wedding, and repenting, is as a Scotch jig, a measure, and a cinque pace: the first suit is hot and hasty, like a Scotch jig, and full as fantastical." This seemed like an enlivening thought to keep in mind while playing the Gigue of the First Cello Suite.

An internet search for Scottish jigs sidetracks me briefly into the arresting world of competitive Scottish folk-dancing. Fascinated, I watch video after video of grim-faced teenaged girls with hairstyles sprayed into the consistency of concrete, frilly tartan mini-dresses, and tans acquired under no Scottish sun. Ambitious parents cheer them on from the bleachers as they go after trophies with a level of ruthless bloodlust I have only ever witnessed in horror movies and classical music contests.

A little disappointingly, Bach's Gigues don't appear to be closely related to this plaid-covered warfare. The dance names might sound similar, but the instrumental forms themselves have significant rhythmical and structural differences. The French Gigue is in compound time with a lilting rhythm; of Bach's six Gigues for cello, only the one from the Fifth Cello Suite falls into this category. All the others are Italian Gigas, an instrumental form that may never even have been used for dancing.[18] Complicated and flashy, they featured long slurring bow-strokes, fast fingers, and other characteristics of Italian-style virtuosity. The Giga-Gigue of Bach's First Cello Suite does all of these things, and more. A gratifying vehicle for display, it allows the cellist to showcase multiple types of articulation, plus humorous gestures such as pretending to be in a minor key only to burst out – surprise! – in major.

37

The Giga form has associations with virtuoso fiddling because the word itself originally referred to a bowed string instrument. In Dante's *Paradiso*, this kind of *giga* makes a cameo appearance in Canto XIV. *"E come giga e arpa, in tempra tesa / di molte corde..."* "And like the *giga* and harp, whose many strings are tempered taut, and produce sweet resonance..." While several English translators of Dante render *giga* as a viol or a lute, it is neither of these things. What Dante most likely had in mind was a medieval fiddle, an ancient precursor to the violin family. The term still exists in the German word for violin, *Geige*.

Does the Giga-Gigue of Bach's First Cello Suite invoke literal dancing, or doesn't it? Does it matter? There isn't a clear answer, because the disciplines of music and dance weren't as separate three or four centuries ago as they are today. As the stereotype of the violin-playing dancing master demonstrates, one person could simultaneously work as a musician and dancer. This might explain the outrage in seventeenth-century France when Louis XIV decided to found an Académie Royale de Danse in 1660. Dancers and musicians had previously been members of the same guild, which they had to share with minstrels, jugglers, magicians, and other entertainers, and the musicians wanted to keep it that way. The dancers, however, liked this plan a great deal, since having their own academy offered certain attractive legal protections. Moreover, they wished to distance themselves from the rag-tag collection of circus performers with whom they had previously been obliged to share a guild.

Musicians, understandably, were peeved. Would dancers now get preferential royal treatment? What would become of their guild now that they couldn't collect membership fees from dancers? Was it even artistically viable to separate dance from music, given the strong connection of the art forms? What, they demanded, was dance without music anyway?

Dancers shot back that "violin is to dance what the drums are to war. The drum stimulates the soldier, the music animates the dancer, but it would be ridiculous to conclude that wars are won by drummers." Then, in a statement shockingly offensive by today's standards, they added "Isn't it true that dancers must have a well-proportioned and beautiful body to express their art to the full, whereas a violinist could be blind, hunchbacked or one-legged without damage to his art? All that was needed there was a good elbow and a good ear."[19]

The separation went ahead, and the dance faction rejoiced, proclaiming that they had outgrown music anyway. Losing such a high-stakes fight must have been painful for the musicians, proud masters of their craft. I find myself sympathizing with their wounded professional dignity.

Bach wrote his Cello Suites only sixty years after the dance vs. music debacle in France, a relatively short period of time in the history of both arts. Though his Cello Suites were never meant to accompany dancers, the dance movements still allude to the graces, seductions, and social shibboleths of the ballroom. Politics aside, boundaries between the two art forms aren't always clear. As William Butler Yeats once demanded of a chestnut tree, "Are you the leaf, the blossom or the bole? / O body swayed to music, O brightening glance / How can we know the dancer from the dance?" Does the essence of a dance exist in dancer, a musician, a score, a choreography, a composer, or a choreographer? Is any component more essential than another? No, because a dance is the sum of many parts.

The journey back through Bach's Cello Suites is still at an early stage, but already I'm convinced that the search for their meaning involves many more people than Bach himself. They've already taken me back through time to King Louis and Lully, resplendent in their dancing costumes, and, going back further, to elegant Monteverdi in Venice. The music of the past, to misquote William Faulkner, is not dead – it's not even past. The Cello Suites are living documents, and as I live with them, they will take me backwards and forwards through history with a cast of characters – cellists, composers, scholars – who have lived with them too.

Part Two

THE NIGHT OF SORROW

Suite No. 2 in D Minor, BWV 1008

Ich lebte mit der Welt in Lust und Freuden,
Und du mußt leiden.

"I lived with the world in joy and delight,
And you had to suffer."

Johann Sebastian Bach, *St. John Passion* BWV 245

I. PRELUDE

The Prelude of the First Suite falls for the most part into repetitive, undulating patterns of widely spaced broken chords. There's something reassuring about the rise and fall of the waves of notes as tensions resolve and journeys end.

The Second Suite's Prelude couldn't be more different.

The first fragile, questioning fragment of melody – built from the ascending pitches of the D minor chord, D, F, and A – stays close together in range. The second fragment, spelling out the dissonant chord C-sharp, E, G, and B-flat, follows suit. A third fragment goes higher, up to the high E – and this gets the motion going. Long chains of notes intertwine and separate, making question-and-answer conversation as Bach deftly shifts the harmony from key to key. The mood is dark. Occasionally a major key surfaces – usually F major, a close relative of D minor – but the hopeful tone doesn't last long.

After a dark interlude in A minor, we're back in the home key of D minor. This is the point at which a lesser composer might have decided it was the end of the movement, but Bach never let us off so easily. The intensity breaks up the closely-spaced motion, and the cello practically slams into a jaggedly arpeggiated chord of C-sharp, A, and G, with the low C-sharp sounding for all the world like a cathedral organist stamping his foot on a mighty bass pedal. It's a genuinely frightening moment. But Bach isn't done – the jagged ascending chord happens again on G-sharp, F, and D, before we launch into a declamatory D-minor section that makes it sound as if we're finally at the end.

Except that we aren't.

Bach cuts us off on the discordant chord of C-sharp, E, and G, a chord that begs for resolution into the home key of D minor, and which Bach doesn't let us have.

There is exactly one rest in the entire D minor Prelude, and it happens right here after the unresolved chord. The surprise is traumatic, because this could – harmonically speaking – have been the end. We, the listeners, expected it to be the end. It isn't the end, though, and what happens next is extraordinary.

As we pick up the broken threads of melody and harmony, the musical line sounds lost, as if it's searching for a key and can't find one. After a measure or two the spinning wheel starts turning again as Bach rebuilds the sense of D minor in our habitual running sixteenth notes. But then, five measures before the end, another surprise comes in the form of five blocked chords, each written as a triple stop in dotted half notes. Up until now, the Prelude has been composed mostly from running sixteenth notes, so the change in texture is striking. What's going on?

I was thirteen years old when Judy Hyatt gave me the Prelude from the Second Cello Suite to learn for my next lesson. I peered at the notes on the page, my fingers stumbling. "This looks like a real finger-twister," I observed.

Judy smiled her twinkling smile. "Oh, but this is the best piece in the world, Miranda." She said this sort of thing about all the pieces I'd been learning lately, like Max Bruch's *Kol Nidrei* and Antonio Vivaldi's C minor concerto.

Before the lesson was over, Judy sat down at her Victorian writing-desk with a piece of manuscript paper and started writing something. "What are you doing?" I said.

"I'm writing down how you should play the last five bars of the Prelude," Judy explained.

"How do you mean?"

"Well, it's thought that Bach only wrote those last five chords in triple stops as a kind of shorthand," said Judy.

"What's shorthand?"

Judy paused to explain what shorthand was. Then she went on "Bach may have run out of time while he was writing, or he wanted to give the performer the chance to add something of his own. People improvised a lot more then, dear. Bach was expecting his cellist to improvise using the notes from the chords."

"Improvise?" I was both impressed and shocked.

"Well, you don't need to do that just yet," Judy reassured me, waving the staff paper. "Someone wrote out this version a while ago, dear. I thought it was pretty good, so let's start by using it. But you might end up writing your own version that you like better."

This was the first I'd ever heard of a piece of classical music where you didn't do literally what was on the printed page. In the Wellington Youth Orchestra, where I was the youngest member, I learned that the printed page was sacrosanct. You had to make sure your bow was always going in the same direction as your section leader, who in turn had to make sure that the cellos' bowings matched those the violins were doing. You had to blend with the section and obey the dynamic and articulation markings. Woe betide you if you surged in at a clumsy *forte* when the score was marked *piano*. You had to count, divide, and subdivide beats. You absolutely, absolutely had to play all the right notes. My parents didn't allow me to listen to any music but classical, so I was only dimly aware of the existence of jazz, and the idea of a score that didn't spell out all the directions was at once terrifying and enticing. It was the first time I'd ever considered a musical score as anything other than an immoveable artifact. The thought that it might be open not just to interpretation, but to improvisation – a kind of recomposition! – was startling. Who was I, a coltish thirteen-year-old with braces, to improvise on the harmonies of the great Capellmeister Johann Sebastian Bach?

*

Twenty years later, Bach's abrupt switch to shorthand still perplexes me, but at least now I have the age, guile, and ten years' worth of university education to negotiate with a score. I've assimilated the research and recordings of the historically informed performance practice movement, and I hope to interpret the Cello Suites in a way Bach might find at least recognizable. How often I've wished for a time machine to take me back to 1720 to ask Bach a thing or two about his intentions. The minute we start conjecturing about them, we're on seriously shaky ground, because a lot has changed since 1720. Instruments, playing techniques, musical languages, musical assumptions, performance settings, social settings, and culture have all evolved into new and different traditions.

The score, though, is a still-living document. What's on a page isn't the end product, since a musical work cannot exist in sound form until the performer has given it a voice. The challenge, of course, is finding that voice when the document is written in a language that we no longer speak. Musical tropes that Bach's Cöthen colleagues implicitly understood are now as unfamiliar to us as the quill pen. That hasn't stopped over-eager performers from claiming that their recordings and editions are "definitive" or "authentic," as if they had a direct line to the eighteenth century. Frustratingly, there is so much we don't know and will never know.

*

After I left Judy's studio to go to university, I was lucky to have many teachers, all of whom had illuminating things to say about Bach's Cello Suites. The most brilliant of all was Alexander Ivashkin. He and his cellist wife, Natalia Pavlutskaya, were my teachers for five years, first at the University of Canterbury in New Zealand, and later in London. Thanks to the Ivashkins' rigorous teaching and even more rigorous exhortations to practice, I was able to progress to the professional level. I came to think of Sasha and Natasha, as they called each other, as my musical father and mother.

Students, of course, were not allowed to call him Sasha; to us he was Dr. Ivashkin or Alexander Vassilievich, the polite Russian form of address. He called me Mirandochka, an affectionate diminutive. While he was personally indulgent and paternal with me, he was also a tough teacher who pushed me hard to improve. "I have loved you as daughter, or probably granddaughter," he once scolded in his idiosyncratic brand of English, "but you are bloody lazy!" On other occasions, he told me crossly that I was "not a *wery* good cellist." *Yet,* I thought, stamping off to the practice rooms for another marathon session of scales.

Perhaps surprisingly for a Russian virtuoso specializing in contemporary music, Alexander Vassilievich was fanatical about historically informed performance practice. He was horrified the first time he heard me attempting to play Bach. "You do not understand this music, Mirandochka," he admonished me, and packed me off to the University of Canterbury library to find the *Neue Bach-Ausgabe,* the complete edition of Bach's music by the publisher Bärenreiter. Standing in the fluorescent-lit stacks, I pulled the volumes containing the Cello Suites off the shelf, not realizing what a revelation they held. One of the volumes was the scholarly modern edition by the musicologist Hans Eppstein – already a great improvement over my dog-eared Starker edition – and another, smaller volume contained facsimiles of the four remaining eighteenth-century copies of the Cello Suites.

I sat down at one of the long wood-veneer tables with these treasures. Source A, the 1728 copy by Anna Magdalena Bach, I'd seen before on Judy's writing-desk. Johann Peter Kellner's 1726 copy, known as Source B, was new to me. Source C, copied in the 1760s by Johann Nikolaus Schober and a second anonymous copyist, and Source D, made in the 1790s by another anonymous copyist, were also unfamiliar. I turned pages back and forth, squinting over the florid handwriting, the blotches where ink had bled through parchment, the crossings-out, the strange slur markings. The four were perplexingly different from each other – different slurs, different trills and ornaments, even different notes. How could Eppstein have figured out how to make his edition at all? How did you decide what was a right note and what was a wrong note when in some cases there were four different choices, and the one manuscript that might have cleared matters up for good, Bach's own, was irretrievably lost?

When I looked up it was dark outside.

Before I studied with Alexander Vassilievich Ivashkin, I had considered the cello a largely melodic instrument. Sure, you had a three- or four-note chord from time to time, but cello was for melody and piano was for harmony, or so I thought. Ivashkin cleared that up for me. He and Natasha directed me to the analytical performance editions by Diran Alexanian and Enrico Mainardi that showed how two or three voices might be going on simultaneously at any moment. It was the cellist's job to demonstrate to the audience which was which. Fragments of melodic lines had to be differentiated from harmonic lines and bass notes, and sometimes there was an overlap that made it hard to tell them apart. Natasha described these fragments as small bricks. "You must find the bricks so that you can put them together in a clever way," she told me. It went without saying that what I was currently doing was not clever.

One of the first steps was to understand what key the harmony was in at all times. "*Vhat* key is harmony in *hyere*? And *hyere*?" My teachers' interrogations sent me rushing for my theory books. I'd yawned through my obligatory classes in harmony, analysis, and counterpoint, doing just enough work to scrape an A, without realizing what they were actually for. Now I understood why the university course catalogue called performance lessons Applied Music – you were supposed to take all that other stuff, the music theory and music history, and apply it to how you played your instrument.

One of the things Alexander Vassilievich did in his lessons on Bach was to improvise an accompanying bassline while you played what was in the score. Much later I learned – from a magisterial dissertation by the cellist John Lutterman,[20] among other sources – that making up basslines to go with a given melody was a technique from seventeenth- and eighteenth-century pedagogy. An integral part of being a cellist back then was to learn and memorize harmonic procedure so that you could independently improvise over it in ensembles. A fact Bach knew by implication when he wrote the last five bars of the D minor Prelude.

Bach wouldn't have thought much of twenty-first century classical musicians who couldn't improvise. To improvise was the norm, to write your improvisations down an afterthought. Composers must have known what a gift they were giving future musicians in writing them down, however, or they wouldn't have done it so much. Most present-day classical music geeks are familiar with the story of Bach's *Musical Offering*, a tale that always makes me want to break into applause. Many years after composing the Cello Suites, Bach went to visit his grown-up son Carl Philipp Emanuel Bach at his enviable position in the employment of King Frederick the Great of Prussia. In his opulent palace in Potsdam, the music-loving king showed Bach an expensive new fortepiano and invited him to improvise a three-part fugue upon it, using as a subject the difficult chromatic theme he had composed for the occasion. In one of the greatest displays of intellectual superiority ever recorded, Bach did just that, amazing his royal host. When I picture this scene – the supercilious king, the nervous son white-knuckling the arms of his chair and hoping his dad wouldn't embarrass him, the elder statesman of music sitting down at the instrument and just *shredding* – I want to punch the air with glee. Papa Bach's still got it! Take that, Your Majesty!

Later, Bach wrote down his *Musical Offering* and dedicated the publication to the king. Sightreading the opening Trio Sonata one day with three friends, I noticed idly that it opened in the same manner as the Prelude to the Second Suite, with the ascending simple minor triad.

*

As my lessons with the Ivashkins progressed, I started thinking of Bach's music as a kind of auditory Magic Eye® image. Before, it had seemed like a mess of hundreds of notes, but when you knew how to look at it, the sound-picture of its harmony came into relief.

The great Romantic composer Robert Schumann understood this. Following the lead of his friend Felix Mendelssohn-Bartholdy, he became part of the nineteenth-century Bach Revival. On another post-lesson trip to the University of Canterbury library, I picked up Schumann's edition of Bach's Cello Suite No. 3, to which he had added a piano part. At first, I assumed this would be a meaningless gloss – why add a piano part to a cello part that already generates its own harmony? – but when I tried it out on one of the clunky upright pianos in a School of Music practice room, I thought I could see what Schumann was trying to do. Unlike the piano accompaniments by more than a few well-meaning nineteenth-century editors, Schumann's is remarkably conservative, even sparse. The rhythm is sensitive to the harmonic shifts, bringing them out so a struggling learner can grasp how the chords and characters change. Like my teacher Alexander Vassilievich, Schumann uses harmonic notes to teach us the concept of the hidden bassline. We might say that Schumann is following the lead of Bach, for whom composing and performing and teaching were so integrated that they might as well be the same thing. In the century and more that had elapsed since the Capellmeister of Cöthen wrote the Cello Suites, his language had been forgotten; Schumann was teaching his contemporaries how to speak and hear and feel it.

That same library shelf turned up all manner of other finds. I dug through everything, seeking all the editions of Bach's Cello Suites I could get my hands on. I had never bothered with looking at old editions of music before, since all my professors were adamant about the need for modern scholarly editions of repertoire, the so-called *Urtext* editions. I had learned to dismiss nineteenth-century editions as awful old-fashioned junk covered with outdated bowings, illogical added dynamics, and fingerings that would cause you to make inapposite sliding noises as you moved from note to note. When I found the earliest editions of the Cello Suites in the library, I assumed they'd be obsolete at best, if not downright intellectually dubious.

What I found caused me to think more kindly of nineteenth-century editors. Many of their editorial changes to Bach's Cello Suites must have been necessary because of changes to instruments and playing traditions over the century since Bach had composed them. In the earliest printed edition by Louis-Pierre Norblin (1824), which appears to be derived from the manuscripts known as Source C and D, we can see careful attempts to make the Cello Suites playable for their contemporaries. In the Prelude to the First Suite, for example, the old bowing pattern for collections of four notes of equal length – a slur of three notes within the same down-bow stroke, then a single up-bow stroke for the fourth note – is replaced with a slur of four notes, plus four separately-bowed notes for the next four notes.

There was a very good reason for this: the hardware had changed. The bow of Bach's time was made from a lightweight, durable wood with the exciting name of *amourette*, otherwise known as snakewood for its snakeskin-like patterning. The tip of the bow had a pronounced point, and the tension of the horsehair attached to it could be adjusted with the player's thumb depending on whether he or she intended to play chords or single melodic lines. By the time Norblin was professionally active as a top player and professor of cello at the Paris Conservatoire, a French bow-maker called François Xavier Tourte had revolutionized the craft of bow-making. Made from heavier Pernambuco wood, with considerably more wood at the tip of the bow and a pronounced concave arch in the stick, Tourte's bow could produce a more projecting, sustained tone in either bowstroke direction. Best of all, the addition of a screw mechanism meant that players could control the tension of the horsehair without putting their fingers on it. To this day, touching bowhair is a big no-no, since the sweat on human fingers interacts with the rosin to create shiny dark patches that won't produce sound. Re-hairing a bow is expensive, so the innovation meant that cellists didn't have to get it done as often. (During my adolescence, my father frequently complained that going by the price tag, luthiers must be getting their bowhair from the tails of unicorns.)

Bowing markings aside, Norblin's edition shows other attempts to normalize an eighteenth-century score for nineteenth-century cellists. He changed the title from "Suites" to the more familiar *Sonates ou Etudes* – "Sonatas or Studies." He renamed all Bach's Courantes as Correntes, even the one from the Fifth Suite that actually is a Courante. Puzzlingly, he insisted that the Bourrées in the Third and Fourth Suites should be termed *Louré*. At one point in the Prelude of the Sixth Suite, five measures are inexplicably missing. Left-hand fingering markings appear regularly, as do suggestions for dynamics, articulations, tempos, and ornamentations such as trills and grace notes. Under the staff at the end of the Prelude to the Second Suite is the suggestion *Arpegio* [*sic*], indicating that Norblin believed the performer should improvise over the chords. He also adjusted the procedure for clefs in the Sixth Cello Suite, which in the eighteenth-century sources appears in a mixture of bass and alto clef. By the nineteenth century, cellists weren't expected to read alto clef any more, and Norblin rewrote the alto clef sections of the Sixth Suite using a treble clef plus the indication to play down an octave from the printed pitch. (This notation convention is now obsolete too, though you occasionally see it in old editions of Antonín Dvořák's chamber music. If you aren't expecting an abrupt switch into treble clef, it can give you quite a shock. The relief of realizing you don't actually have to whiz up to the stratospheres of the cello's range doesn't quite make up for the near-heart attack.)

Subsequent editions are more than mere curiosities; on the contrary, they teach us a lot about the evolution of cello playing conventions. A couple of years after Norblin's edition came out, a 43-year-old member of Dresden's royal orchestra called Justus Johann Friedrich Dotzauer produced the first truly practical performance edition of Bach's Cello Suites.

Dotzauer is a name familiar to anyone who has studied the cello, because he wrote dozens of technical exercises. Judy Hyatt, who was much addicted to the etude-book, gave me a new one to learn every week between the ages of nine and twelve. Like other young players, I didn't like them much until I started picking up a few private students of my own and realized just how useful they are. We can see how intimately Dotzauer understood the capabilities of cello technique and the tendencies of human learning in the notes of his *113 Etudes*. In this remarkable work, Dotzauer covers every aspect of musicianship and technique with forward-thinking thoroughness: in places where he knows inexperienced players will screw up the notes, he discreetly adds a courtesy fingering or bowing marking to jog their memories. Looking at these considerate reminders through the eyes of a teacher fills me with gratitude and nostalgia. Dear Dotzauer!

His edition of Bach's Cello Suites shows the same scrupulous attention to detail. It's clear that Dotzauer made it with reference to Source B, the eighteenth-century manuscript by Johann Peter Kellner, or more likely a now-lost copy of it,[21] though how he got his hands on it is uncertain. While Dotzauer's markings show an attempt at standardizing and normalizing the bowing to make it playable for nineteenth-century cellists, he didn't – to his credit – iron out the "three-plus-one" bowing practice into four-note slurs. Unlike Norblin, he called a Bourrée a Bourrée, and let Bach call a Corrente a Courante. His suggestions for fingerings and articulations are still practical today, as is his procedure in the Sixth Cello Suite of rewriting high pitches in the tenor clef instead of treble clef. It's clear that Dotzauer was no impro-viser, however, since the last five measures of the Prelude from the Second Cello Suite appear as straight chords in dotted half notes, with no mention of arpeggiation or improvisation of any kind.

Even if Dotzauer was a pedagogue and not a scholar, his edition was one of three used by the musicologist Alfred Dörffel for the 1879 *Bach-Gesellschaft*, a scholarly edition of Bach's complete works. By now, Anna Magdalena Bach's manuscript had come into the possession of the Berlin Royal Library, where it became Dörffel's chief source. Dotzauer's edition, however, was still reliable enough for Dörffel to use it in places where Anna Magdalena Bach's work had been ambiguous.

Dotzauer's successor as the frontrunner in German cello playing was the notorious Friedrich Wilhelm Ludwig Grützmacher (1832–1903). Here was another name I recognized right away. Grützmacher is chiefly known in modern times for his many technical etudes, and also for an eccentric, patchwork-like arrangement of Boccherini's B-flat major concerto that for decades was part of the standard repertoire. He made two editions of Bach's Cello Suites in the 1860s, one a so-called performance edition, the other a more conservative rendering. The second I already knew, because Judy and John had had a copy of it in their music cabinet. It was, she told me, the same edition that the thirteen-year-old Pablo Casals had found in a second-hand shop, "and the rest is history, dear." To call it conservative, however, is only accurate in comparison with Grützmacher's other efforts. His nineteenth-century tastes abounded in his additions of dynamics, articulations, tempo directions, and bowing techniques that didn't exist in the time of Bach. To give him credit, he acknowledged certain Baroque stylistic traits that were no longer current in the middle of the nineteenth century, including those troublesome last five measures of the Prelude of the Second Suite. His written-out improvisation was the same one Judy had written out for me on staff paper years ago. Looking over it again, I thought it stood up quite well.

Grützmacher's "performance" edition, on the other hand, is better termed an arrangement than an edition. Evidently Grützmacher thought contemporary editions of Bach hadn't gone far enough, and set about recomposing the Cello Suites until he had changed hundreds of notes, chopped 33 measures out of the Prelude of the Fifth Cello Suite, and transposed the entire Sixth Cello Suite from D major to G major. Admittedly, the latter wasn't a bad idea, since Bach had composed the Sixth Cello Suite for a now-obsolete five-string cello, meaning that the notes were playable on a four-string cello, but often went into high registers that were difficult for less advanced players. By transposing the Sixth Cello Suite down to G, Grützmacher did increase its accessibility. The problem was that his rendering of Bach was so extreme, it was almost unrecognizable as Bach.

Even in an era when editors regularly made huge "improvements" to Baroque compositions, there were musicians who thought Grützmacher had gone too far. In a letter to his publisher, Grützmacher pronounced defensively "My main purpose has been to reflect and to determine what these masters might have been thinking, and to set down all that they, themselves, could have indicated.... Regarding this activity, and relying on my long musical experiences, I feel *I have more right than all others to do this work*... Who could possibly see anything in my work but a great deal of care and love, since it cannot be thought that it is done from a lack of knowledge... My concert version of the Bach Suites, which you likewise mention, cannot also be a subject of reproach since, in editing them, I not only tried to follow the *same intentions* of which I have just spoken, but I succeeded at it. I have reaped much success in presenting this edition in concert, something that would have been impossible with the bare original in its primitive state."[22]

Poor Grützmacher. All that work on the performance edition was in vain, since it never really caught on, and to this day no one has recorded his reimagined "Bach." And yet, even if his methods were overzealous, I can see what he was trying to do. He was improvising, a skill that by now was less common, and he wrote the improvisation down. We ought perhaps to be grateful to him for giving us a glimpse of a now-lost art.

More happily for Grützmacher, his "conservative" edition sold widely and influenced several future editions. Two of the best-known are by Julius Klengel (1900) and Grützmacher's student Hugo Becker (1911). Both were top cello teachers in major German cities, Klengel in Leipzig and Becker in Berlin. Everyone who was anyone wanted to study with them, and their alumni included most of the top players of the early twentieth century. To our eyes, their Bach editions seem old-fashioned and full of fingerings that would cause a player to make ungainly sliding noises when moving from note to note. This was in fact deliberate. Hardcore cello nerds sometimes collect digitally remastered early recordings of both venerable professors, and the evidence bears out their slide-y predilections. (Klengel's 1928 recording of the Sarabande from the Sixth Cello Suite, complete with piano accompaniment, sounds very strange to modern ears. It takes several hearings to deduce his exquisite intonation and purity of sound through the crackling of the ancient recording.) Even if Klengel and Becker's playing styles are now outdated to the point of incomprehensibility, they still have something important to teach us about the performance history of Bach's Cello Suites.

It's worth noting that Klengel and a handful of other nineteenth-century editors, including Brahms's friend Robert Hausmann (1898), were still suggesting written-out "improvisations" for the last five measures of the Prelude of the Second Suite. The later practice of playing them as straight chords appears to have started later, perhaps with Pablo Casals. Even if he got his start using the Grützmacher edition, Casals abandoned many of the performance practices in it that had come down directly from Bach's time, including the direction in the Fifth Cello Suite to tune the cello A-string down to a G.

No one could dispute Casals's importance in the history of cello playing, but the exaggeration of his so-called discovery of Bach's Cello Suites is one of my pet peeves. His biographers and admirers repeated his claim that no one before him had played the Cello Suites or recognized their greatness, but this isn't entirely true. If it were, we wouldn't have all these nineteenth-century editions by the top cellists of the time. Dotzauer and his successors possessed some of the finest musical minds in Europe, and were friends and collaborators with the greatest composers of their age. To suggest that they didn't properly appreciate Bach is misleading, to say the least.

I secretly didn't enjoy Casals's recordings of Bach, and felt embarrassed about it in case this was a sign of ignorance. Wasn't Casals supposed to be the god of cello playing? The long lines of his phrasing seemed to skip over the rhetorical gestures of Bach's counterpoint, while his frequent emphatic pauses on notes disrupted the pulse. Casals's signature intonation system, an exaggerated version of Pythagorean intonation in which he deliberately pushed the third and seventh degrees of the major scale sharp, sounded unbearably forced. Later, in my string quartet days, I started wondering why Casals had insisted on this raised third/raised seventh intonation at all times, when another system might have worked better for chords. Just intonation, for example, in which the third degree of a major chord is deliberately made flatter rather than sharper, would have produced more harmonious results. Casals's recordings of other pieces – the great concertos, Romantic miniatures and so on – were incomparable. Why, then, did his Bach seem so artificial?

So it was with some satisfaction that I read the polemical musicologist Richard Taruskin's opinion of Casals's Bach. Taruskin didn't much like it either, writing "Resonance is the thing the Casals manner has always killed." To him, Casals's tone was "deliberately scratchy, ugly, effortful."[23] (Oh my God, *thank you*.) I reflected on all the Casals-influenced recordings of the mid-twentieth century that I'd listened to. Though I revered the great mid-century cellists Casals, Pierre Fournier, André Navarra, and Paul Tortelier for their supreme mastery of cello playing, I no longer wanted to listen to their Bach. I didn't want to hear Bach's rhetoric steamrolled into long slurs. I didn't want ponderous Sarabandes. I didn't want operatic vibrato, multi-note chords executed like gunshots, or any of the other overplayed tropes of the twentieth century. This musical dialect no longer held meaning.

When I told Alexander Vassilievich of my guilty dislike of mid-century Bach playing, he handed me the second of Anner Bylsma's two recordings and told me to come back when I'd listened to it several times. Sitting cross-legged on my bed with my Discman, the facsimile of Anna Magdalena Bach's copy, and a pounding heart, I realized I – we – could never go back to Casals's Bach. Bylsma, playing on gut strings with a Baroque bow, made quicksilver magic of Bach's language and gesture. He gave the Preludes a sense of architecture that was missing from older interpretations, and the dance movements sounded not like a herd of elephants but like the gallant courtiers of the king's ballroom. Back in Alexander Vassilievich's office, I effused "I've been longing for this all my life."

When Alexander Vassilievich bought Bylsma's book *Bach, the Fencing Master*,[24] he excitedly shared it with me. In reproducing parts of Anna Magdalena Bach's copy and adding his own annotations, Bylsma showed that we could and should take eighteenth-century bowing conventions seriously. His recordings of the Cello Suites put this conviction into practice. They weren't so much a breath of fresh air as an entire oxygen tank. His playing was so remarkably free of built-up layers of twentieth-century overplaying that in his hands, the Cello Suites sounded like different pieces. In carefully observing Anna Magdalena's manuscript, he had formed an interpretation that sounded as if he were making up the music on the spot.

Anner Bylsma set the stage for other cellists who sought to interpret Bach through reimagining the musical languages and performance practices of the eighteenth century. His Prelude from the Second Cello Suite contains a convincing improvisation over the last five chords, and we can hear in many subsequent recordings that other cellists followed his lead. Some of these players are stalwarts of the historically informed performance movement, but others who aren't primarily "historical" players show his influence too.

I was almost afraid to ask Alexander Vassilievich what he thought of the 1995 recording of the Cello Suites by his mentor Mstislav Rostropovich, but when I did he smiled. "Mstislav Leopoldovich said he decided to record Bach when he completely changed his interpretations from before," he told me. But Mirandochka, I have listened to them and they are *exactly the same*."

*

Our conversations about Bach were interrupted one day when I showed up at my lesson time to find a note pinned to his office door. The Ivashkins had had to leave abruptly for Russia because their great friend, the composer Alfred Schnittke, had died. When they got back to New Zealand a couple of weeks later, Alexander Vassilievich looked much older than his fifty years, the lines of loss and grief written on his pale face.

"Were you sorry to leave Russia again?" I asked him, knowing that he had only emigrated in the first place because of the unbearable political pressure on musicians in the former Soviet Union.

"No, I am always glad to return to New Zealand," came the reply. "I like Christchurch. I hope to die in Christchurch."

I thought Christchurch was stuffy and Wellington far superior. "But Alexander Vassilievich," I said, "how could you tell whether you were dead or alive in a place like Christchurch?"

That got him to smile again for the first time, that snaggle-toothed but luminous grin of his. "Little witch," he said affectionately. "*Vhy* you are not practicing? You must practice."

Soon after arriving back, Alexander Vassilievich presented a concert in memory of Alfred Schnittke in Christchurch. Last on the program was Sergei Prokofiev's unfinished Cello Concertino, for which Schnittke had written a cadenza. The cadenza itself was unfinished, and it had fallen to Alexander Vassilievich to compile one according to Schnittke's wishes. The result was a composite of one of Schnittke's quasi-mystical cello solos and a rewritten version of the viola da gamba solo from Bach's *St. John Passion*. "It is from the aria about the last words of Christ," Alexander Vassilievich told me. Reviewers of his biography of Schnittke had criticized him for attributing what they called "Christ-like irreproachability" to his friend, but Alexander Vassilievich really did believe Schnittke to be irreproachable. At the concert, when the moment of the cadenza came, Alexander Vassilievich's trademark intense vibrato died away to almost nothing as he began Bach's melody. His face was ghostly pale, like an effigy of a medieval saint, and his glasses kept sliding down his nose. The melodic line dropped relentlessly downwards, downwards, like slow tears, and I felt my own tears running down my face. How I loved him then, this magnificent, sad man, my musical father.

II. ALLEMANDE

When you spend a great deal of your life walking around airport terminals with a cello on your back, you meet amiable strangers who want to talk to you about it. Sometimes they tell you that they've always wanted to play the cello. "Why don't you start?" I ask them. "It's never too late."

"Oh no," they demur, "I don't have time. I don't have the money. I'm not musical. In fact, I'm tone deaf."

Other times, I cringe when yet another jovial elderly man bellows "Have you got a dead body in there?" or "Bet you wish you played the piccolo!"

I always want to narrow my eyes and snarl back "Well, aren't you amusing and original!" I cannot do this, of course, because I am a New Zealander and therefore too repressed to shout at senior citizens, so I smile weakly and move on.

The other classic is "Bet you can't get that under your chin." To which I could actually respond "That's what *you* think, buddy."

One of the biggest surprises to me on my mid-life journey through the Bach Cello Suites was the realization that my definition of a cello and Bach's might be radically different. The cello of Bach's day might have been nothing like our modern conception of what a cello is and how you play it. Size, number of strings, string tunings, instrument hold, and bow hold – none of them might correspond to what we do now. In fact, Bach's contemporaries really might have put their cellos under their chins.

Stringed instruments in in early eighteenth-century Europe were still evolving, and varied greatly in size, stringing, nomenclature, and manner of playing, It would be many years before they were standardized. We know that Bach himself owned instruments that he called *violoncelli* (violoncello being the cello's full name), because an inventory after his death recorded two, plus something called a *bassetgen* that might have been a cello too.[25] What were they like? How big were they, and what were their string tunings? Did Bach, a fine violinist and violist, play them himself? Or did he have them on hand for a side gig in instrument rentals? Like so much else to do with the Cello Suites, we can't say with certainty.

In Bach's compositions, he is known to have specified two types of cellos. For the Cello Suites and numerous ensemble works, he asks for "violoncello," and in several of his cantatas he calls for a "violoncello piccolo," meaning "small cello."[26] In the Fifth Cello Suite, he specifies the string tuning C-G-D-G (as opposed to the usual C-G-D-A), and in the Sixth, the addition of a high E-string. There is no other clue to tell us the size of the instrument he was expecting to be used or how you might play it. Was it the same small instrument he used for his cantatas, or something else altogether? Frustratingly for us, Bach never wrote down a definition of what "cello" meant for him and his colleagues.

Fortunately, a source not a million miles from him did. Bach's contemporary Johann Mattheson (1681–1764), in addition to being a composer, singer, harpsichordist, critic, journalist, lexicographer, and sometime lawyer, was a prolific writer on all manner of useful topics, including the cello. (He also nearly killed George Frideric Handel in a swordfight over who was going to play the harpsichord at an opera gig, but luckily for history, a large button on Handel's coat obstructed Mattheson's sword and the two went back to being the best of friends.) In Mattheson's entertainingly opinionated book *Das Neu-eröffnete Orchestre* (1713), he offered this intriguing definition: "The outstanding violoncello, the *bassa viola* and *viola di spalla* are small bass violins in comparison to the larger ones with five or six strings, upon which you can do all sorts of things, variations and ornaments, more easily than on large machines. The *viola di spalla* or shoulder viola makes a great effect in the accompaniment, because it projects strongly and can express the notes purely. A bassline can never be brought out more distinctly and clearly than on this instrument. It is attached to the chest with a band and thrown on the right shoulder, so it has nothing to stop or prevent its resonance in the least."[27]

See? You *can* get it under your chin.

Then there's the matter of the *viola pomposa*, which disappointingly doesn't mean "pompous viola." A few of Bach's early biographers repeated a story that Bach himself invented this instrument, reportedly a sort of small shoulder-cello or large viola.[28] This sounds like a neat solution to the problem, except that the story might not be true. In another of the perplexing mysteries surrounding this topic, Bach himself never used the term in his scores or correspondence.

The only thing we can be sure of is that in the 1720s, the cello was still a newish instrument, a low-voiced member of the violin family that had only appeared midway through the previous century. The people who made them and played them still hadn't quite settled on its name yet, as we can see from glancing at the early manuscripts of the Cello Suites. While Anna Magdalena Bach calls it a *violoncello*, the manuscript by Johann Peter Kellner says *viola de basso*, a bass viola. He wasn't confusing it with a modern-day viola, and neither should we: lots of instruments of the violin family were called violas. The bass-voiced member of the family was called a *violone*, or "big viola," and scholars have never unanimously agreed on exactly what that was either.[29] A big cello? A small double bass? A bass viol? Or something else entirely? Reading the work of warring musicologists on this subject always fills me with an impish desire to push them all into a closet, lock the door, and announce "All right, you lot, you're staying in there until you've sorted it out."

Since the suffix "-cello" means "little" in Italian, the word "violoncello" would appear to mean "a little big viola,"[30] to the delight of modern-day viola players. There's convincing evidence from several countries that bassline players used big violas or small cellos held violin-style with the aid of a strap, and that the modern cello-hold was a later innovation.

It wasn't until 1741 that we can be reasonably sure of what musicians meant when they used the term "violoncello," or how they expected it to be held and bowed. In the engraved frontispiece to his confidently-titled method book *Theoretical and Practical Method for Learning the Violoncello to Perfection in a Short Time*, Michel Corrette sits grandly astride his cello in a beribboned wig and frock-coat in front of what appears to be an erupting volcano. Having presumably survived the lava flow, Corrette offers these instructions on holding the instrument: "To play the cello well, you must sit on a chair...you must place the cello between the legs, hold the neck in the left hand and lean a little to the left, and hold the bow in the right hand... Not only is this posture the most beautiful, it's also the best for playing difficult passages."[31] On the next page, he gives instructions for an "overhand" bow-hold comparable to that for the violin.[32] If none of this sounds strange, it's because it's approximately what we do today. By 1756, Leopold Mozart, new father to little Wolfgang Amadeus and an early prototype for helicopter parenting, was able to state "In the past, [the cello] had five strings; now you only play it with four. It is the most common instrument for playing basslines, and although there are some bigger cellos, there are smaller ones."[33] He continued "These days the cello is also held between the legs,"[34] implying that this was a recent change from an older practice.

At the time Papa Mozart was writing, Bach had only been dead six years. A lot had happened in the decades since the Cello Suites.

The fast rise of the cello happened at the same time as the slow decline of another instrument with "viola" in its name, the viola da gamba or bass viol. Being approximately cello-shaped, this ancient and noble instrument is often mistaken for an ancestor of the cello. Since the cello is a member of the violin family, however, it's more or less unrelated, even if their histories run side-by-side for a while. Placed next to each other, the instruments look markedly different. The cello's shoulders are rounded, the viola da gamba's sloped. The cello has four strings, the viola da gamba six or seven. The cello's bridge is rounded, while the viola da gamba bridge is flatter, making it easier to play multi-note chords. Like a guitar, the viola da gamba has frets, which to a cellist looks a lot like cheating. Unlike the cello bow, the viola da gamba bow is held underhand, like some modern-day double bass bows.[35] There had once been viols in all shapes and sizes too, but by Bach's lifetime the brighter, louder violin family had superseded the smaller ones, leaving only the bass viol in common usage.

This left composers with a choice of two competing instruments for basslines, or more, if you count the mysterious violone. An interesting social dynamic surrounding both instruments led to a class-laced controversy about which was better. The violin family didn't just have associations with dancing masters, but also with tinkers and ne'er-do-wells at the very bottom of the class hierarchy. (Imagine the Pied Piper, only with a violin.) The viola da gamba, by contrast, was the instrument of upper-class amateurs, including Bach's boss Prince Leopold. Bach composed for both instruments, and often made a viola da gamba part for the prince to play in ensemble music such as the famous Brandenburg Concertos.[36] At this transitional point in music history, plenty of musicians played both instruments before the eventual decline of the viola da gamba. Michel Corrette's treatise on cello playing even offers advice for those making the switch to cello: "For those who play the viol, they will have more trouble in the beginning because the bowing is opposite…but a bit of practice easily surmounts the difficulty, for even people who play the viol will have some advantage with the cello, being already in the habit of playing bassline instruments. Three or four months with a good teacher will sort it out."[37] How many viola da gambists, I wonder, shed a few tears as they kissed the carved scroll of their viols for one last time before putting it away in the case and consigning it to dust and history?

Others weren't giving up without a fight. As late as 1740, an enraged French lawyer and amateur viola da gambist called Hubert Le Blanc published a polemic called *Defense of the Bass Viol Against the Enterprises of the Violin and the Pretensions of the Cello*. Determined to set people straight, Le Blanc compiled a lengthy list of all the famous and important people who had praised the viola da gamba. Another section enumerates the godlike qualities of top viola da gamba composers Jean-Baptiste Lully, Marin Marais, and Antoine de Forqueray, though Le Blanc heaps scorn upon Arcangelo Corelli for his vulgarity in composing for the violin. "The elegance of musical discourse," he hectors, "comes from making the thinning of the sound follow a reinforcement, like the well-formed leg of a lady, which the Queen of Navarre noticed has such power over the heart of the man."[38] (Blimey!) This isn't even the weirdest bit. In the second part of the book, the increasingly apoplectic author casts the violin and the viola da gamba as characters in a bizarrely racist role-play in which "Sultan Violin, a little runt and a pygmy" has the gall to challenge the "monarchy" of the viola da gamba.[39] The reader is left feeling as if the violin family have committed regicide.

In a way, they had. Like the French aristocracy, the viola da gamba was on the way out, and Le Blanc knew it. The cello was simply louder and more robust, which you wanted if you were going to play in any space larger than a small chamber. The gamba-playing Prince Leopold must have known this, because he employed players of both instruments in his court ensemble, a cellist called Christian Bernhard Linigke and a gambist called Christian Ferdinand Abel. Both men have been named as possible first performers of the Cello Suites, but yet again, we don't know for sure. All that's for sure is that for now, cello and gamba were – uneasily, perhaps – coexisting. Bach's Cello Suites, six long and difficult pieces for a solo instrument that can generate its own melody *and* multi-voiced harmony, might be unprecedented in cello repertoire, but we can see and hear in the music of the past how much they owed to the ancient tradition of viola da gamba playing.

*

The year I was fourteen, a film called *Tous les matins du monde* came to a film festival in Wellington. It had been made some years previously, but like most things from abroad it took a while to make it to New Zealand. Because it was about music and because I was studying French at school, my parents decided it would be educational for me to see it. Together with a small group of my friends and their parents, we made an evening of it. I'm not joking when I say that this film is one of the reasons I decided to become a professional cellist.

The great French actor Gérard Dépardieu starred as the seventeenth-century gambist and composer Marin Marais, with his dishy son Guillaume as the younger version in flashbacks. Set in a spectacularly verdant part of rural France, the film tells the story of brash Marais, the son of a shoemaker, who ambitiously desires to break into the music scene at the French court. He seeks the advice of the reclusive Monsieur de Sainte-Colombe, a crotchety, aristocratic widower who wants nothing to do with him. Luckily Sainte-Colombe's older daughter takes pity on Marais, gives him a few gamba lessons, and helps him eavesdrop on Sainte-Colombe practicing in the garden shed. Seduction, betrayal, tragedy, and redemption follow, all with a soundtrack of viola da gamba music by both composers.

The voluptuous melancholy of Marais's *The Dreaming Girl*, Sainte-Colombe's *Tears*, and Marais's *Tombeau*, played gorgeously by Jordi Savall and the instrumental ensemble Hespèrion XXI, moved my heart in a way music had seldom done. This was also absolutely the sexiest film I and my friends and I had ever been allowed to watch, which was slightly awkward given that we were all sitting between our parents, passing a bucket of popcorn back and forth. Nevertheless, we all clamored to be allowed to see it again, chaperones or no chaperones, since the music had enthralled us all.

For my birthday, my father went to the Parsons Bookshop on Lambton Quay and special-ordered the *Tous les matins du monde* soundtrack, which had to be imported from France at great expense. I was thrilled and listened to the disc every dark winter morning as I tugged on the cashmere tights, check skirt, and scratchy blue sweater of my school uniform. After that, I took my cello out of its case and practiced for two hours before school. After school, I hurried home to get another two hours in before dinner and homework. Gone were the days when my mother had to shake me awake at five in the morning and shout at me to practice. If music had once been a chore, the biggest and least optional component of my mother's expectations for me, it was now something I loved for its own sake. It had becoming compelling, addictive, fascinating. "It's music or nothing," I announced at the family dinner table one evening. "I'm going to be a cellist whatever it takes."

My mother beamed.

I didn't actually want to switch to viola da gamba. I'd put too much into the cello for that, and besides, you couldn't play the viola da gamba in orchestras or string quartets, two of my favorite activities. No, what I wanted to do was make my cello sound like a viola da gamba when I played Bach. By now, I'd learned the first three Cello Suites, and I set about trying to play them with some of the marvelous poetry and rhythmic freedom I heard in Jordi Savall's recordings. I wanted to imitate the plangent tone of his viola da gamba, a sound that at once suggested despair and sensuality. Bach's Second Cello Suite, being in a minor key, seemed like a good vehicle for it. I experimented with a straight, pure tone without a trace of vibrato. I tried "releasing" the bow on the string after the initial articulation of a note, rather than the *sostenuto* bowing I'd been taught. Discarding the choppy modern-day "two-and-two" technique of breaking three- and four-note chords, I broke them instead in exaggerated rolling arpeggios. I wasn't specifically trying for historically-informed performance practice, though as the daughter of two musicians I was familiar with the concept. What I was seeking was the heightened expressiveness that had so moved me when I watched *Tous les matins du monde*.

A year later the great Jordi Savall came to play at the New Zealand International Festival of the Arts along with his wife, the soprano Montserrat Figueras, plus Hespèrion XXI and the vocal group La Capella Reial de

Catalunya. My mother got tickets for the two of us to go and see them perform in the Wellington Town Hall. It was a good thing she booked well in advance, because it was sold out. We had front-row seats next to Rosie Salas, the choir teacher from my school and a friend of the family. Rosie was as excited as I was. "This is the chance of a lifetime," she told me.

Up close, Savall's personality seemed to fill the whole hall. He and Figueras, clad in long robes, appeared to be not quite of this age, but larger-than-life figures, a king and queen from ancient times. I'd expected viols, but not harps and drums too. The program featured Catalonian, Spanish, and Italian music from the sixteenth and seventeenth centuries. It was the first time I'd heard any of it, and one piece in particular made me feel as if I'd been stabbed in the heart. It was Claudio Monteverdi's *Lamento della ninfa*. With her angelically lovely, almost girlish voice, black hair cascading over frail shoulders, and a pale oval face, Figueras didn't just sing Monteverdi's nymph, she *was* the nymph. Alongside her, three male singers punctuated her distraught outbursts with sympathetic interjections of *dicea*, "she said," and *miserella, più no no*, "You poor girl, oh no." Alongside them on his bass viol, Savall sounded the hypnotic descending bassline of the passacaglia, A-G-F-E. Those relentless pacing footsteps, the endless circular repetitions of the harmonic pattern, showed the nymph's prison of heartbreak more than any picture could. *Make my love come back as he used to be.* I might be only fifteen, but I'd felt the nymph's agonies of love and rejection in teenage break-ups and the pain of being the only girl in my class not to have a date to the school ball. *You will never receive from those lips/Kisses as sweet as mine/ Nor softer.* I had a sudden flash of realization that Monteverdi *knew me*. His music was about my life. I felt my eyes fill and I was embarrassed, but when I sneaked a glance at Rosie she was weeping openly.

Afterwards, the audience leapt to their feet and cheered uproariously, a thing Wellington's urbane audiences did not often do. We called them back to the stage again and again. One encore wasn't enough – they ended up doing thirteen.

Such a concert could not be forgotten quickly. I couldn't stop thinking about how Monteverdi's *Lamento* and how it had shaken me to my core, and I felt a passionate yearning to make music that could do *that* to the audience. I found myself coming back again and again to Bach's D minor Allemande, rejoicing in the opening D minor chord and cascades of descending sixteenth notes in two-note slurs that followed it. I loved the little vignette in F major, like a hope that so soon would be crushed by D minor again. When you weren't in a hurry – I imagined gambists never hurried anywhere – it was positively blissful to negotiate your way around the detours and diversions on the way to a modulation into the dominant key of A. Those dissonant double-stops just crying out to be resolved back into consonances – and the agonizing wait for that resolution! And then just as you expect resolution onto A, a surprise D-sharp and a sort of flourishing cadenza – Bach always keeps us guessing. Finally, you're allowed your cadence into A, but Bach can't help himself, he has to decorate that too, with a kind of mini-cadenza that takes place after the cadence. The second half is rather longer than the first, which is usual in Bach's binary dances. This is because once you've modulated to a secondary key, you have to get yourself back again, and it's much harder to return home than it was to leave in the first place. A metaphor for life, perhaps.

*

Almost two decades later, I learn that I wasn't wrong to associate Bach's Allemande from the Second Cello Suite with the viola da gamba and Marin Marais. In David Ledbetter's engrossing book *Unaccompanied Bach: Performing the Solo Works*, I read about the clear intertextual relationship between Bach's Allemande and Marais's Allemande and Double in D Minor from his first book of *Pièces de Viole*. But while Marais's Allemande is "fundamentally melodic in intention," Ledbetter observes that Bach's is "more in the sonata than the dance tradition."[40] Sonata is an Italian word, and in the eighteenth century it referred to an instrumental work, such as the church and chamber sonatas of Arcangelo Corelli – a known influence on Bach's music. Bach was not so much eclectic as sponge-like, absorbing everything he heard, bringing together French dances and Italian sonatas and his own native German traditions into this miraculous amalgam, the Cello Suites.

As I relearn the Allemande, I start thinking about the viola da gamba again. I've played Baroque cellos in early music ensembles at the universities I attended, but never a gamba, and the idea won't leave me alone. Sometimes ideas are persistent for a reason, because a mere few weeks later

I serendipitously find myself in possession of not one but two violas da gamba. Lois Blackburn, a retired string music education professor, calls me to ask if I'd like to buy her viola da gamba. She's about to move to another state and doesn't want to take all her instruments, so she's selling it cheaply.

"Would I!" I exclaim, grabbing my car keys.

The gamba is a six-stringer, well set up and ready to play. Lois shows me how to cradle the lower bouts of the instrument between my calves, and demonstrates the underhand bow-hold. I had always imagined that there would be a lot of crossover between cello and gamba technique and that it would be reasonably easy for me to pick up the gamba, but my first scratchy attempts teach me that this is an entirely different instrument. So much for Michel Corrette and his optimistic assurances.

"Don't worry, you'll figure it out," says Lois. "Think of it as a cello crossed with a double bass crossed with a guitar."

Little over a week later, another viola da gamba appears in my life. I'm practicing in my office when one of my undergraduates knocks on the door. He's a little out of breath and holding a very dusty instrument in a canvas case. "Dr. Wilson, I found this in the back corner of the music library behind a bunch of stuff. It looks sort of like a cello but it's not a cello. It has *frets* on it. Do you know what it is?"

We open up the case and I crow with laughter. "It never rains but it pours," I say. "It's a viola da gamba. I wonder who it belongs to."

I make inquiries, but nobody seems to know where it came from or who owns it. "Finders keepers," I say to myself, deciding that it's not stealing to store it in my office until someone claims it. (No one ever does.) It needs a good dusting, some new strings, and new hair on the bow, but is otherwise in good condition.

The students are fascinated with the violas da gamba. They're rural Pacific Northwest kids, good players but musically sheltered, and most haven't ever seen a professional opera or symphony concert. The viola da gamba is something they've only read about in books, so to have two to play with feels like Santa Claus has visited. All of our attempts are clumsy, though the double bassists have more success than the cellists since the string tunings and bow-hold are more like those of their instrument. I go off into a daydream about starting an early music ensemble here, remembering what fun it had been to play in one when I was a graduate student at the University of Texas. Why, we could write a grant to get a whole chest of viols – a soprano, an alto, and a tenor to go with the two bass ones – and we could play Renaissance music for viol consort. I go off into a daydream about a group of us in a circle with our viols, bathed in a glow of light on the stage of the university's Victorian Gothic auditorium, playing Henry Purcell's *Fantazias for the Viols* as the snow falls gently outside. Wouldn't it be bliss?

Before I can do any of this, however, I need to learn to play the thing, and my progress is slow. I acquire Alison Crum's excellent self-teaching guide *Play the Viol* and set about working through the instructions. As Michel Corrette warns us, the bowing is upside down, and I find this quite a mental shift. In modern string playing, the "down-bow rule" is one of those near-immutable playing conventions. The strong beats of the measure demand strong bow-strokes, so you use a down-bow, the pulling stroke where the arm comes away from the body. On weaker beats, you use the weaker up-bow, the pushing stroke that makes the arm come back to the body. Judy drummed the down-bow rule into me in childhood, and since then it's become as instinctive as breathing. Because the physical characteristics of the viola da gamba, its bow, and its bow-hold are so different from the cello, bowing goes in the opposite direction. It might be logical, but for a lifelong cellist, it's not at all intuitive.

My goal is to get good enough to play Bach's three sonatas for viola da gamba and harpsichord, but right now I can barely manage a scale. Aside from the maddening bow direction problem, the flatter bridge of the instrument means I constantly bump into wrong strings and fudge notes. Of course, the bridge is the very thing that allows for the sonorous chordal playing that I've always loved in the viola da gamba. It's a bit like strumming a chord on the guitar, but with a bow. Now if only I could manage to play in a way that's more elegant, less elephant.

I'm frustrated, but I tell myself what I tell students: that everyone is bad when they first attempt a new skill, and that it can be humbling to be bad at something for a while because it makes you break the skill down into manageable tasks and really understand how it works. "Failure is the wellspring of creativity," I say to the reflection in the studio mirror, using my best lady professor voice. Then I have to tune my viola da gamba again, because the wretched thing goes out of tune literally every ten seconds. "I can see why the cello won," I whisper nastily into the viola da gamba's peg-box, and it retaliates by making all the pegs pop at the same time.

III. COURANTE

My viola da gamba experiment becomes more than just a nerdy hobby when the opportunity arises to play it in public. My colleagues and I are preparing to perform Bach's *St. John Passion*, and I'm going to play the cello part throughout *and* the viola da gamba obbligato in *Es ist vollbracht*, the alto aria to which Ivashkin introduced me years before. For an ambitious project like this to work here in tiny Moscow, we need all hands on deck. Several local choirs will come in to bolster our university singers, and faculty members from both universities – the University of Idaho and Washington State University in Pullman, fifteen minutes away – will populate the small instrumental ensemble. Our vocal faculty will sing some of the solos, and guest artists will come to sing those we can't cover in-house.

I've been looking forward to this for a long time, because the *St. John Passion* is one of my favorite compositions by Bach. It's a sacred work, of course, but Bach's dramatic depiction of the confrontation between Jesus Christ and Pilate is almost operatic in scope. Playing continuo, the bassline accompaniment, will be fun but exhausting. In the arias and choruses, the cellist underscores the harmony while the harpsichordist fills out the chords. In recitatives, cellist and harpsichordist become a kind of punctuation for the singers. Having worked alongside my father many times now, I'm fairly adept at accompanying voices, and I can't wait to get started.

While practicing the *St. John* cello part is taking up a lot of my time, I'm still working my way through relearning the Cello Suites. With all the basslines going on in my brain, it seems appropriate to get started on the Courante from the Second Suite. Its opening features a highly characteristic Bach bassline, but that isn't immediately obvious to the listener, or to the player for that matter. It's an Italian Corrente in the literal sense of the word – running – and at first glance seems like a mass of dashing sixteenth notes.

Now that I've been living with Baroque basslines for so long, though, I find that it's getting easier to tease out the implied basslines in what on the surface looks like a mostly monophonic movement. David Ledbetter points out that the opening bassline of the Courante – D, C-sharp, D, B-flat, A – comes from another of Bach's compositions in D minor, the great Chaconne from the second Partita for solo violin. [41] Of course, the bassline doesn't keep repeating as it does in the Chaconne, otherwise it too would be called a Chaconne and not a Courante. Chaconnes are always a set of variations over a repeating ground bass, and if this sounds a lot like passacaglias, that's because Baroque composers sometimes used the two terms interchangeably. This greatly irritated certain twentieth-century scholars who liked musical forms to have specific names. The musicologist Susan McClary notes with a certain glee that "most seventeenth-century musicians cared much less about generic boundaries than do historians."[42]

The idea of a bassline in the Courante puts a different perspective on the movement for me. When I've played it before in my teens and twenties, its difficulty seemed like an annoying road-block, and truthfully, I skimped over it in practice, eager to move on to the passionate Sarabande. Now I want to take another look at the Chaconne, so I download Bach's autograph copies of the Sonatas and Partitas from the internet, listen to my favorite recording of the Sonatas and Partitas by the Baroque violinist Rachel Podger, and do some homework by looking up Chaconne form in *Grove's Dictionary.*

Soon I'm shaking my head in wonder that I've somehow managed to amass ten years of university education and actually played several Chaconnes without figuring out that a Chaconne is a dance. And not a polite courtly one either. Originally called the Chacona, it was another disreputable Spanish import from the New World, "like syphilis," as McClary helpfully points out.[43] If you wished to dance the wicked Chacona in sixteenth-century Spain, all you had to do was shout "Vida, vida, vida bona! Vida, vámonos á Chacona!" ("Life, life, good life! Life, let's go to Chacona!")[44] Thus summoned, everyone in the vicinity would rush towards you and gyrate to the seductive click of castanets. One castanet tended to lead to another, and this so scandalized the Pope that he banned the Chacona in 1615 for its "irredeemably infectious lasciviousness."[45]

In this way, the Chacona seems to have been the heir to the similarly shocking Sarabande. It was too late to suppress it, however, and no doubt the Pope ground his teeth and shook his head at the sheer impertinence of all the composers who immediately seized upon the Chacona as a musical form, writing Italian Ciacconas and French Chaconnes. By Bach's time the outrage had died down, of course. Reading about the Chacona's checkered history, however, makes me want to hear some earlier Chaconnes, and so I spend a pleasant few hours doing just that. I already know Monteverdi's *Zefiro torna*, a jaunty pastoral ode to the west wind, the coming of spring, and the attendant opportunities for illicit frolicking. Lully's *Amadis de Gaule* is new to me, and after reading about it in Susan McClary's delicious *Desire and Pleasure in Seventeenth-Century Music* I'm eager to listen to it. In this immensely complicated opera – plots, sub-plots, sorcerers, deities, demons, magic forests, and above all, ballet – the chivalric protagonist is one of Lully's many thinly-disguised suck-up portrayals of King Louis himself. The entire last scene is a long Chaconne where the assembled cast, repenting of their demonic ways, sing serenely in praise of love and making good decisions, implying perhaps that past ones had left something to be desired.

Possibly because I didn't realize a Chaconne was a dance, or because so many violinists play it so dolorously, I'd always thought of the Chaconne from the D minor Partita for violin as a solemn, churchy piece. There's also the matter of a myth that built up around it over the past couple of decades after a German musicologist named Helga Thoene claimed that Bach composed the Chaconne as a *tombeau* for his first wife, Maria Barbara Bach.[46] As evidence, Thoene pointed to what she believed to be excerpts from Bach chorales, spellings of Bach's own name in musical letters, and numerical symbolism embedded within the notes of the Chaconne. Her imaginative theories might have remained in obscurity if the violinist Christoph Poppen and the Hilliard Ensemble hadn't seized on them. Together, they recorded a bestselling disc called *Morimur* (*We Will Die*) in which movements of the D minor Partita appear in a kind of mash-up with rhythmically altered chorale excerpts. The musicianship of the performers makes for a highly persuasive interpretation, and Thoene's conspiracy theory caught on like wildfire among violinists and Bach fans. The only problem was that Thoene's analyses are, well, a bit far-fetched. In a thought-provoking essay for the *L.A. Review of*

Books, Michael Markham points to the *tombeau* story as a kind of musical *Da Vinci Code*, a good yarn that appealed to the popular imagination but did not, alas, stand up to scrutiny.[47] Another scholar, Benjamin Shute, likewise rejects Thoene's work as unprovable, but is unable to resist speculating that the Italian-ish title Bach gave his Sonatas and Partitas, *Sei Solo* (usually corrected in printed editions to *Sei Soli* or Six Solos), might in proper Italian mean You Are Alone. Is the grieving widower Bach talking mournfully to himself in the second person? Or does he address the lonely figure of Christ on the cross?[48]

I hate to be a killjoy, but sometimes I think Bach was just bad at Italian.

Reflecting that Chaconnes might then suggest equal measures of sorrow and desire, I turn back to the Courante of the Second Cello Suite. Since we don't know which Bach composed first, the Cello Suites or the Sonatas and Partitas for violin, it's impossible to say whether he's alluding to the violin Chaconne in the cello Courante. What's more important is making the bassline clear in the harmonic texture. In the past I've always tried to take the Courante at breakneck speed, and I still think it should run quickly. The structural framework of having a bassline to refer to makes this a lot easier, however, and I'm able to invent all kinds of exercises to teach myself to play it cleanly at high speed.

All this athletic cello playing stands me in good stead for our monster four-hour *St. John Passion* rehearsals. We have several hours of music to prepare, all of it complicated. While the woodwind players and even the upper strings can sometimes be excused from rehearsals of the movements they don't play, the harpsichordist Elena and I have to be there for every one of the forty-odd movements. It's physically and intellectually exhausting.

The first thing that happens is that we realize there won't be enough room on the university auditorium's stage for me to have a cello and a viola da gamba at my disposal, or at least, not if there is to be a second and third cellist. Since a second cellist is essential and a third very desirable, I regretfully decide to play the viola da gamba solo for *Es ist vollbracht* on my cello. Remembering my teenage experiments in gamba-esque tone colors in the Second Suite, I decide to play *Es ist vollbracht* without vibrato, placing my bow far away from the bridge for a spectral, *flautando* effect. I meet with Lexa, my mezzo-soprano colleague, to decide what we're going to do with the aria. The sheer emotional beauty of her voice astounds me, and I see right away that it wouldn't work to attempt to imitate it on the cello. "What do you think about having you as the human voice, and me as the inhuman one?" I ask her. "You get the almighty word, and I get the thing that words can't say. You can be the one who's gorgeous and sorrowful, and I'll be like the otherworldly ghost voice." Lexa tolerates my weird ideas with equanimity, and we rehearse together for an hour or so before heading to the auditorium.

Playing the *St. John* is an all-absorbing experience. Far from being just accompaniment, the instrumental ensemble are just as much part of the drama as the singers. The very beginning is darkly menacing, the cello's relentless bassline of repeated Gs underpinning a swirling, brooding figure in the low registers of the violins. Storm clouds are gathering, there's trouble. Flute and oboe lines appear, criss-crossing each other's middle registers in chains of dissonances.

The choir enters and the storm breaks loose as their voices call us three times into the presence of God. *Herr. Herr. HERR!* This isn't the harmless, Jesus-is-my-boyfriend God of contemporary worship songs, but a fierce and terrible God, the one who sends floods and plagues and locusts. It's one of the most awe-inspiring moments in all of classical music, and playing it the hairs stand up on the back of my neck every time. Looking around at the faces of my colleagues in the front stands of the string section, I can see they feel it too.

One of the things that surprises first-time *St. John Passion* listeners is that Jesus isn't actually the main character. That role falls to the Evangelist, a high tenor voice. It is he who declaims the Gospel of John in recitative, punctuated with bass notes by yours truly. This keeps the narrative going in between choruses, arias, and the drama of the trial. Jesus, sung by a low-voiced man, is actually a relatively small role, considerably smaller than that of the disciple Simon Peter. Perhaps the role is less prominent because of the inevitability of what we, the audience, know is about to happen. When the mobs attack Jesus with weapons and torches, he already knows the answer to his question "Whom do you seek?" His recitatives tend to be short sentences, and he has no aria of his own. Arias by the soloists – soprano, alto, tenor, and bass – work as a kind of emotional commentary on the catastrophic events of the last days of Jesus's life.

Part Two of the *Passion* starts with the trial, where Bach's setting of the dialogue between Pilate and Jesus virtually sparks with electricity between the antagonists. Accompanying the extended recitative sections is one of the hardest gigs I've ever had as a cellist, and I can't lose concentration for a second. The rhythmically flexible nature of human speech means that the singers must be free to slow down and speed up as they see fit. Elena and I joke that you have to keep one eye on the vocal score and the other eye on the conductor as if your life depends on it, going slightly cross-eyed in the process. While I love the fast-paced, exciting nature of recitative, I'm also terrified I'm going to mess up. Singers are a headstrong bunch, and chasing them around a recitative can be like the world's scariest game of Whack-A-Mole. You absolutely can't get lost, because you'll never get back on again. Worse, you could also mess up the singer, who is the center of the audience's attention and therefore the most vulnerable person on the stage. To prepare, I've studied the score for hours, translating all the German in the margins so that I can imbue every note I play with the emotion and meaning of the words. It's hard to practice the notes of recitatives without a singer present, so I attempt to sing them myself while I play. It's hilariously untuneful, and I doubt my opera singer father would be impressed, but by doing it this way I learn the rhythms and nuances of the German well enough that I can stay on top of my game in rehearsal. I don't think recitative will ever be a stress-free activity, but at least I feel that I know what's going on well enough to fix anything that goes amiss.

It gets to the point that I start dreaming in recitative. Not the *St. John* recitatives exactly, but some strange hybrid of the Evangelist and my own anxiety dreams about missing trains and exams. I play the opening bass note, and the Evangelist sings *Und Pilatus sprach*…and then Pilate informs me indifferently that *Die Prüfung war um neun Uhr. Du bist zu spät!* As I play the cadence from F to B-flat, my framed degree certificates fall off the walls and crash to the ground.

*

I'm laughing about this on the phone with a friend as I walk in my front door late at night after rehearsal. Just then another call comes in from a British number I don't know. "I'll call you back," I tell my friend, and answer the caller.

It's Rebecca, a cellist friend from my student days in New Zealand and Britain. She is calling with the horrible news that Alexander Vassilievich Ivashkin is dead.

IV. SARABANDE

If there's a more poignant musical depiction of human remorse than the aria *Ach, mein Sinn*, I don't know it. Just as his teacher foretold, Peter has denied Christ three times before cockcrow. "Then Peter thought of the words of Jesus," the Evangelist tells us, "and went out, and wept bitterly." In another of the paradoxical sacred-secular pairings that are everywhere in Bach's music, *Ach, mein Sinn* is set in the form of a Sarabande.

*

The only inkling I had of Ivashkin's illness is a puzzling text four months ago from a mutual acquaintance in London who wonders if I've been in touch with him recently. No one's heard from him, and he's canceled all his concerts. Alexander Vassilievich is the sort of person who wouldn't cancel a concert if his arms fell off. "Everyone says he's really ill. Do you know anything?"

I'm cold all over. I rush to the computer and start an email. "Dear Alexander Vassilievich, they tell me you are very ill. I wish you all the best for a quick recovery. I want you to know how much I love and admire you. Miranda." As soon as I click send, I regret it. How would it feel to receive a letter like this, a virtual declaration that someone thinks you're about to drop dead? I go hot and cold with shame.

I call my great friend Rachel Johnston, another ex-Ivashkin student and cellist of the Australian String Quartet, to see if she knows anything. She tries to talk me down from the ledge. "Look, it's probably just an embarrassing little case of prostate cancer or something," she reasons. "Practically all men get prostate cancer. I've heard that if you have to get cancer, that's the one to get. They say it's painless and it's an easy fix. He just doesn't want to talk about it. Would you, if you were a man? I'm sure he'll be as good as new in no time."

"You're probably right," I agree.

Alexander Vassilievich emails me back a week or so later. He carbon copies Natasha, which is strange because Natasha isn't really one for email. The message is one line. "Thank you, my Mirandochka!"

The cause of death, Natasha tells me later, is complications from pancreatic cancer. Pancreatic cancer is not painless. It is not an easy fix.

*

All I want to do when I hear Rebecca's awful news is to fall into my husband's arms and heave with sobs, but I can't do this yet. Alexander Vassilievich's death will be in the British newspapers in the morning, and we want to make sure our friends know so they don't have to find out about it on social media. Through tears, Rebecca and I put together a long list of the "Ivashkin diaspora," the generation of New Zealand cellists taught by Alexander Vassilievich and Natasha during their ten years at the University of Canterbury. There are so many of them, and they are scattered all over the world. We agree that Rebecca will track down the Canterbury graduates in Britain and Europe, and I'll find the ones in America, Asia, New Zealand, and Australia. We say some loving words to one another, and hang up.

I have never grieved before.

In the morning the light is far too bright. I have to teach a class at half past eight, but I'm so nauseated with grief that I decide to call in sick. How can I teach students when I'm like this? How can I even speak? I can't talk. I can't go. I will stay at home in bed and cry.

No I won't. This is not how Alexander Vassilievich Ivashkin would behave. Alexander Vassilievich would show up and do his best no matter how much he was suffering.

First I have to dig my car out of the snow that has fallen overnight, and then it won't start. I curse and smack both hands against the steering wheel, which hurts. Out of options, I have to make the long walk to the university in snow boots. It's freezing but brilliantly sunny, and all the world looks white and shiny and new.

I can remember nothing of the day's lectures. Somehow my body does what it's supposed to.

It's getting dark by the time I leave to walk home. About halfway along the creekside trail, I realize suddenly that I've gone the wrong way. Sean doesn't like me walking this way at night. Not so much because of shady characters, we don't really have those in Moscow, but because young moose sometimes venture into Paradise Creek. If you get between a baby moose and its mother, you can expect to be trampled. I don't know whether I should go back or onwards. I sit down on a park bench and weep.

Back in the house, with the aid of a sleeping pill, I finally get some sleep, but I dream that Alexander Vassilievich is trying to call me and I can't get to the phone in time. I wake up sobbing. I don't want to wake Sean, so I go down to the basement and sit on the sofa with a blanket. "I'm angry at you, Alexander Vassilievich," I say out loud. "Why didn't you give me the chance to say goodbye to you properly?"

Everything is silent.

What would he say to me right now?

I know the answer right away. "And *vhat?*" He never learned the expression "So what?" correctly and I never had the heart to tell him.

"I don't know what to do, Alexander Vassilievich. I don't know how to be."

"Oh, Mirandochka. *Vhy* you are asking me this stupid question? You must practice. Really."

Yes, I must practice.

*

The Sarabande to the Second Suite draws more heavily on viola da gamba tradition than any of the other movements. One of the ways is the characteristic Baroque texture of *style brisé,* the broken style. In pieces for viola da gamba, lute, and harpsichord in particular, composers sometimes arpeggiated chords in jagged, unpredictable order instead of sounding them simultaneously or in a more routine arpeggio. Bach's D minor Sarabande is such an extreme example of this brokenness that I can almost imagine it as a conversation between two violas da gamba, one playing the heart-searing melodic line, the other gloomily intoning the bass notes.

Bei der Welt ist gar kein Rat, und im Herzen stehn die Schmerzen... "There is no counsel in all of the world, and in my heart stays the pain..."

"Honey," Sean says, after patiently listening to me play the Sarabande about twelve times over, "is this really helping anything?"

I consider the question, and decide that it is.

*

Musical works often contain marked similarities to other works, even when we aren't sure whether the composers are aware of each other. Given that Bach's *St. John Passion* was still unpublished at the time Beethoven wrote his A major cello sonata in 1809, how then can we explain the sudden appearance of the viola da gamba theme from *Es ist vollbracht* in the middle of the first movement? Under the circumstances, it's practically impossible that Beethoven could be quoting Bach. And yet, we want it to be possible, so we start reasoning with ourselves that the themes are far too similar for it to be a coincidence. Excitable now, we start asking what this might mean for an interpretation of the sonata. What was Beethoven doing in 1809? Let's see, profoundly deaf and perpetually unlucky in love. Under these circumstances, of course he'd like to quote a Bach aria about the last words of Christ on the cross. We imagine the rumpled Beethoven sitting bolt upright at his desk and knocking over his inkstand as he shouts "I know! I'll cryptically quote a theme that no one in my own time knows yet, so that two hundred years from now, people who really understand me will know the loneliness I feel and the solace I take in Christ's suffering. It will make them play my sonata very passionately, just as I want it. Yet another brilliant idea, Ludwig!"

It's a great story. It's also probably not true. I kind of wish it were.

Bach's Sarabande from the Second Suite appears to have a few quotations in it too. More than one scholar has pointed to a very similar Sarabande in D minor for solo viola da gamba by one Monsieur Demachy, whose first name hasn't made it to modern times. Mark M. Smith finds an apparent quotation by Bach of a sonata of 1712 for two violins, two violas da gamba, and continuo by François Couperin. Intriguingly titled *La Sultane*, Couperin's sonata laments the death of the wife of a Turkish Sultan, Turkish music being all the rage in France at the time. Smith further contends that Couperin wrote *La Sultane* to mourn the death of the young Dauphine Marie-Adélaïde, and that Bach deliberately quoted it in the Sarabande to the Second Suite as a *tombeau* for his own first wife Maria Barbara.[49]

The desire to look for secrets between the notes of a score is hard to resist. I try to keep an academic's skepticism, but I catch myself at it all the time. How often have I played Bach's music imagining intrigues in the

Prince's ballroom, or the lonely figure of a viola da gambist looking out over a tangled garden? The question perhaps shouldn't be why we feel the need to invent stories, but how on earth we could restrain ourselves from doing so when music is so stirring to our emotions. It's how we performers keep ourselves excited about music during the long slog of daily practice. It's how we form interpretations that we hope may move the hearts of the audience. Cellists may not ply our trade with words, but we're storytellers all the same.

*

I've barely eaten or slept in days and I have to perform the *St. John*. I will be playing for two and a half hours with no breaks and people are counting on me, but I'm so, so tired. In the bathroom underneath the university auditorium, I peer at my panda-eyed reflection in the mirror and decide to give her a stern talking-to. "You are allowed to be like this for exactly one minute," I say. "Then you're going to fix your mascara and go out there."

Backstage, the familiar, reassuring rituals of performing take over and I find that my body walks itself onto the stage just fine with the rest of the orchestra. I know how to do this, I'm trained to do this, I'm good at this, it's happening. I even get that little thrill I always feel when I look around the circle of string players in the front stands. *They're here!* It's time to tune to the oboist's A, check that my endpin is securely anchored in the floor, and make last-minute adjustments to the tension of the bow hair. The choir walks on, and after that we all stand up for the conductor and soloists. *It's time!*

A strange calm comes over me. I have the score, the conductor, and the soloists in a perfect line of sight. I can switch seamlessly between characters, from the rabble shrieking *Jesum von Nazareth!* to Jesus's dignified "I have told you that I am he." It's going so well, it's almost as if the cello is playing itself. I couldn't miss a beat if I tried. I make it through Simon Peter's inexplicable violence upon the ear of the High Priest's servant Malchus, his three denials of Christ, the cockcrow, his guilty weeping, and the aria *Ach, mein Sinn*. In truth, I've been dreading this aria, but in the moment I'm completely composed.

Es ist vollbracht is harder.

I've always had a horror of over-the-top emotional displays in performance. Gyrations and face-pulling are superfluous to expression; the music itself should be enough. I've learned this lesson at first hand while listening to recorded performances that in the moment, I thought were the most emotional I'd ever given. In recordings, they invariably sounded disappointingly sloppy and inaccurate. I'm determined, therefore, to keep my composure and let Bach's music speak clearly.

And yet, when I hear Lexa's unbearably beautiful voice singing "The night of sorrow now counts out its last hours," playing without weeping is one of the hardest things I've ever had to do.

Afterwards, as I'm putting my cello in its case, my colleagues approach me to say kind things about the solo. I thank them as graciously as I can. They're all going out to the only bar in Moscow that's still open at this hour; do I want to come? I plead a headache and, hefting my cello onto my back, walk out into the dark parking lot. It's only once I've laid the cello down over the backseat and climbed in the driver's door that I can safely let the tears come.

"It's finished," I mutter.

Silence.

"And *vhat*?"

I put my head down on the steering wheel. "I don't want *anything*."

V. MENUETS

The thing about relearning pieces you've played before is that your fingers remember how difficult they were the first time around. Aged thirteen, and even eighteen and twenty-three, I could barely play Menuet I of the Second Suite because I couldn't get my fingers around the triple-stopped chords. No matter how hard I tried, I couldn't reliably land on the pitches in tune. Trying again now, I feel my hands pinch into the neck of the cello and the frog of the bow, my shoulders rise, and my neck hunch forward into old, tense habits that I learned years ago to release. (Alexander Vassilievich, in moments of frustration at my lack of body awareness, used to bellow "Re-*lax*!" in lessons, even though he must have been able to see he was having exactly the opposite effect.) Revisiting this Menuet reminds me of the cellist I used to be before I learned to use my body more effectively in the service of music. If I'm going to drag this piece into the present, I'm going to have to change the way I play it.

The first chord, I now realize, isn't so hard. Interestingly, it's the same simple D minor triad that we had at the start of the Prelude, only on this occasion the three tones are played nearly simultaneously in a triple-stop. The real killer, it transpires, is the second chord, C, E, B-flat. There isn't really a way of playing it in a triple-stop because it doesn't work with the natural spacings between the fingers. You can try to contort your hand into it, but it hurts. In the past I've tried to fudge my way through it with finger-hops and arpeggios, but something always goes wrong and it's out of tune or slides about inelegantly between pitches. I experiment with trying to get the B-flat with the side of my left thumb, but even when I can get it in tune, the C and E are only sporadically and unreliably in tune. I puzzle over this for a while until it occurs to me that I could try to get the C using the natural harmonic note at the mid-point of the cello's C-string rather than attempting it on the G. Natural harmonics are located at points on the cello strings that don't require the finger to push the string all the way down for them to sound, so taking advantage of this buys me a split second to get two other fingers down for the E and B-flat. Brilliant! It may be a small victory, but it pleases me immensely.

It's only after figuring out this vexing chord that I notice another of Bach's signature basslines, the passacaglia. D, C, B-flat, and A are right there as the lowest notes of the chords in the first phrase of the first Menuet. I have to smile at this, since it seems the other thing about relearning a piece from long ago is that you notice things you couldn't see before because you were too busy tying your fingers in knots.

But first there is the matter of the second Menuet, a piece I've never really loved. The Second Suite is an almost unrelievedly mournful composition, contrapuntal and chordal in texture. It's complicated music, and to juxtapose it with a second Menuet in the bright key of D major, linear in delivery and entirely lacking in dissonant harmony, seems out of keeping with the character of the rest of the Suite. What was Bach thinking?

It's only when I try to imagine an implied bassline for the second Menuet that I start to understand what threads the two Menuets together. I have basslines on the brain these days and I look for them everywhere, and it suddenly occurs to me that you could make a case for a major-key passacaglia bassline in the first half of the second Menuet – twice over, if you manipulated it a bit. To check that I'm not mistaken, I play D, C-sharp, B, A on the cello while I sing the melodic line. And there it is, that footstepping passacaglia, taking us on a surprise detour.

*

It's spring at last, and now that it's staying light later in the evenings, I've started to take my dog Cyril for two- and three-hour walks along the nature trail that goes by our house. It runs for miles and miles between several small Idaho and Washington towns, the vestige of an old railroad line that used to transport Idaho farmers and university students to Spokane in the nineteenth century. Eventually and inevitably, the automotive industry took over, and the government pulled up the tracks and paved over the old route. I'm grateful they kept it as public land for hiking and cycling.

Cyril is delighted with this plan, and the exercise helps work off some of my restlessness. Taking pleasure in exercise is a relatively new experience for me, because as a child I was bad at sports and desperately shy. Other children made fun of me for it, and for liking things like books and classical music. At my school, sports were king and the arts regarded with suspicion, so I was always lonely. My brother fared better since he was athletic as well as arty, and my parents also enjoyed healthy New Zealand pursuits such as hiking up near-vertical slopes. Dragged along on these walks, I often griped that every New Zealand trail seemed designed to go uphill both ways. Exercise was still too tied up with the pain of social exclusion for me to enjoy it, and by the time I was a teenager, I had truanted from so many physical education lessons that my high school principal stopped trying to make me attend them. My mother was dubious, but I sold her on the idea by promising to spend the extra hour practicing. After this victory, I didn't exercise or even own a pair of sneakers until vanity compelled me in my late twenties to acknowledge that I might not always be so naturally thin. I plucked up my courage to start going to a gym, but although I noticed its health benefits almost immediately, I can't say it ever became a pleasure.

With all of this emotional baggage about exercising, I'm surprised to find how much I enjoy my walks that spring. Being outside and moving seems to calm my acute grief as well as some of my habitual anxiety. Every day the lentil fields get a little greener until they attain the hard bright color of highlighter pens, the same color as New Zealand grassland.

Bach was a big walker too, but perhaps not so much by choice as by necessity. His 250-mile hike from Arnstadt to Lübeck to study with the composer Dieterich Buxtehude is well-known. On the course of my walks, I listen to an entertaining BBC radio documentary by Horatio Clare, a travel writer who retraced Bach's steps in a series of podcasts before writing a book about it.[50] Clare's descriptions of the landscape fill me with a restless yearning to get on a plane to Germany and see Bach's hiking trail for myself. Since this option is not, alas, possible, I look up the route on Google Earth and find scenery not unlike my Northwest landscape: rolling green hills, farmland, low mountains, picturesque little towns. On my screen, I follow the walking trail up to Brocken, the highest summit of the Harz mountain range that Bach had to cross on his way north in the autumn and south in the spring. Uphill both ways; the New Zealander in me has to grin at that.

What did he think about as he walked? Music, doubtless. Did the rhythm of his footfalls inspire compositions? Did he make up preludes and passacaglias to pass the time and forget the ache in his feet? Did he think about his parents, both of whom had died by the time he was a child of ten? Or about the stressed and distracted older brother who was obliged to take him in after his new stepmother couldn't cope with widowhood? Did he think about grief? Did he think about girls? Like so many other things about Bach, we don't know much about what he thought, at least not in any personal way. If he ever wrote a diary or intimate family letters, they haven't survived. His early biographers built up the myth of the virtuous composer whose music transcended mortal human feelings. Bach's true thoughts are anyone's guess.

Of course, people have tried to guess them. A filmmaker once decided to make a biopic about Bach, and sought consultation from the great Bach scholar Arthur Mendel. According to Robert L. Marshall, Mendel advised the man "not to bother: you could not make a film about Bach's life. There was nothing exciting about it – except for the making of the twenty children, and you could not show that."[51] As disappointing as this must have been for the filmmaker, it was better to hear the blunt truth before he attempted a script. Just as famous sportspeople and Hollywood actors seldom have anything interesting to say in interviews, Bach might not have been personally fascinating. His music, of course, is the thing that makes him most interesting. Perhaps it's better for posterity that he spent his time writing music and not tell-all diaries.

*

The word passacaglia itself originally came from two Spanish words, *pasar* and *calle*, meaning "to walk" and "the street."[52] The name apparently came from the guitarists who roamed the streets of the cities, strumming improvisations over a descending bassline. I picture them as louche, mustachioed fellows whose wicked grins and wickeder chord progressions impelled the matriarchs of Granada and Madrid to cover their daughters' eyes when they strolled past.

Not all passacaglias, then, were about sorrow and mourning. For every woeful passacaglia like Bach's cantata *Jesu, der du meine Seele*, whose narrator warns of "the devil's dark cave," there's a suggestive passacaglia like Act Five of Lully's *Armide*. In this depraved scene, a sorceress and her retinue of demon-sycophants imprison a hunky medieval knight and dance alluringly around him, purring things about *doux plaisirs* and *heureux amants* that you'd think would have made Bach blush. It's rather a surprise, therefore, to learn that the passacaglia from *Armide* was almost certainly the model for *Jesu, der du meine Seele*.[53] In one of those paradoxical Bachian blurrings of sacred and secular, we learn that a passacaglia can symbolize anything from the entrapments of spiritual warfare to those of amorous enchantment.

Bach's walks and mine eventually come to a place where we must turn around and go home, but the way back looks different. The *da capo* return to Menuet I is shaped by all the things we've seen, things that have changed us.

You can't just go back and play it the same way you did the first and second time. You need to change it up, improvise some ornaments such as a trill or two, just make it different. The manuscript of Johann Peter Kellner is significantly different from that of Anna Magdalena Bach here, and I find it useful to play Kellner's version on the "way home." Are the elaborate ornaments in his version Bach's ideas, or Kellner's? Maybe it doesn't matter. What matters is that we have at our disposal a little glance at a written-out eighteenth-century improvisation by someone close to Bach, and that may be as close as we get.

VI. GIGUE

Throughout the Cello Suites, Bach finds ingenious ways around the problem of creating harmonies on a solo instrument whose most natural voice is linear. In the Second Suite alone we can hear triple- and quadruple-stopped chords, mellifluous arpeggios, angular "broken style" harmonizations, and imitative melodic lines that chase each other around so effectively that we can imagine the presence of other voices. We might think of these harmonizing techniques as borrowings from the vocabulary of other instruments – violin, harpsichord, lute, viola da gamba, even organ.

In the Gigue that concludes the Second Suite, Bach uses all of these techniques, and more. For the first time in the Cello Suites, but not the last, he adds harmony using an effect reminiscent of the drone on a bagpipe. To create it, the cellist must place the bow on two strings at once and use the left-hand fingers to make a scampering, capricious melodic line on just one of them, while the other string is "open" and doesn't change pitch.

As a New Zealander of Scottish descent, I have a sentimental weakness for bagpipes. If I had my way, I'd have walked down the aisle to their stirring music if a certain cranky American bridegroom hadn't vetoed this plan, saying he couldn't tolerate such a din. Prince Leopold of Anhalt-Cöthen likely couldn't either, but he might have been more favorably inclined to the musette, a daintier upper-class version of a bagpipe. This instrument was played not with the mouth but with a small bellows under the player's arm, and its bucolic charm made it a favorite trope of pastoral music. In ballets at Versailles, aristocrats delighted in dressing up as shepherds and shepherdesses to praise the wholesome simplicity of country life, oblivious or indifferent to the reality that Europe's peasantry were currently starving. Just as courtiers didn't want to know about wretchedness of actual people, neither did they wish to observe the ugly facial contortions of bagpipers, hence the bellows.[54]

It might be a less efficient means of sound production, but at least no one looked inelegant.

Bach's father Johann Ambrosius had been a violinist and town piper, so Bach was certainly familiar with the pastoral associations of woodwind instruments, and it's no accident that he wrote so many solos for flute and oboe. If the presence of horns symbolized hunting and drums meant war, flutes and oboes were inextricably tied up with pastoralism. Bach wasn't inclined towards cute baby animals or coy love songs, however – for him, a shepherd wasn't just a shepherd, he was the Good Shepherd. Once the Good Shepherd got involved, the conversation habitually turned quickly to death. While this might sound gloomy, it wasn't necessarily so. Bach's Lutheran worldview held that death was both a release and a blessing.

Perhaps this is why Bach's settings of texts about human mortality so often use the woodwind instruments, major keys, and lilting compound meters of the pastoral idyll. If you didn't know the text of Bach's cantata *Liebster Gott, wenn werd ich sterben?*, you might think it was about a party. A pair of oboes d'amore swoop joyfully around each other in the opening chorus, with a piping piccolo that sounds for all the world like the first bird-song of spring. The words, though? "Dearest God, when will I die? My time is running out." The patterns of twenty-four repeated pitches in the piccolo part aren't birdsong, they're hours. And bells, representing the death-knell.[55]

Conversely, the slightly more life-affirming text in Cantata 175, *Er rufet seinen Schafen mit Namen*, appears in the type of setting I start to think of as Bach's "dark pastoral." In this respect, it's similar in character to the Gigue of the Second Suite. "Come, guide me," sings the alto, "my spirit longs for green pasture! My heart languishes, groans day and night, my shepherd, my joy." Long held notes in the bassline part make me think of the drones of the Gigue. The Cello Suites date from about five years before either of these sacred cantatas, and I can't help wondering if the Gigue has more in common with them than with anything you might find in a ballroom.

*

We have no need to long for green pasture in Idaho, because the hills are covered in it. It's May, and the campus is pink and white with apple blossom. I finish my last practice session of the day with the vigorous cadence that ends the Gigue, and put my cello in its case. After all the morbid yearning in the religious texts I've been reading, it feels strange to go outside into the sunshine. It's the day of the end-of-semester department picnic, and it's also my thirty-second birthday. I've recently made some progress on a few of my own rather more optimistic yearnings, and I notice the teasing smiles of colleagues when I turn down a can of beer. "What kind of Bach scholar doesn't like beer?" one of them asks, and I make some joke about my great-great-grandmother's membership in the New Zealand Christian Women's Temperance Union.

Part Three

A THOUSAND HAPPY DAYS

Suite No. 3 in C Major, BWV 1009

Sehet in Zufriedenheit
Tausend helle Wohlfartstage,
Daß bald bei der Folgezeit
Eure Liebe Blumen trage!

"May you see with satisfaction
A thousand happy days,
So that soon afterwards
Your love may flower!"

Johann Sebastian Bach, *Weichet nur, betrübte Schatten* BWV 202

I. PRELUDE

Carl Philipp Emanuel Bach, in his father's obituary, had this to say about his keyboard technique. "All his fingers were equally skillful; all were equally capable of the most perfect accuracy in performance. He had devised for himself so convenient a system of fingering that it was not hard for him to conquer the greatest difficulties with the most flowing facility. Before him, the most famous clavier players in Germany and other lands had used the thumb but little. All the better did he know how to use it."[56]

Anyone who has ever had piano lessons will find the thought of playing without thumbs strikingly odd. After reading Carl Philipp Emanuel's words, I go to the piano and attempt the "easy" C major Prelude from the *Well-Tempered Clavier* to see if I can do it the no-thumbs way, and it transpires I can't. At first I keep forgetting I'm not supposed to use them, so I fix my gaze on my hands and will myself to remember. This time I can do it, but I'm clumsy and inaccurate and it makes my hands hurt. How extraordinary it seems that a centuries-long tradition of keyboard playing could have developed without its occurring to anyone that the largest and strongest digit of the human hand might be deployed in its service.

Around the same time that Bach came up with his logical fingering system for the keyboard, cellists too must have been glancing thoughtfully at their thumbs. While the small size of the violin made it reasonably straightforward for the player's left-hand fingers to stretch between even quite widely spaced pitches, the cello was much bigger and its playing technique less agile. One flamboyant passage in the middle of the Prelude of the Third Suite contains stretches so large that most players can't reach them using the first and fourth fingers (as the index and pinky are called in string instrument fingering). Bach appears to have lifted the harmonic progression wholesale from a violin sonata by Arcangelo Corelli,[57] but such copying wasn't frowned upon in the eighteenth century. Rather, Bach was adapting a violinistic passage to encourage cellists to extend their technique. He asks a lot of us, however. To execute this passage, we have to take the left thumb away from its usual resting place on the back of the cello's neck, bring it around to the fingerboard, and use the outer side of the distal phalanx to depress the strings. Pushing a cello string down to the fingerboard requires around two pounds of weight, and doing so on the thin skin near the nail-bed is just as uncomfortable as it sounds. Before attempting the Prelude of the Third Cello Suite, cellists must therefore study a great many preparatory exercises to learn a correctly rounded hand position and build strength in the thumb so that their joints won't buckle under pressure. No one knows beyond a doubt who first came up with the idea of thumb position, but it's likely to have been an Italian cellist, Italy being the cradle of virtuoso string playing. Michel Corrette was the first person to write about thumb position technique in his method book, by which time it must have been standard practice.

Such innovations make the Third Cello Suite quite a jump up in difficulty from the Second, and Bach knew this. One of the rewards of virtue in the practice room is exhibitionism in the concert hall, and the Prelude of the Third Cello Suite feels an awful lot like a vindication of all the hours you spent on technical exercises by our old friends Dotzauer and Grützmacher. This piece sure isn't for wimps – it's long and tiring and difficult, but getting it right fills you with glee. C major is the most resonant possible key for the cello, since all the notes of the open strings – C, G, D, A – are part of the C major scale and therefore ring sympathetically with most of the fingered pitches. The melodies are composed of scampering scales and arpeggios in repetitive round-and-round patterns that can really tire you out. You have to make sure to place your fingertips on the string very precisely, but also mindfully relax and release them whenever you can so that you'll have the stamina to get through the suite without injuring yourself. The bow has to dance around the strings in a similarly circular fashion without straying too far towards the less powerful upper half of the stick. For optimal friction between bow and string, you also need optimal balance, and this isn't at all easy when you're attempting, as I am, to follow Anna Magdalena Bach's articulation markings.

I like to play the Prelude of the Third Suite very fast, partly because I don't like ponderous playing but mostly so that the audience can understand the large-scale architecture of the movement. Like so many passages in Bach's works, much of the Prelude is composed from a type of chord progression known as the circle of fifths. Bach didn't invent the concept; it had been around for a few thousand years since Pythagoras, perhaps during a break from measuring triangles, worked out the ratios for dividing an octave into twelve pitches. It wasn't until the nineteenth century, though, that the procedure became a codified law of music theory. Astonishingly, Bach and Mozart didn't know they were writing textbook harmony – it wasn't until after their deaths that theorists decided to base the rules on their work. Because of the rationality of the mathematical principles that govern music, these rules aren't hard to learn, and if you happen to forget them, you can find them again on the posters plastering every high school music room. These often have helpful circular graphics that show us how many sharps or flats are assigned to key signatures, but in a pinch you can work it out by furtively muttering the musical alphabet while counting on your fingers. The rule of fifths is also what determines the order of sharps and flats in key signatures, and we teach this to small children using delightfully bloodthirsty mnemonic devices such as "Fat Cats Go Down Alleys Eating Birds" for the order of sharps and "Before Every Animal Dies, Girls Cry Forever" for the order of flats. (Music pedagogy is red in tooth and claw.)

In the Prelude to the Third Cello Suite, Bach uses the circle of fifths procedure to get from key to key in the form of phrases that sound like questions and answers. It's how he transports us from the home key of C major to a secondary key of G major using a roundabout but rapid trip through F-sharp, B, E, A, and D. On the way to the Corelli-inspired central event, he uses a different circle of fifths pattern to get from C to A to D to B to E to C to F to D and finally to G, and there we stay, relentlessly hammering that bass note of G until we can stand the prolongation no longer and the harmony is prepared for a triumphant ending in C major.

The Prelude is 88 measures long, but so skillful is Bach's harmonic preparation that the movement could conceivably have ended after 82 measures, or even 71. But Bach never just gets to the end and goes home. Instead, he gives the cellist an ornate coda-cadenza featuring some sweeping four-note chords and, in an outrageously flashy flourish, a double trill. Back when I first learned the piece aged sixteen, it took me ages to learn to do this finger-twister of a technique, and now that I've finally mastered it, I can hardly keep a smile off my face when I play it. "Herr Capellmeister," I say to the picture of Bach on my office wall, "that's just showing off." I have always been a terrible show-off, and I rather wonder if Bach was one too.

After this last-minute show of bravado, it really is the end, and Bach ends with the same descending scale with which he began. Full circle – the end is the beginning and the beginning is the end.

*

I'm in the middle of recording the Prelude on my phone when there's a hesitant tap at my office door. It's early fall, and the faculty are all in last-minute preparations for the new semester. Right on cue, the department photocopier has broken, and the bookstore calls in a panic every half hour with some new textbook problem. It's harder these days for me to get up out of chairs, but I hit pause and make it over to the door in time to find my choir colleague Mike standing outside. "I'm starting a Bach festival," he tells me. "Do you want to do this with me?"

For a moment I look down doubtfully at my baby bump. Everyone's been telling me to learn to say no to things, to reserve my energy for juggling career and motherhood. As if in response, the baby delivers a kick worthy of a rugby player, sending ripples through the fabric of my maternity smock. I feel a great *yes* bubbling up and I can't stop the huge grin spreading across my face. "Hell yeah," I tell him.

II. ALLEMANDE

The Bachs were a family who stuck together. Bach's first biographer, Johann Nikolaus Forkel, describes their "clannish attachment to each other." At annual family reunions, "music was their sole recreation. As those present were either Cantors, Organists, or Town Musicians, employed in the service of the Church and accustomed to preface the day's work with prayer, their first act was to sing a Hymn. Having fulfilled their religious duty, they spent the rest of the time in frivolous recreations. Best of all they liked to extemporize a chorus out of popular songs, comic or jocular, weaving them into a harmonious whole while declaiming the words of each."[58] Ever discreet, Forkel does not disclose the subject matter of these choruses, whose interestingly vulgar lyrics go some way to explain how and why the Bachs tended to have a lot of children.

In 1735, at the age of fifty, Bach began working on a genealogical document, *Origins of the Musical Bach Family*. It was no accident that he began the project after this milestone birthday, since he was now the age both his parents had been when they died. An orphan from age ten and sufferer of many family bereavements, it was small wonder he wanted to document the achievements of the clan.

To be a Bach in Thuringia was practically synonymous with being a musician, and *Origins* reads like a union membership roster. It was not an exhaustive list, though, and contained some conspicuous omissions, such as one Hanns "the Jester" Bach.[59] Poor Hanns – he must have been the black sheep of the family, even if he was the life of the party at their bawdy singalongs.

Also excluded are the women. This is curious, because practically all Bach women made music in one way or another, some of them professionally. Did Bach not consider their achievements worth mentioning? Did male pride or class-consciousness prevent him from mentioning their contributions to household finances? Perhaps the Bach *Frauen* were philosophical about being left out, but I find it hard to put this injustice into a historical picture-frame or to console myself that "things were like that then."

Another unmentioned fact is that Bach No. 14, Johann Michael (1648–1694), a first cousin of Bach's father, was also Bach's first father-in-law. Marrying a second cousin was not a usual practice in the Bach family, even if the royal families of Europe did it all the time. While such a match would raise eyebrows today and possibly did even then, it also made sense. Johann Sebastian and Maria Barbara were orphaned members of the same tribe, and perhaps they longed to recreate a stable family unit as husband and wife, father and mother. Beyond the unbeatable convenience of Maria Barbara's not having to change her last name, they had a lot in common: religion, music, and family traditions. It must have been like marrying a childhood sweetheart. They had known each other for so long as cousins and comrades, and then perhaps one day they looked at one another in a different light as man and woman, and that settled things.

This, in effect, is what my own parents did. They weren't related, I hasten to add, but they had known each other since the age of about ten from inter-church sporting events. That they hadn't met earlier in the small southern city of Dunedin was probably because my father went to a private school and my mother, the daughter of a poor clergyman, didn't. The paths of their ancestors hadn't crossed either, as far as we know, even though they had all emigrated a century before from the same parts of lowland Scotland to the so-called Edinburgh of the South.

Music has a way of softening boundaries. My parents might not have been members of the same circles, but once they caught each other's eye across the madrigal choir at the University of Otago, that was that. In more ways than one, it was a strange attraction of opposites, since Gillian was shy and Roger sociable to the point of exhibitionism. I think my mother admired my father's fluency with music and words, and that built-in confidence that comes with social privilege. My father, for his part, admired her in equal measures for her soulful piano playing and her enormous brown eyes. From their late teens on, they were seldom apart. He helped her translate German articles for her dissertation on Arnold Schoenberg's *Transfigured Night*, and she helped him scrub up his music theory when he decided he'd like to give up studying European languages and become an opera singer instead. They went to Germany for graduate studies at the Musikhochschule in Cologne, moved into a romantically decrepit medieval townhouse, and married hastily in a registry office when their parents in New Zealand found out about the cohabitation. They moved back to New Zealand and settled in Wellington, not Dunedin, because it was a bigger city with more opportunities for musicians. They bought a big white house by the sea and had two children, my brother and me.

And so we became the Wilsons of Wellington. Not quite the Bachs of Thuringia, but there were noisy family gatherings, singalongs around the piano, and plenty of silly in-jokes. Most of our extended family were musicians or artists of some kind, and everyone sang and played instruments. Partners in life and music, my parents performed together often, rehearsing at night after my brother and I were in bed. Drowsy and warm from our hot baths and flannel pajamas, we fell asleep to the sound of Schubert Lieder slugging it out for supremacy against the spin cycle on the washing machine.

*

At its heart, the harmony in the binary dance movements in Bach's Cello Suites can be reduced to a kind of fundamental conflict between the so-called tonic and dominant, the tonic being the chord of the home key of the movement, and the dominant the chord built on the fifth scale degree of the home key. Wherever you find the tonic, the dominant won't be far away, and vice versa. Even if they oppose one another, they also can't do without one another. I think of this relationship as a kind of yearning. Human beings are motivated by their desires, and so is harmony. It's what makes music appeal to us. Once more, we have Pythagoras to thank for this, since he was the first to teach the principles of the harmonic series. This is the heart of the inextricable relationship between music and mathematics – two subjects so integral to each other that we might even say they're two sides of the same thing. The chords used in Western and non-Western musics are not the random invention of an excitable composer; they're determined by the very nature of sound itself.

The tonic-dominant relationship is why we instinctively know that the mid-point of a Bach dance movement is the middle and not the end. We don't yet have our resolution and fulfillment. Listeners can hear this even if they don't have the words to explain it. Even if tonic and dominant live in perpetual conflict, they also can't do without each other. They're ineluctably drawn to one another.

I think of this strange oppositional attraction every time I play the Allemande of the Third Suite. It's an interesting foil for the Prelude, because both of them are built from C major scale constructions, but where the Prelude rushes about almost entirely in regular sixteenth-note rhythms, the Allemande's rhythm and melody go off into endless twists, curlicues, and diversions. It's the first movement in the Cello Suites to contain a long chain of double-stopped notes, a scale played simultaneously in two voices a third apart. As a teenager, I found this technique almost impossible to play reliably in tune because it meant moving the first and fourth fingers around at irregularly spaced intervals, a maneuver that perplexed me even in the cellist-friendly key of C major. These days I can take it in my stride, using my knowledge of the overtone series to feel my way around the pitches on the cello's fingerboard. I also notice a harmonic feature that had eluded me before, the fact that this passage gets us from the home key of C towards the dominant key of G by means of a disruptive F-sharp. This two-voiced scale is what links the two endlessly conflicting, endlessly attracted keys.

When I teach tonic-dominant harmony at the university, I always tell students about the feelings of yearning it provokes in me, and I see in their faces that they feel it too. "Notice that F-sharp. It's not random. It's what draws us towards G," I say. "F-sharp is powerful. We have to follow it now." Is it romanticizing to draw an analogy between harmonic progression and human desire? Love can be the most powerful and destructive of emotions, and sometimes we can't resist it even when we know what wreckage it can cause. But would we really want to resist it, after all? To live without it would be like only listening to elevator music, a genre in which the tonic-dominant conflict is conspicuously absent. That's why it never reaches a cadence, and why it's so boring.

*

The first time Bach married, it was to a woman he had known for a long time. He met his second wife, Anna Magdalena Wilcke, the way so many musicians meet their spouses – at work. Anna Magdalena, the daughter of a trumpeter, was a singer at Prince Leopold's court. She must have been a good one, too, because apart from Bach she was the highest-paid musician there.

Bach didn't marry out of desperate need to find a stepmother for his children the way his own father had done, since he already had his sister-in-law and a maid to take care of his home and family. It might well have been a love match and a marriage of true minds, since Anna Magdalena was a professional woman in her own right. Did they start to feel something for one another as they rehearsed recitatives for the Prince's cantatas? Like Dante's ardent Francesca and her Paolo falling in love over a book in the *Inferno*, did Bach and his Anna fall in love over a score?

Once they were married, Anna Magdalena kept her career, and Bach seems to have supported her ambition, since they continued to work together at the court for the rest of their time in Cöthen.[60] Though Anna Magdalena held no professional position when they later moved to Leipzig, she remained Bach's partner in life and music until his death.

My husband and I aspire to this kind of partnership. Like Bach and Anna Magdalena, we too met at a rehearsal. I wish I could say that we were playing Bach's second Brandenburg Concerto, with its spectacular piccolo trumpet solo, but in fact the repertoire was Beethoven's First Symphony and Ottorino Respighi's *Pines of Rome*. The University of Colorado, where my string quartet had a postgraduate residency, asked my colleagues and me to play a concert with the university symphony since they were short of string players that year. We'd been traveling so much on the concert and competition circuit that we hadn't yet had time to meet many of the students. As principal cellist, I seldom had a moment to look away from my score, since the string section typically plays almost all the time in orchestral music, but Sean, the principal trumpeter and a doctoral candidate, had plenty of multi-measure rests. Having ample time to look around the room, he saw me before I saw him.

Before one rehearsal, he appeared seemingly out of nowhere to hold a door open for me as I struggled through with a cello, a laptop bag, and a large binder full of scores. It was the first time I'd noticed him, this big blond man with fearless blue eyes.

"Thank you," I exclaimed.

Sean lost no time in starting a conversation. "I enjoy working with you," he told me. "It's great to have a principal cellist who knows the score so well and is so prepared for rehearsals."

I didn't hate this adulation one bit. "Thank you," I said again, bestowing what I imagined to be a ravishing smile.

After that I seemed to bump into the blond trumpeter everywhere, and it wasn't long until he asked me for a date. Although I enjoyed the flattering knowledge that he liked me, I wasn't sure that I wanted to have a boyfriend. When the day came, I showed up fifteen minutes early so that I could buy my own coffee, meaning that it didn't have to be a date if I didn't want it to be. This attempt at evasion didn't put Sean off. With supremely informative self-assurance, he began telling me of his likes and dislikes, his religious and political preferences, and the reasons he had broken up with his most recent ex-girlfriend. His confidence and optimism seemed indestructible.

At the end, he pulled out a smartphone – he was an early adopter of all technological innovations – and scrolled through his calendar app. "I enjoyed our date very much," he told me, "and I would like to do it again. I'll pick you up on Thursday at half past five."

On the second date, we talked about our careers and ambitions. On the third date, he informed me that he intended for us to attain advanced ages together and be buried side by side aged ninety-nine.

My quartet colleagues were not happy that I had a boyfriend. I had said in the past that I had no intention of finding a husband, and I think I meant it. I saw myself as a cross between Hildegard of Bingen and passionate Madame Suggia from the portrait by Augustus John, a mystical prophetess devoted not to religion but to music. I relished solitude and spent my tiny amount of spare time dreamily reading poetry and walking in the foothills of the Flatirons. Cello was and had always been my life. I hadn't imagined that I would ever be allowed a partner or a home life, since being in a string quartet involved eighty-hour work weeks and a grueling travel schedule.

Soon I became aware that my colleagues were having serious discussions about my relationship and what it meant for the quartet. Our second violinist started to refer to Sean as "Yoko," only half in jest. It would be hard to imagine anyone with less physical resemblance to the woman accused of breaking up the Beatles, but my colleagues clearly saw him as a threat to our tight-knit, workaholic group.

They were right to worry, because I was falling in love hard. Sean was an outsized personality, the personification of American ambition and American success. Unlike me, he was hyper-organized and entirely without sentimentality. His life was a relentless campaign of self-improvement, goals, and checklists. He was always firmly abreast of the contents of his email inbox. He had an artist's appreciation of beautiful things, whereas I had lived out of a suitcase for so many years that I thought a cardboard box covered with a scarf was an acceptable item of furniture. It was both bizarre and blissful to date a man who refused to sleep on any sheets but Egyptian cotton, collected crystal glassware, and enjoyed researching and purchasing orthopedically designed mattresses and enormous television sets. I admired him right away for all these qualities, but I grew to love him when I realized he was the most sensitive and intuitive person I had ever known. He knew and understood me down to my bones, and for some reason wanted to be with me anyway.

We were married in secret in a registry office less than a year after that first date. Leaving the quartet had also meant the cancelation of the visa that permitted me to live and work in the United States, so marrying was the only way to regain legal immigration status. Without my meager quartet salary, neither of us had a job or any income other than Sean's doctoral stipend, though Sean was serenely confident we would win university positions. This was the most reckless thing I had ever done.

III. COURANTE

In the course of relearning Bach's Cello Suites from a facsimile of Anna Magdalena Bach's copy, I spend a lot of time daydreaming about her. I picture her sitting at a messy desk, or at the family dining table, surrounded by ink-pots and coffee mugs, copying her husband's manuscripts while yelling children ran around her, tugging on her skirts, asking her to play with them and fix their snacks. I follow the swirls and flourishes from her quill pen, the ambiguous blotches where ink leaked over more than one line of the staff, the irregular slur marks. In knowing her handwriting so well, I imagine I know Anna herself. I can hear the scratching of her quill pen on parchment, see the ink stains on her apron, and look into her tired young face as she squints over her parchment in the candlelight.

Even if my fingers are racing through the frantic up-and-down arpeggios and *bariolage* of the Courante of the Third Cello Suite, the third trimester of pregnancy has finally slowed the rest of me down. I've had to make some adjustments to my endpin and seated stance so that I can play the cello around my bump, and I'm grateful to have long arms so that I can still reach the strings with the bow. Sitting with an enlarged photocopy of the facsimile, I find myself wondering if Anna Magdalena were pregnant too at the time she made her copy. She spent almost all her fertile years pregnant or looking after small children, and presumably nursing, cooking, and doing the housework as well as copying her husband's music, so it's not unlikely. I feel a sisterly kinship with her when the baby boots me so hard I fear the cello might go flying. Before pregnancy, I lived so much in my imagination that I barely remembered I had a body, but now I'm growing another human in it, my aching hip-bones won't let me forget. Under normal circumstances, I never walk if I can run, so my slowness and queasiness and need for frequent naps frustrate me immensely. When I get irritated, I remember that my mother went through this for my brother and me, and Anna Magdalena Bach went through it for thirteen babies in twenty years. It makes me forgive my mother any lingering childhood resentments, and Anna Magdalena for the errors in her copy.

I've almost given up on using editions of Bach, because even the ones that claim to be faithful to Anna Magdalena's score have trouble with her calligraphy. One of the best attempts is by August Wenzinger, a Swiss cellist and pioneer of historically informed performance. His 1967 edition[61] has never been out of print and is still considered the standard version. It's what I use myself when I'm teaching Bach to college students, since most of them aren't yet ready to grapple with eighteenth-century manuscripts. The thing that makes Wenzinger's work so practical is also what now frustrates me about it: his perfectly understandable initiative to make some sense out of Anna Magdalena's articulation markings such as the slurs above the staff. This, in effect, is what all editors of the Cello Suites have done, including the creators of other scholarly performance editions such as those by Hans Eppstein[62] and Kirsten Beisswenger.[63] It seems hard to resist the urge to craft editorial consistency out of a written language that is inherently inconsistent.

In saying this, I don't mean to disparage Anna Magdalena's musicianship, or her handwriting. Like so much else about Bach's Cello Suites, her copy is an intimation of an old musical language that we no longer natively speak. With this thought uppermost in my mind, the one edition I return to – which isn't even really an edition – is Anner Bylsma's *Bach, the Fencing Master* and its companion volume *Bach and the Happy Few*.[64] Bylsma may have lived with Anna Magdalena's copy longer and studied it more than anyone else. His commentaries intersperse excerpts from her manuscript with Bylsma's own whimsical, stream-of consciousness thoughts on their interpretation and performance. "Bowing is gesticulating," he asserts. "Bow-strokes are eloquent gestures, especially up-bows. For example: an inhaling up-bow on the first beat of the bar, with the eyes turned up towards heaven, or an up-beat up-bow like a rhetorical gesture, a salutation."[65]

When Alexander Ivashkin first handed me his copy of *Bach, the Fencing Master*, Bylsma's commentaries seemed so eccentric that I barely knew what to make of them. His overriding point is a serious one, though. Unlike just about every performance editor of the Cello Suites, Bylsma insists that we should take Anna Magdalena's bowing markings literally. He demands: "What if Bach had been exploring new ways for the bow, new paths which were not followed, being too difficult and irregular…?"[66] Where most editors and most cellists throw up their hands in horror at Anna Magdalena's slur markings, Bylsma practices what he preaches. We can hear it in his recordings of the Cello Suites. A lesser player could not do what he does, and almost everyone is a lesser player than Bylsma, but I admire and revere the singularity of his determination. "The bowings in what is called Anna Magdalena are by Johann Sebastian!" he insists. "Who else could have thought of such meaningful and magnificent irregularities, if not he?"[67] If this sounds pedantic, it isn't. Bylsma acknowledges the difficulty of reading Anna Magdalena's articulation markings, and his own struggle in coming to terms with them. His work seems truly open-minded in a field of performance practice that is often riven with dogma.

Inspired by his example, I set about trying to move the bow in the way he does. I've internalized modern bowing convention for so long that to disrupt it feels counter-intuitive. Still, Bylsma's "best guess" suggestions can make for though-provoking results in the Courante of the Third Cello Suite. It's hard to peel back all the layers from editions I've used and playing conventions I've practiced, but starting afresh like this brings different nuances to these familiar melodic lines. I realize that in my haste, I've been "playing over" parts of the line that really ought to come out of the texture more. Anna Magdalena Bach only applies slur markings to the melodic parts of the line, while the harmonic parts, the arpeggios and *bariolage* passages, don't have slurs at all. This suggests an inherent color contrast between the two voices, the linear melodic voice and the arpeggiated harmonic voice. Once more, Bach pulls off a melodically and harmonically complete composition using just one single line of notes.

When I first read Bylsma's books, I couldn't imagine how he remembered all these wild, irregular bowings when playing from memory. Now that I've attempted to give Anna Magdalena Bach's bowings the serious consideration Bylsma demands, I realize how eloquent they can be. This is why Bylsma's recordings of the Cello Suites are so poetic, and so profoundly unlike any that had come before.

Even if Bylsma's work has revolutionized the way we think about Bach, not everyone agrees with his literalist approach. The cellist and Baroque improvisation expert John Lutterman calls his attitude "the most extreme example of text fetishism,"[68] comparing it to "the religious fundamentalist's dogmatic, literal reading of sacred scriptures."[69] The comparison makes me think back to my days as a graduate student in London, where I followed the Ivashkins after they left New Zealand. In twice-weekly three-hour discussions, musicology professors asked my class to discuss what a musical composition actually was. Was it a printed page? Was it a first performance conducted by the composer? Was it a wholly imaginary thing? What kind of authority could we invest in a score? Was the page a primary document for performance, or a jumping-off place for the performer-interpreter? What was more important, a score or a contextual knowledge of performance practices that we might draw on for interpretation?

I rarely spoke in these discussions because I was afraid of being ridiculed, whether for my New Zealand accent or for what I assumed to be my idiocy. The musicology majors launched fluently into a discussion of *Werktreue*, work-concept, a term I'd never heard and which made my head hurt when one of them tried to define it for me. They wanted us performance majors to argue with them about it, but we were mostly pining for this exercise in intellectual vertigo to be over so that we could get back to the practice room. ("Where we actually make music instead of going *blah blah blah* about it," one of my friends grumbled.) Now I wish I'd paid more attention to the discussion. Even if their conversational style can be a little intense, musicologists are our best friends in the search for musical interpretation. With Lutterman's work as a starting point and many recordings by historically informed performance practitioners in my streaming playlist, I find myself seeking a middle ground. Perhaps we can have both – Bylsma's serious-minded faithfulness to the text *and* historically researched improvisatory practices *and* something of our own as individual performers. Abandoning all notion of the definitive can liberate us to new possibilities.

Bylsma may have been certain of Anna Magdalena's accuracy, but experts on Bach's ink, paper, and handwriting have other ideas. The Bach scholar Yo Tomita proposes that even if Anna Magdalena copied as well as she could, the lost original document itself might have been full of revisions and difficult to read.[70] Zoltán Szabó argues further that Johann Peter Kellner's copy of the Cello Suites came from a different and superior autograph manuscript altogether.[71] I find Szabó's reasoning persuasive enough to set aside for the time being the question of which surviving manuscript copy is "better." In any case, we can now compare all our primary documents in Bärenreiter's synoptic edition, in which Source A, Source B, Source C, Source D, and Source E, the first printed edition by Louis Norblin, appear side by side. (I order this marvelous publication the moment it comes out, and when the FedEx driver brings it to the door I greet him like a child meeting Santa Claus.)

Surely the strangest take on Anna Magdalena Bach's work comes from the British-Australian scholar Martin Jarvis, who made headlines with his book *Written By Mrs. Bach*.[72] To the derision of Bach scholars worldwide, Jarvis makes the extraordinary claim that Anna Magdalena herself authored the Cello Suites. I have my doubts even before reading the reviews, if only because the Cello Suites are so similar in style to many other compositions verifiably by Johann Sebastian. Still, I borrow the book from the library and read it. The entire project seems to have started with an unverifiable "hunch," and grown into the evidence-free conjecture that Bach cheated on his first wife Maria Barbara with the teenage Anna Magdalena Wilcke. Maria Barbara, Jarvis concludes, committed suicide.

The popular press goes wild over Jarvis's book – who doesn't love a good conspiracy theory? – but such lurid speculation makes me queasy. It's with some relief, then, that I read the rebuttals of Jarvis's theories. Christoph Wolff and other scholars "extensively refuted the basic premises of the thesis, on grounds of documents, manuscript sources, and musical grounds. There is not a shred of evidence, but Jarvis doesn't give up despite the fact that several years ago, at a Bach conference in Oxford, a room full of serious Bach scholars gave him an embarrassing showdown."[73] At this point, I start feeling a bit sorry for Jarvis, since such a stinging rebuke must have hurt.

*

By the time of our inaugural Idaho Bach Festival, I'm just days away from giving birth, but nothing will stop me throwing myself into the event with all the energy I've got. Our guest artist is none other than John Lutterman, whose work I've admired for so long. As part of a scholarly paper, he performs an intriguing improvisation in the style of Bach. Under these circumstances

I feel some trepidation about performing the Third Cello Suite, in which I've been trying out some improvised ornaments, but he's kind and encouraging.

For the final festival performance, our faculty ensemble performs the cantata *Weichet nur, betrübte Schatten*, "Depart, you troublesome shadows!" Written in 1721, the same approximate time as the Cello Suites, this so-called Wedding Cantata might have been a wedding present for Prince Leopold. Or could it have marked Bach's own wedding to Anna Magdalena? Whatever the occasion, its hyperactive continuo basslines make it a joy to play. Mark M. Smith points out their remarkable similarity to the Courante from the Third Cello Suite,[74] and once I hear this the two compositions remain forever connected in my mind. Racing up and down the Courante's exhilarating scalar and arpeggiated lines, I think of the words from the second aria of the cantata: "Phoebus hurries with fast horses through the newborn world, yes, because it pleases him, he himself will become a lover!"

IV. SARABANDE

"The eye can follow and encompass the lines of a painting or architectural structure in all their directions, breadth and relationships," wrote the German music theorist Heinrich Schenker, "if only the ear could hear the background of the fundamental structure (*Ursatz*) and the continuous musical motion of the foreground as profoundly and extensively."[75] Schenker's pioneering methods of seeing and hearing music reduced it to its unadorned fundamentals, and by doing so, illuminated them.

When I was an undergraduate, I thought Schenkerian analysis was a pointless exercise in trying to reduce music like boiling jam to show that it was made of tonics and dominants – so what? Now, while reading everything I can find on the Bach Cello Suites, I come across a reference to an analysis Schenker made of the Sarabande of the Third Suite. Due diligence, I think, and set out to hunt through the library stacks for the ancient collection of theoretical essays that contained it. But when I heave my nine-months pregnant form into a carrel to skim-read Schenker's study, I realize I've been wrong all along about him.

Declaring a truce with the great theorist doesn't come without some grudging feelings, since Schenker didn't exactly go out of his way to be lovable. Dogmatic to the point of absolutism, he was given to long rants about composers who violated what he considered the immutable laws of composition, that is, those expressed by Bach, Beethoven, and Brahms. He singled out Berlioz and Wagner for especial disapprobation, but he also scorned world music, atonality, music from any European nation but Germany, jazz and everything else from America, and above all English music. In an essay with the alarming title *The Mission of German Genius*, he thunders "No Anglo-Saxon, French, or Italian mother could ever carry in her womb a Moses, a Christ, or a Luther...nor yet a Bach, a Mozart, a Goethe, or a Kant."[76]

("Well, that's all right then," I think, patting my bump, "I'm a Scottish New Zealander, so perhaps there's hope for you.")

Looking at Schenker's study of the Sarabande, though, I feel my heart softening towards his method. The study cuts to the very heart of the Sarabande, showing that its fundamental line, seemingly obscured amid the many voices of the texture, is the descending C major scale. The same scale, that is, that began the opening measure of the Prelude and was central to the Allemande too. In essence, the C major scale functions as a unifying link between dramatically contrasting movements in the Third Cello Suite. We might even say that the Sarabande is a descendant of the Prelude.

As I read and re-read Schenker's study, I start to hear the Sarabande of the Third Cello Suite with new ears. It's like having an auditory Google Earth where I can zoom in and out. This giddy sensation makes me realize how easy it is for performers to get so caught up in the close-up, small-scale details of a composition that we lose perspective on large-scale musical architecture. Schenker, himself a fine pianist, understood the performer's dilemma from a practical as well as academic viewpoint. His tone may be abrupt, but his passion for Bach is that of a performer. "By varying the degree of light and shade," he tells us, "the performer can bring the phrases and motives to life, thus enabling the ear to hear their relationship to the various structural levels."[77]

There's something powerfully moving about the Sarabande. That characteristic "one-*two*-three" meter often seems exaggerated by discordant harmonies and distinctive rhythms on the second beat. In a movement of three broad sections, the second departs from the multi-voiced style of the first and third in a kind of solo cantilena in the cello's upper register. The effect is, in Schenker's expression, an "enchanted world."[78] Mark M. Smith hears the brief foray into the "death-key of D minor" as a glance back at the anguished Sarabande of the Second Suite.[79] Allen Winold points to Bach's musical monogram, B-flat – A – C – B-natural, in the bassline.[80] There is much below the surface.

*

The obstetrician has told Sean and me to report to the hospital at four o'clock in the morning. I'm in my office until eight the night before, and on my way out of the building some students follow me, asking me questions. "I'm so sorry," I tell them, "I have to go because I'm about to give birth." But even when the nurses wheel me into the operating room, I'm puzzled when I see a bassinet in the corner. What's that doing there? "Oh, there's going to be a baby!" I exclaim to myself. Throughout this hard-won, high-risk pregnancy, I haven't dared to let myself believe there will be a baby at the end of this.

An anesthesiologist pushes an enormous needle into my spine to make me numb from the chest down. Adjusting tubes and syringes, he cheerfully tells me that I'm the calmest person he's ever seen in this situation. "I couldn't sleep all night, so I meditated instead," I tell him.

"I'm going to give you some uppers," he replies.

Our daughter is born at dawn. There's a curtain over the lower half of my body and we can't see anything, so when we hear a strange quacking noise the first thing I say is "Is there a duck in here?" But of course it's not, it's our little daughter taking her first breaths.

I hear the surgeon telling the pediatrician that he's about to hand her the baby, and I crane my neck to see. She's here! She's real! Then she's surrounded by nurses examining her and I can't see her any more. I sink back down into the stretcher, and when I look up, I see the acoustic tiles on the ceiling float away like rose petals and there, dazzling and magnificent, is heaven.

"They're here," I say in wonderment. "They came."

"Who came, honey?" says Sean.

"The angels," I say.

"There aren't angels," says my husband. "You've just had a lot of medicines today."

"But I can hear them," I insist. "They're singing."

My husband is silent for a moment. "What do they sound like?"

"Like music," I tell him. "Like music, but better."

To medieval philosophers, *musical instrumentalis* was the lowest form of music. Made by humans, it was also the only kind the human ear could hear. Up one level was *musica humana*, the music made by mathematics. Highest of all was *musica mundana*, the music made by suns and moons and planets, a music so pure and perfect that no human ear could hear it. "It's the music of the spheres," I insist. "I can hear it!"

Which should go down in history as the nerdiest thing anyone has ever said while giving birth.

The nurses bring our perfect little girl to us wrapped in a striped hospital blanket. Someone has put a pink knitted cap on her head. I'm allowed less than a minute with her, because I have to have several hours of surgery. Sean leaves the operating room with the nurses and I'm alone with the doctors. The anesthesiologist asks me if I want to go to sleep now. "No," I say. I don't want to forget anything about this moment, because I have seen God and the angels and I never want to stop listening to their unearthly music. I lie still and rapt until gradually the ceiling closes back up again and the singing stops.

V. BOURRÉES

As every music student knows, Bach fathered twenty children. Any mention of this usually elicits smirks and wisecracks about passionate Protestants. I always knew that some of the children hadn't made it out of infancy, but it isn't until I'm researching my Bach project that I learn just how many of them died. With Maria Barbara, Bach had seven children, and of those, three died in infancy and one in early adulthood. Anna Magdalena bore Bach thirteen children in nineteen years, and lost seven of them within seven years. *Seven.*

Before I was a mother, I'd supposed that people who lived in a time of high infant mortality would try to have as many babies as possible under the assumption that they would lose a few, and knowing this, try not to get too attached until the little ones got strong enough to survive. Now, holding my daughter, I realize how wrong I was. It would be impossible to look into this little face, or feel her tiny pink-nailed fingers wrapped around my thumb, or kiss the top of her head, and not get attached. She is as much a part of me as my arm or leg.

We name her Eliana for her grandmother Gillian, and Grace because we hope she will be graceful. Only later do we learn that Eliana is a popular name in infertility circles because of its Hebrew meaning, "My God has answered me." When she gets old enough to ask why she has one brown and one hazel-green eye, we tell her that we wished for a little daughter with skin as white as snow, lips as red as blood, and eyes two different colors like David Bowie's. "And look what happened!" we finish, triumphantly.

There would be no more children. Multiple infertility surgeries and a cesarean section had left me resembling nothing so much as a patchwork quilt of scraps and fragments, just enough to make one baby. From my first glance of her in her little pink hat, I knew I would do anything for her. How had Johann Sebastian and Anna Magdalena felt as they went through this love and pain again and again? It occurs to me for the first time that perhaps their deep Lutheran faith was not simply a habit or a cultural by-product of their East German upbringing, but something they really needed to be true. If it were not true, how would they bear the never-ending tragedy of bereavements and hopes crushed?

Perhaps this is why Anna Magdalena's *Notenbuch* contains so many copied-out "death-lullabies."[81] One of them, "Bist du bei mir" – not actually by Bach, but often attributed to him – treats death as a kind of heavenly sleep in a mother's loving arms. Small wonder it appealed to Anna Magdalena enough for her to copy it out in full; it must practically have jumped off the page at her.

These thoughts weigh heavily on my mind as I sit at home with my new baby in my arms. I cry a lot for no reason. I've heard that you're supposed to sing to your baby to improve her brain development, and I'm too tired to sing. Then I panic that my inaction will disadvantage her brain, so I mutter weakly and tunelessly through "Mary had a little lamb," crying with exhaustion while she looks up at me with those strange different-colored eyes. When we take her back to the hospital for her first check-up, we learn that she has lost a significant percentage of her body weight. The nurse calls a lactation consultant in, and that's when I learn that I barely produce milk. "But my latch is perfect," I protest. "The nurse in the hospital said so." I'm not used to being bad at things, and this feels like an outrage.

The lactation consultant appears not to be listening. She picks up a telephone and calls our pediatrician, who gives the approval for us to start feeding the baby formula.

At first I object to this plan. "Your baby has to eat," says the lactation consultant. I keep arguing, since I've read everywhere that breast is best. What's more, I dread having this conversation with my mother, who is vocally opposed to formula feeding.

"Fed is best," the lactation consultant tells me firmly.

I'm not giving up without a fight. Even if I'm a weeping wreck, I'm still a know-it-all professor, and I like to have the last word. "You're a lactation consultant," I say reproachfully. "You're supposed to tell me to lactate."

It only occurs to me a few days later that without the privilege of our modern medical care, something really terrible could have happened. When the lactation consultant makes a house call to check on the baby and me, I ask her what people used to do before science came up with a product nourishing enough to substitute for breastmilk. Surely I can't be the only mother whose body has calamitously let her down when her baby needed to eat.

"They lost a lot of babies," she says.

After the lactation consultant drives away, I grab *The New Bach Reader* from the bookshelf and flip through to the chapter on Bach's family tree. "Twins, Maria Sophia and Johann Christoph, b. February 23, 1713; son d. at birth, daughter buried March 15, 1713…Ernestus Andreas, baptized October 30, 1727; d. November 1, 1727…Christiana Benedicta, baptized January 1, 1730; d. January 4, 1730…Johann August Abraham, baptized November 5, 1733, d. November 6, 1733…"[82] No causes of death are recorded, but the thought that some or all of these tiny children might have starved to death for lack of mother's milk sends me into one of my increasingly regular anxiety attacks. Sean tries to console me by reminding me that Eliana is happy, healthy, and nourished, but my inability to feed her with my body taps into some primal maternal fear. It takes me several years to recover from the shame and terror of that time.

After those first panicked days are over, we adapt well enough to our new normal, that is, chronic sleep deprivation. The hardest thing for me, once I get treatment for my post-partum anxiety, is losing the use of my arms. When I'm holding the baby, I can't pick up anything, least of all a cello. Temperamentally restless, I find myself missing and mourning the ability to pick things up – forks, books, my hairbrush. I even miss housework. I go for days without washing my hair, and often neglect to eat because it seems like too much effort.

The one thing I can do successfully while holding the baby is watching television. I watch it all day and most of the night. I work my way through costume drama after costume drama, and one day Netflix suggests a film called *Valmont*, an adaptation of the novel *Les liaisons dangereuses* by de Laclos that had the misfortune to come out in the same year as *Dangerous Liaisons*, an adaptation with a much bigger budget. In it, a young Colin Firth stars as the depraved nobleman Valmont. "You had me at Colin Firth," I say to the television. To Sean, I add "That's the only other man you ever have to worry about, darling." He pulls a face and leaves the room.

The film is terrible, but it does apparently have good music and dance consultants. In one scene, Valmont – the only gentleman present – is obligated to dance with every lady in the room. First he does a stately Courante with his elderly aunt, Madame de Rosemonde. Next, a rowdy Gigue with little Cécile de Volanges, who in this adaptation is a tomboyish teenager. With his co-conspirator the Marquise de Merteuil, he dances a well-behaved Menuet, which seems fitting for two amoral aristocrats who pretend to behave well, at least when others are watching. When the virtuous Madame de Tourvel stands up to dance with him, the filmmakers give them a Bourrée. This is a pivotal point in the story, because it's the moment where Valmont stops wanting to manipulate Madame de Tourvel for Madame de Merteuil's amusement, and falls in love with her instead.

What is it about the Bourrée that made the production team choose it as Valmont's falling-in-love dance? Wouldn't a Sarabande or Chaconne fit the bill better? This thought sends me back to the ever-amusing Johann Mattheson's *Der volkommene Capellmeister* to see what he has to say about Bourrées. As usual, I can't tell if he's being funny or serious. "The word *Bourrée* in itself actually means something filled, stuffed, solid, strong, weighty, and yet soft and delicate," he informs us, "which is more suited to shoving, sliding or gliding, than to lifting, hopping or springing."[83]

"Are you messing with me, Herr Capellmeister?" I say to the book, and pull out my phone to find an etymological dictionary online. Sure enough, Mattheson is telling the truth about the origins of the word. To stuff, though. Stuff what? He makes it sound like a soup dumpling. What are we to do with that? I assume that like most dances of questionable origin, the doughy Bourrée became more refined once French royalty got hold of it.

Before having the baby, I read a book on getting newborns into a clockwork-like routine so that their superwoman mothers could glide seamlessly back into professional life once their maternity leave is over. In reality, I'm unable for several weeks even to identify what day or time it is, so any thought of a schedule is out. Six weeks pass before I can pick up the cello again in time for my return to work. I've never taken a break of more than one day from practice unless I had the flu or was on an international flight. To my horror, my fingers feel as soft and helpless as the baby's. When you're used to having callused pads of thick skin on your left fingertips and the kind of grip strength that can defeat the most tenacious jam jar, it's dismaying to realize how quickly you lose them if you don't use them. I'm woefully clumsy, stumbling around my scales and arpeggios with poor intonation and a scratching tone. How on earth am I going to whip myself back into shape for work? For a moment I'm tempted to put the cello away and go to bed and cry. The only thing that stops me is the supportive presence of my husband, who has come home from work early to hold the baby so that I can practice.

After this unsatisfactory warm-up, the first piece I attempt is the Bourrée from the Third Cello Suite because comparatively speaking, it's easier than the other movements. Teachers often give it to children to learn long before they tackle any of the rest of the Third Suite. That was my experience, and coming back to it as a university student meant listening to it with new ears so that I could play it with a better understanding of theory and context. Even so, it still seems childlike to me – or rather, the first of the two Bourrées does. There's something sweetly innocent about it. Perhaps Mattheson's right to call it "soft and delicate."

Another thing I imagined about new motherhood was that the baby would lie cooing quietly in a Moses basket next to me while I practiced for as long as I liked, but again this turns out not to be the case. Once I start back into regular practice, she isn't impressed at all. She flails her way out of her swaddling cloth and howls, red-faced, until I pick her up, so I can only snatch a few moments of practice at a time. I do notice, though, that she fusses less when I'm playing Bach's Third Cello Suite. Is this because I played it so much in my last trimester of pregnancy? Maybe I've created a Bach-loving baby.

The Bourrée of the Third Cello Suite isn't really as easy as we imagine, of course. One of the challenges is to bring out the color contrast between the first and second Bourrées before repeating the first again at the end. Bach does part of this for us by putting the second Bourrée in the parallel minor mode, but thematically it's not that different from the first Bourrée. Some cellists get around this by playing the second Bourrée much slower and with an air of tragedy. By choosing to play high up on the D-string in preference to the brighter A-string, they can get a darker, more muted color. It's also quite common to stretch the phrases into long, slurring bow-strokes, but this is a much later, more Romantic style of playing than anything Bach would have expected to hear. Going back to the eighteenth-century manuscripts, we can see quite clearly that they don't contain any long slur markings. As always, I find that relearning Bach movements means peeling back generations of performance traditions and assumptions.

The question of contrast still needs addressing, though, and after many experiments it occurs to me that I could actually try playing it without any marked contrast in tone quality or tempo in the second Bourrée. Even if we separate the two Bourrées into "major" and "minor" sound-worlds, the fact remains that quite a few measures of the first Bourrée are in minor modes, while the second Bourrée has a significant section in the major mode. They are also melodically related, as opposed to the stark contrast between the pairs of Menuets in the First and Second Cello Suites. Here, the paired dances present joy and sorrow side by side throughout. What would happen if we interpreted them both as different sides of the same emotion, like the comic and tragic muses of the two-faced Greek theater mask? The reappearance of the first Bourrée at the end, sneaking in on the E-natural that signals the return to the major mode, reminds us of the possibility of hope after anguish. There is no ambiguity, no open-endedness. Bach always answers his questions.

VI. GIGUE

Slowly and gradually, I edge back into the routine of work. One morning, when the baby is seven weeks old, I take her into daycare and drive up the hill to the School of Music parking lot. I turn the engine off and burst into tears, having at least managed not to cry when I handed the baby over to the teacher. I'm not sure I'm ready to go back to teaching, but I can't afford to stay away any longer. I have no idea what I'm doing and I'm so tired I barely remember the baby's name. I might even have trouble remembering my own. I'm supposed to give a lecture on cello pedagogy in ten minutes, and while I'm prepared – I wrote a semester's worth of lesson plans and quizzes while I was pregnant so that I wouldn't have to do them now – I currently doubt my ability to speak in full sentences. A panicky voice in my head shrieks "I can't do this!"

The outburst appears to summon Alexander Vassilievich. "And *vhat?*"

My mother's voice chimes in, firmly: "It will get easier."

It does. Somehow my body finds its way up the steps into the music building, then along the corridor and up the stairs to my office. I gaze around the room at my big bookshelf full of scores, my New Zealand art prints on the walls, the photographs of my quartet and some of my teachers, the cello chair in the middle of the rug, the oversize practice mirror. I'm still me.

In the classroom, some reserve of strength takes over and my body remembers how to teach. The students welcome me back, and the lecture goes well. The boost to my self-esteem from doing my job well feels like a blood transfusion. The life is flowing back into me after these blurred, confused weeks of new motherhood. I mightn't be mother of the year, but at least I'm good at being a professor.

My department chair insists on moving a large reclining armchair into my office so that I can nap during my lunch hour, and this turns out to be enough for me to function through studio lessons and lectures. My graduate teaching assistant offers to do my photocopying before classes so that I can come in a few minutes later, and the students smile understandingly when I space out in the middle of conversations. Best of all, I can now summon up the strength to get two practice sessions in every day. I'm too tired to do as much as I did before the baby came, but it's enough to start work on Bach again.

So much of the passagework in the movements of the Third Cello Suite reminds me of the turning of wheels in a great machine. Repeating patterns carry the harmony round and round from one key center to another, while embellishments encircle the important pitches of phrases. The Gigue does this more than any other movement in the Third Suite, excepting the much longer Prelude. Three distinct textures are at play here – unaccompanied monody at the outset, a two-voiced *bariolage* as Bach starts to move towards G major, and two-voiced double stops as he approaches the ends of sections. When I first learned this Gigue in my teens, my right arm was so tense that I could barely play the *bariolage* section. You'd think relaxation would be natural and easy, a default setting for the human body, but paradoxically it's one of the hardest things to learn on any instrument. Coming back to the Gigue now, I take pleasure in feeling the weight of the bow in my fingers, and balancing it so that it can take on most of the hard work of the *bariolage* while my loose-jointed arms, wrists, and hands just move in sync with the bow's trajectory. My weeks away from the cello have made me love it more than ever. What a friend and comfort it is, and always has been.

It occurs to me as I work on the three textures of the Gigue that the word *texture* itself comes from the same root as *text* and *textile*. All of them are related to *texere*, the Latin word that means "to weave." A signature feature of Bach's musical language – his text – is the *Fortspinnung* or "spinning out" of melodic material. Through long sequential chains of short repeating ideas, he invents an entire musical structure. The fabric of the Gigue comes together like this, and now when I play it I have the irresistible mental image of a spinning wheel. Hypnotically rhythmical, its gliding circular movements weave fragments of melody into a seemingly endless thread.

When my daughter is old enough for bedtime stories, she always wants the Sleeping Beauty. I hesitate over this, since I'm not sure I approve of helpless princesses who need princes to rescue them, but my daughter insists. After the umpteenth reading, I start to wonder whether we should rethink the princess's tussle with the spindle. Have we unjustly maligned the bad fairy all along? By cursing the princess, she spared her – at least for a time – the realities of society's expectations for adult princesses. Even as it sends the princess into her century of sleep, that hidden, forbidden spinning wheel might symbolize a kind of awakening.

This thought plays through my mind as I practice the Gigue's reckless dives from high to low pitches. The sections of intense *bariolage* demand perfect looseness of the joints so that the bow can execute string crossings with exquisitely controlled circular movements. With this technical workout, Bach is preparing us for the demands of what's coming next.

Part Four

CROSSROADS

Suite No. 4 in E-flat Major, BWV 1010

Welt, ich bleibe nicht mehr hier,
Hab ich doch kein Teil an dir,
Das der Seele könnte taugen.

"World, I will stay here no more,
I possess no part of you
That could matter to my soul."

Johann Sebastian Bach, *Ich habe genug* BWV 82

I. PRELUDE

The Fourth Cello Suite is music for grown-ups. Even if the First Cello Suite is playable by advanced children, and teenage cellists master the Second and Third, a child who could give a mature performance of the Fourth Suite would be very unusual indeed. If I ever doubted that part of Bach's intention in composing the Cello Suites was to extend the instrumental technique in ways that compelled players to get better, the Fourth Suite is proof. Every Cello Suite from the Second through the Sixth represents a significant jump in difficulty from the preceding work, such as the finger-contorting double stops in the Second Cello Suite and the hard string crossings in the Third, and the Fourth Cello Suite demands all of these and more. Compounding every difficulty is the key of E-flat major.

All the Cello Suites but the Fourth are in keys that correspond to one of the open strings of the cello – C, G, D, and A. The First Suite is in G major, the Second in D minor, the Third in C major, the Fifth in C minor, and the Sixth in D major. When you have an open cello string that corresponds to your home key, this simplifies many decisions about the pitches of the notes. If you're in C major, for example, you can tune any C on the cello to engage the sympathetic resonance of the C-string. This not only takes the guesswork out of tuning, but makes the cello ring in a gratifying manner. In the absence of an E-flat string, cellists have to find the pitch of E-flat by relating it to the open strings.

This isn't as straightforward as it sounds, because there's more than one way to tune an E-flat depending on the intonation system you're using. It's easier for pianists, whose instrument sits immutably in equal temperament. In this famous tuning system, the octave is divided into twelve equal semitones, which sounds promising, except for the problem that it's not really "in tune." As Ross W. Duffin explains in the delightful *How Equal Temperament*

Ruined Harmony (And Why You Should Care),[84] modern piano tuning is a compromise that allows pianists to perform compositions in any key without wincing in pain at out-of-tune intervals. A successful compromise, to be sure, but not an entirely satisfactory one.

Equal temperament was in use during Bach's lifetime, and we can find it mentioned in the writings of the great organ builder Andreas Werckmeister. "It says much about the Lutheran mentality of the time," comments David Ledbetter, "that what finally convinced him [Werckmeister] of the validity of equal temperament was an unnamed theologian deriving its proportions from the biblical description of the construction of Solomon's palace."[85] Bach, for his part, was sensitive to the possibilities of several intonation systems. It's therefore tempting to assume that he used equal temperament for the forty-eight Preludes and Fugues of *The Well-Tempered Clavier*, which cycles twice through the twenty-four possible major and minor keys, since this would mean not having to get up to tune the harpsichord in between pieces. Inconveniently, this may not be true. Some present-day harpsichordists enjoy experimenting with different tunings, and I've attended more than one performance of the *Well-Tempered Clavier* in which the audience has waited patiently between the end of a Fugue and the start of the next Prelude while the harpsichordist re-tunes. The resulting performances were convincingly and amazingly characterful, and made me wonder what heightened expression we might accomplish if we didn't constantly have to compromise with equal temperament on the modern piano.

We cellists can vary the tuning of our pitches with the slightest adjustment of a fingertip on a string, meaning that any approximate system such as equal temperament is unsatisfactory. We're happy enough to adjust to a piano's intonation in the cello-piano repertoire, but in Bach's Cello Suites we can do better than this compromise. In relearning the Fourth Cello Suite, I start thinking of my instrument as a *well-tempered cello*, since I don't have to be wedded to any particular choice of intonation system.

The fact is that we have several choices for intonation, all of which must relate to the pitches of the open strings if we're to get any resonance out of the cello. In linear, melodic playing, it can work well to use Pythagorean intonation, where the third and seventh degrees of the major scale are pushed a little sharp in relation to the first scale degree. This means pitching the

E-flats rather flat so that they are close to the seventh degree of the scale, D, which corresponds to the cello's D-string. Then again, when you have to play a lot of E-flat major chords – a thing that happens again and again in the Fourth Cello Suite – it makes more sense to use just intonation, where the third degree of the major scale is pushed flat in relation to the first scale degree. This means pitching the E-flats rather sharp so that they will sound good against the third degree of the scale, G, which corresponds to the cello's G-string.

If this sounds complicated to the point of bewilderment, it is. On my first few attempts to learn the Fourth Cello Suite, aged about eighteen, the matter perplexed me so much that I declared I "didn't like" the piece and refused to perform it in public. Picking it up again now, I'm thankful for the years I spent in a string quartet, where arguing about intonation was an all-day-every-day activity. Now that I've played Beethoven's String Quartet Op. 74, Mendelssohn's Octet, and several other chamber music works in E-flat major, I feel better prepared for experimenting with E-flats in Bach. The worrying question is whether I may end up doing it more than one way. Will people in the audience notice if I make the E-flats flatter in the linear textures of the Allemande and first Bourrée, but sharper in the chordal Sarabande and the second Bourrée? Will it sound as if I don't know what I'm doing? *Do* I know what I'm doing? Suddenly I feel as daunted as my eighteen-year-old self, and it takes some self-control to stop myself getting up out of my chair and going off to get a coffee or a long walk or pretty much anything other than a practice session in E-flat major.

The other thing about playing in E-flat is that it's exhausting. The left hand often has to stretch using a technique known as the extended position, which enables us to reach the frequent E-flats, B-flats, and A-flats on the fingerboard. If there's any tension or locking in the fingers and thumb, this can cause painful injuries like tendinitis. When I first start to relearn the Prelude of the Fourth Cello Suite, I feel an unpleasant strain in the webbing between my first and second fingers. It's only a mild injury, but enough to make me abstain from playing anything in E-flat for a couple of days. All musicians fear injury and try to prevent it by rethinking their technique, and my own temporary brush with pain causes me to re-examine the way my fingers and thumb move around the fingerboard and neck of the cello.

After I've recovered, I realize that my thumb has to be more moveable so that it can gently oppose whichever finger is depressing the string, since an "anchored" thumb isn't going to work when the stretches between the notes are so wide. Once I've worked on this new method for a day or two, I notice that my agility and intonation have improved in every key, not just E-flat. Perhaps Bach knew this all along and wanted us to learn from it?

It's not just the left hand that gets tired in the Prelude of the Fourth Suite. In this "pattern Prelude," where chords are repeatedly broken in regular eighth notes, we have to figure out a way to articulate the bow strokes. It's here that I find I need the biggest rethink of all. The recordings I grew up listening to made the Prelude sound sustained, booming, and majestic. Pablo Casals, Pierre Fournier, and especially Paul Tortelier go at slow speeds, with long, smooth bowstrokes and sustained vibrato. They sound for all the world as if they're trying to imitate the sound of the organ, an instrument Bach loved. Indeed, he didn't have a good one to play on in Cöthen, where his job didn't require his skills as an organist or composer of sacred music.

When I first attempted the Prelude of the Fourth Cello Suite as a student, I tried and failed to play like the great "organist-cellist" interpreters. The problem with trying to sound like an organist in this particular piece is that you don't get to play those mighty bass notes on an open string. Instead, you have to try to get the low E-flat to ring as much as possible before you take your bow off it, since the resonance disappears right away. Relearning the Prelude now, I still don't sound anything like an organist. I try to imagine Bach's foot – clad in soft kid leather shoes with shiny buckles, silk stockings underneath – slamming down onto the E-flat pedal, while his powerful hands manipulate the manuals and stops of his titanic instrument. The sound should fill up a magnificent cathedral, but mine doesn't. It's no use, I can't make this work.

It's only after re-watching *392*, Pieter Wispelwey's documentary about his third compact disc recording of Bach's Cello Suites, that I feel as if I finally have permission to abandon the cello-as-organ idea. "It sounds awful on a Baroque cello," Wispelwey observes. "Why organ? Why not lute?" Using pizzicato instead of the bow, he plucks the opening of the Prelude on his cello, lute-style. "I'm in lute land! I'm going to use my bow as if I'm plucking the string."[86] He demonstrates this, and it sounds marvelous, like a gorgeous waterfall of notes. His bow-strokes have a lightness that perfectly suits the *style brisé* of the chordal patterns. I pause the DVD and rush to the cello to start trying out both the pizzicato version and the pizzicato-like bow-stroke, and I love it. I can never go back to the heavy, organ-imitating interpretations of the past – to do so would feel like trying to swim in a pool full of thick custard.

The Prelude of the Fourth Cello Suite is unusual in many respects. As a pattern Prelude, it's comparable in some respects to the Preludes of the First and Third Cello Suites – arpeggiated chord patterns, a burst of improvisatory virtuosity in the middle, and a return to patterns at the end – but it's far more complicated. In the First and Third Preludes, Bach shifts dutifully around the key centers you expect and arpeggiates the chords in the way you expect. In the Fourth Prelude, the key centers are sometimes surprising and the *style brisé* is, well, much more *brisé* than in earlier Suites. Before, in the Prelude of the Third Suite, Bach arpeggiated the chord patterns in a closed, round-and-round manner, but here in the Fourth, the pattern is one of unsettling up-and-down leaps of huge intervals, the interior voices criss-crossing each other in a tangle of harmony.

Aside from the home key of E-flat, the main secondary key is G minor. This is an unusual move from the viewpoint of the music theorist, but makes sense for the cellist because it makes resonant use of the G-string. Once the shift to this key is achieved in the middle of the movement, the bass notes of the chord patterns clearly and unmistakably start to descend in the familiar passacaglia bassline. G, F, E-flat, D...and suddenly, where we might have expected a return to G for another round of this, Bach instead takes the bassline down to the low C-sharp. In doing so, he jolts the musical line right out of chord patterns and into a dazzling *toccata* that sounds for all the world like something Bach might have improvised on the spot to impress an emperor.

Let's go back to that low C-sharp, which analytically speaking is a very strange note to feature so prominently in a composition in E-flat major. In terms of musical relationships, E-flat and C-sharp are complete strangers. Its function here is essentially – after a few brilliant diversions – to get us back to D and then G before the long journey home to E-flat. It's a striking moment, and one that inspires even music theorists, normally a reticent sub-group of music scholars, to flights of creative interpretation. In his Schenkerian analysis of the Prelude of the Fourth Cello Suite, Carl Schachter points out that the German word for "sharp" is *Kreuz*, a word that also happens to mean "cross." Apologetically, Schachter writes "I usually refrain from swimming in such sharp-infested waters," but once he's started he can't seem to stop. "Bach does sometimes use sharps as cross symbols... The climactic C-sharp-E-flat-D in the upper voice...makes a particularly vivid chiastic shape." For him, the "jaggedly descending arpeggios" of the opening "might then all stand for the fall of sinful humanity," while what comes next "could represent steps in the believer's path toward salvation."[87]

Schachter's passionate reading of the Prelude of the Fourth Suite changes everything for performer-interpreters. In pointing out cross imagery, he brings sacred and secular together for us. The pious Bach might well have nodded his approval of such a viewpoint: this was, after all, the composer who scrawled *SDG* at the end of musical works, an abbreviation of *Soli Deo Gloria*, or "To the glory of God alone."

Once you start looking for religious messages in Bach's music, you find them everywhere. Some scholars, such as Benjamin Shute, have written entire books on religious metaphor in Bach.[88] Tucked into the back cover of Anner Bylsma's *Bach, the Fencing Master* is an extraordinary essay by Gé Bartman, "Christian Symbolism in the First Three Preludes of Johann Sebastian Bach's Six Suites For Cello Solo," that claims to unearth some very well-hidden numerological and alphabetical references to Christ, the Crucifixion, the Holy Trinity and King David.[89] Even if you don't buy Bartman's theories, they make for compelling reading. For a performer mired in the daily slog of practice, thinking about the extrinsic meaning of a composition can keep your creative imagination going while you pursue a convincing interpretation of it.

But the further I get into Bach's Cello Suites, the more I have to face up to my unease with Bach's religion and what it means for the cellist and the audience in the present day.

II. ALLEMANDE

"Is it morally acceptable," I ask the class, "to listen to the music of a composer whose worldview is unacceptable to us?"

This is a classic topic of discussion for music undergraduates. The obvious composer to debate is Richard Wagner, the genius of whose compositions may or may not compensate for the repulsiveness of his anti-Semitism. It isn't unusual for students never to have previously listened to any Wagner, and often all they know about the composer are his penchants for monstrously long operas and monstrously bigoted opinions. Laurence Dreyfus – a scholar of Wagner as well as Bach – recalls arguing in an undergraduate essay that Wagner had foreshadowed the Nazis. He was "about to submit it when I put on a recording of *Tristan und Isolde*. The shock of the musical experience forced me to admit that my denunciation was hypocritical. Much to the dismay of my professor...I appended an "afterword" challenging my own conclusions..."[90] This kind of dilemma happens a lot in the university classroom. It takes about five minutes of blasting the love duet from *Die Walküre* through stereo speakers to draw students into Wagner's transfixing sound-world. Its effect is written on their faces. It might be impossible to listen to this music with indifference, and in musically sensitive young people the reaction is often one of awe. This sets us up for some conflicted and uncomfortable emotions. Allowing ourselves to feel those emotions is part of a musician's journey.

It's harder to have this debate about Bach's music versus his worldview. Wagner, whose behavior could veer into almost cartoonish villainy, is easy to despise. Bach, the industrious Capellmeister and family man, is not. And yet there is plenty to trouble us in his settings of religious texts. Michael Marissen doesn't think much of "those aesthetes, typically knowing next to nothing about the Bible or Luther and very little about Bach, who say things like 'Well, yes, Bach, you know, was a *great* composer, and, ahem, we can, and indeed *should*, simply ignore all that unpleasant talk in the text – which, to be sure, *Bach* didn't write – about "the Jews" and their shouting for the death of Jesus… Bach's *music*, you know, is *so* magnificent!'"[91]

I'm abashed when I read this, because I know I'm guilty of such intellectually lazy platitudes. In our performance of the *St. John Passion*, my colleagues and I decided to follow the common modern practice of changing the libretto to replace the word *Juden*, Jews, with *Leute*, people. This, we agreed, was the right thing to do. But was it? Were we wrong to sanitize Bach's text, particularly given that most of the audience weren't German speakers?

Entire musicological and theological conferences continue to debate the subject. Even setting aside for now the possible offensiveness of the *St. John*, what to make of the much more overtly anti-Semitic texts in other compositions? According to Michael Marissen, author of *Bach and God*, "the Lutheranism of Bach's heritage unambiguously and, more often than not, strongly contemptuously taught that those who ultimately are not turned from their Judaism will be appointed their portion with the unbelievers."[92]

Even if Marissen concludes that the *St. John Passion* doesn't necessarily promote anti-Judaism, he points to two other compositions that unmistakably do. One of the cantatas in question, *Schauet doch und sehet*, ostensibly laments the destruction of Jerusalem, but Bach's setting of it leaves little doubt as to its message. "Without even employing the word *Jews* or *Judaism*," Marissen writes, "Bach's cantata appears simply, if more abstractly, to dismiss Old Jerusalem as temporally downfallen, *irreparably* out of God's favor, and covenantally condemned." While we might expurgate the even more odious text of the other cantata, *Am Abend aber desselbigen Sabbats*, by changing *Jüden*, Judeans, into *Verfolgern*, persecutors, we still know who the author is talking about. It's sickening to us, the present-day listeners, because we know how this ends. It's hard to excuse historical anti-Semitism when we also know the history of the Holocaust. I can't imagine that Bach would have endorsed Hitler's murders – I can't even think this of Wagner, for all the ugliness of his prejudices – but I also can't stomach the contempt embedded in the very notes of these two cantatas. Can I hate the composition, though? No, I can't hate anything Bach composed. I am incapable of listening to Bach and remaining unmoved, and somehow that's the most disturbing thing of all.

*

One of the most consoling features of the Allemande of the Fourth Suite is its very equilibrium. You might not necessarily get this from listening to the movement on its own, but when you juxtapose it with the preceding Prelude, it seems like a moment of repose. The Prelude symbolizes the very notion of conflict, with its relentless about-turns from pattern preluding to improvisational flourish and back, plus all manner of weird diversions to far-flung keys. (C-flat major, anyone?) Next to this, the Allemande is the epitome of order and regularity. The rhythm is one of perfectly regular running eighth and sixteenth notes, and the harmony does nothing outlandish – E-flat goes to B-flat in the first section, and in the second, brief detours through C minor and G minor take us back to the circle of fifths so that F can take us into B-flat and then E-flat. After the Prelude, this straightforward harmony comes as a welcome relief.

*

Having previously lived only in cities – Wellington, Christchurch, London, Austin, Boulder, Denver – my decision to accept a position in a small Idaho town surprised my friends. It even surprised me. The evening before my campus interview, a kindly piano professor showed me around the charming town center and insisted on stopping at an organic foods store. With the cello on my back, I followed her up and down the aisles, puzzled as to why she wanted to show me nineteen brands of organic rice. It wasn't until later that I realized she was trying to sell me on Moscow.

I'm still not sure why she thought I'd need persuading, because Moscow isn't difficult to love. Walking around campus is a daily joy, thanks to the nineteenth-century Gothic Revival buildings and landscape design – created, locals will proudly tell you, by the Olmsted firm who also designed New York's Central Park. Moscow's downtown is quaint and leafy, with Christmas lights strung up about the trees and storefronts all year long. Owing to a city ordinance, chain stores aren't allowed in the central part of town, so when you stroll up and down Main Street, every business is locally owned. On Saturday mornings, the city blocks the street off for a bustling farmer's market. Artists, writers, and musicians congregate everywhere.

Every university town has its own particular town-and-gown dynamic, and Moscow is no exception. Co-existing uneasily with the state land-grant university is the headquarters of a growing fundamentalist Calvinist church, whose central tenets include classical education, complementarian gender roles, homeschooling, prolific stay-at-home motherhood, and filial obedience. While there is some interaction between the university and church communities, the two sides regard each other with suspicion. Some church members attend the University of Idaho, while others opt for a small unaccredited college affiliated with the church. In so small a town, the two institutions make for strange bedfellows. While the city council is strict about not allowing "campus creep," these rules don't seem to apply to the church authorities, who eagerly purchase former nightclubs, empty plots of land, and disused grain silos when they're available. The leader of the church makes no secret of his goal to make Moscow a "Christian town," and needless to say, many members of the university community don't like this plan.

One of the few things both parties seem to agree on is the organic foods store my pianist friend was so determined to show me on that first night in Moscow. In the produce section, well-heeled professors rub shoulders uneasily with churchwomen in bonnets and prairie dresses as we measure out our organic local lentils into recycled paper bags. I try not to stare or make assumptions about these women on the basis of their Laura Ingalls Wilder-esque uniform, reasoning that to them I might look like I'm in a uniform too.

Love of lentils aside, there's mistrust between communities. While I'm anxious to give a welcoming, inclusive impression, some of my encounters with church members make me aware of the chasm between our cultures. When I launch a children's music program at the university, the father of one family asks me to change a policy that states children must practice their instruments daily. "In our belief system, Sunday is a day of rest," he explains apologetically. "My children can only practice six days a week. I promise they will practice diligently."

Realizing I've blundered, I apologize too. "How about 'students must practice as directed by the teacher'?" I suggest. This appears to satisfy everyone, and the subject is closed.

On another occasion, I decide to order t-shirts for the children to wear at outreach events. When I announce this to the parents, a mother approaches me to request that the shirts be "modest."

At first I don't understand what she's asking me for. "There won't be any bragging slogans on it," I assure her.

"No," she says, "I mean that we need them to have sleeves and a high neckline for our girls' modesty." We stare at each other in mutual incomprehension.

Intuition dictates that this is not a viewpoint I should challenge. Until now I've never heard of modest apparel, but an internet image search reveals an entire industry devoted to long denim skirts and loose blouses. I call the t-shirt company and change my shirt order to long sleeves. It costs more, but there are dozens of church families in the program and it's not worth alienating them over shirtsleeves.

The conflict goes both ways. One day, Sean and I unwittingly anger a neighbor when we suggest holding our annual homeowners' association meeting in a popular downtown coffee shop owned by a family who attend the church. "I will not support the business of *those people*," she snaps. When we want to know why, she tells us to Google it.

We do, and learn about a scandal involving sexual predators, cover-ups, and not a little victim-blaming by the church. We come across church-endorsed blogs whose sexism and homophobia make for painful reading. We read that the church has ties to Confederacy apologists. How, we wonder, can anyone support this?

There's a lot of discussion among our progressive friends about whether it's right to eat and drink at *their* restaurants and bars, or allow *their* banks to profit from our money if it means that some of it might indirectly go towards the tithes they pay to the church.

And yet, the church doesn't seem to be boycotting me. It transpires that along with classical education, the church values classical music. Church families are often in attendance at our university concerts, even though buying tickets for eight or ten children can't be cheap. What's more, we couldn't run the children's music program without them. With their flexible schedules, homeschooling families are easy to work into the teachers' lesson schedules, and the parents make sure the children cooperate with practice expectations. Every Christmas I get cards thanking me in beautiful cursive for the "blessing of music." Even if their church's positions dismay me, the people themselves are lovely.

Most people are, when you get to know them. Many young members of the church come to study at the university, and music tends to be a popular major in their community. In the music department, the one-on-one nature of the instruction means that professors and students get to know each other well, and we talk about all sorts of things besides music. While I prefer not to tell students my own political and religious leanings, they sometimes want to tell me about theirs, and I'm willing to listen. One young woman from the church community, an excellent student who contributes intelligently to class discussion, comes in one day with news of her "courtship." She talks excitedly about the procedure, which appears to be entirely managed and stage-managed by her father. When she marries, her father will remove the so-called purity ring from her finger so that the groom may replace it with a wedding band.

Listening in silence, I try not to show my astonishment at the transactional nature of the ritual. Would it be overstepping for me to tell her that she doesn't have to do this? Yes, says my intuition. Hold your tongue, don't mess with this. I'm still trying to process my feelings when I realize that the student shows no sign whatsoever of feeling oppressed. On the contrary, she's looking forward to her wedding as a rite of passage.

*

"Someone should start a refuge for the women so they can leave that cult," says a friend when I tell her about the conversation.

"Isn't that a bit patronizing?" I say. "Lots of cultures have arranged marriages. I don't know why this one is bothering me so much. Maybe it's because my family used to be from a Calvinist background, so it all seems a bit close to home."

"They're completely brainwashed," says my friend. "They don't get a choice. It's beaten into them. Then they literally beat it into their own children."

I've always been opposed to physically punishing children, and now that I'm a mother the thought of anyone hitting a child's tender flesh fills me with visceral horror. How could they? I realize I'm too cowardly to ask any of the church members I know about this. If I did, they might tell me, and I might not be able to bear hearing it.

"Can we blame women for any of this, though?" I say. "There are a lot of rewards for meeting your family's expectations. People want to have the approval of their community, don't they?"

After all, haven't I made life decisions of my own based on keeping my mother's approval? It wasn't that I was forbidden from studying anything other than music, but there had been a lot of pressure. After the money and effort she put into my education, it wasn't unreasonable to expect a return on her investment. Everyone in our family was a musician. Like the Bach family, it was what we did. If you were a Bach, you were supposed to be a musician, and while becoming a court jester might not mean social death, it did mean you were left off the family tree.

Surprisingly, it's my mother who helps me work through my conflicted feelings. When I tell her about my student's upcoming marriage on one of our weekly Skype conversations, she tells me "You shouldn't think you can rescue her."

"Well, I don't want to rescue her, exactly, but…"

"You can't change people's minds," my mother says firmly. "People don't really change, so you just have to look for the things you have in common." She reminds me that she was once friends with a well-known Catholic doctor, now deceased, whose activism included an adamant opposition to birth control. It was an unlikely friendship, since my mother has never made a secret of her progressive views.

"Didn't you ever discuss the birth control thing with her?" I say.

"Heavens no," says my mother. "What would be the point? We talked about music, of course. She adored music. I sometimes sat with her at concerts."

"Didn't you get offended when you read things she said in the newspaper?" I persist.

"Of course," says my mother, "but if we only focused on our differences with other people, we wouldn't have any friends, would we?"

*

I decide that I'm still going to go to the Christian-owned coffee house. Whenever I go in, a German word comes into my mind – *gemütlich*, cozy. Worn Victorian floorboards creak agreeably under your feet, and the walls are lined with philosophy and history books. Glass cabinets display apple pies and chocolate layer cakes. The coffee is excellent, the beer even better. Bearded seminarians sit outside, smoking old-fashioned pipes and debating Zwingli and Melanchthon. Baroque music plays on the stereo all day, and in the evenings musicians play jazz on an ancient upright piano. Dogs are allowed, though I don't bring mine since he tends to yap. I can imagine Bach himself enjoying this place. He'd be a regular, stopping by several times a week for a glass of ale, a theological chat, and maybe – if pressed – an improvisation session. "Ah well, all right. Here's a little musical offering I thought of just now."

The thought occurs to me that Bach also might have felt more at home in Moscow's church community than in the secular university. Aside from the obvious matter of his deep religious feeling, he clearly valued abundant childbearing and gendered distribution of labor in his family life. It's easy to put this in the picture-frame of history and excuse it because "things were like that then," but as my mother has reminded me, people don't really change.

*

Relearning the Fourth Suite, I have the idea of gathering together all the pieces I can find by Bach in the key of E-flat. The first one that occurs to me is the opening Sonatina movement from the cantata *Gottes Zeit ist die allerbeste Zeit*, "God's time is the very best time." At university, a music history professor had given it to the class as a set piece. "This cantata is about preparing for death," he told us. "Bach wrote it when he was about your age." As we listened, I was overcome by the beauty and simplicity of the opening Sonatina, a small instrumental piece for two recorders, two violas da gamba, and continuo. The bassline – my part! – was all in eighth notes, steady as footsteps. I felt my arms come up in goosebumps. To me, that bassline seemed to say "I will stay with you, I will walk beside you while you go through this, I will never leave you." Orphaned at just ten years old,

Bach had already suffered loss after excruciating loss by the time he wrote *Gottes Zeit* aged twenty-two. How comforting it must have been to imagine the soft footfalls of a faithful companion on his journey.

Remembering the feeling of hearing it for the first time, I decide to introduce *Gottes Zeit* to the cello studio at our weekly score study meeting. I bring scores and translations of the text for the entire cantata, and ask if anyone knows where Bach got it from.

One student instantly puts up his hand. "Psalm 90, Isaiah, Mosaic Covenant, Luke," he says. "And some things that aren't actually in the Bible. From Lutheran hymns, maybe?"

"Very good!" I say. The histories of Western music and Christianity are so intertwined that it's useful to have people around who know their Bibles inside out. "Now, let's look at the instrumentation of the Sonatina. What do you notice?"

The students peer at the full scoring for two recorders, two violas da gamba, and continuo. "The two recorder parts. They seem to...to finish each other's sentences."

"They overlap."

"Bach's crossing the parts! I thought you weren't supposed to cross the parts in voice-leading."

"That's in four-part chorales. Maybe he can do it in cantatas because..."

"Well, you know what also crosses," says another student who hasn't yet spoken. The others turn to look at her. "You know, like, a cross," she finishes.

"I think you're onto something," I say. "Shall we listen?"

I play the students my favorite recording of the Sonatina by Ton Koopman and the Amsterdam Baroque Orchestra and Choir, and they follow along with their scores. At the end, there's complete silence. When they finally lift their heads, I see in their faces that all of them are profoundly moved. Bach's music tends to have that effect on people. I'm not naïve enough to imagine that his music is powerful enough to reconcile our communities, much less bring about world peace, but for one hour in one classroom a group of believers and non-believers shared a sense of awe in his creation.

III. COURANTE

Bach's long melodic phrases often fall into three distinct parts. The first is an opening idea, a fragmentary hint at the characters Bach will create. The second is a repetition of the first, usually not an exact one – Bach might put it on a different chord, for example. The third, longer part of the phrase is the one that goes somewhere. After some twists and turns and diversions, it finishes off with a cadence, precise as the period at the end of a sentence. Three-part phrase structure makes me think of the fairy tales where a hero, on his way to a princess or treasure or both, finds himself at a three-way fork in the road. The first path initially looks attractive, but it's a trap to weed out the foolish heroes. The second path is a trap too, perhaps a less obvious one than the first, but a trap nonetheless. The third way, which is the longest and most arduous on account of being covered with thorns, brambles, and monsters, is where the princess and/or treasure live. The reward is there for you to find, but you have to work for it.

The Courante of the Fourth Suite is mostly constructed from this type of three-part phrase. The up-and-down nature of the melodic line might look back to the jagged broken-chord patterns of the Prelude, but that's where the similarity ends. There is no shape-shifting through fantastical key-changes here, just clear beginnings and endings and rational chord progressions. The cellist gets to swoop up and down chains of sequences, question-answer phrases, and elaborate voyages around the circle of fifths. Bach also introduces the concept of triplet divisions of the beat, which makes for an interesting textural contrast with the more regular duple and quadruple divisions. In the three-part phrases, the third part often transitions out of pairs of eighth notes into running lines of tripletized ones, giving us a sense of speeding up even when the overall pulse hasn't changed.

Going back to the very fundamentals of the staff, we can find more threes. E-flat major has three flats in the key signature, and Courantes are always in triple meter. It's tempting to read some kind of symbolism into this, and into the idea of threes in Western music in general. Take Mozart's opera *The Magic Flute*, where the composer and librettist practically smack us over the head with three of everything – ladies, boys, temples, and hunks of cut-up serpent, and that's before we even get to the preponderance of movements in E-flat major. For Mozart, three was significant because of its connection with Freemasonry, while for other composers the Holy Trinity had a lot to do with it.

Is this what's going on here? My recent preoccupation with searching for religious metaphor in Bach makes me want to look for a symbolic subtext, but I'm not sure the number three is the place to look for it. Going through the score with a pencil in preparation for relearning it, I find myself lightly drawing lines between the heads of the notes to make cross shapes, the way you see in so many analyses of Bach's music. Once you've started looking for them, it's hard to stop even when you suspect that sometimes a melodic line is just a melodic line.

It's the beginning of another fall semester, and we're preparing for another massed ensemble concert at the university. This semester, the repertoire is Bach's cantata for Ascension, *Gott fähret auf mit Jauchzen*, "God goes up with jubilation." This piece brings me special joy because it has a virtuoso part for the piccolo trumpet, and Sean is joining the Idaho Bach Consort to perform it. We've always thought it was a pity there's so little chamber music featuring both cello and trumpet, probably because of the decibel-producing differences between the instruments, so it makes us particularly glad to be able to perform orchestral repertoire together.

Whenever I accompany singers, I try to be conscientious about studying and translating texts so that I can support the meaning of the words with my choice of articulations, dynamics, and tone colors. I try to imitate vowels and consonants with my fingertips on bow and strings. Going through the text of *Gott fähret auf*, I notice there are three iterations of the line *Ich stehe hier am Weg*, "I stand here on the road." The first appearance comes at the end of a recitative for the alto soloist, ending "I stand here on the road, and look after Him joyfully." Bach sets the first half of the statement to dissonant chords, and in the second half resolves the dissonance into a consonant cadence. The second appearance of the text is at the end of the alto aria that comes next: "I stand here on the road, and look after Him longingly." This time the first part of the statement is uttered on a single pitch – a literal standstill – while a pair of oboes weave a complicated *obbligato* around the words. The second part is in an extraordinary dissonant melisma on the word *sehnlich*, "longingly." The text appears for the third time in a recitative for the soprano soloist: "I stand here on the road, and call after him thankfully." For this final iteration, Bach sets the text syllabically, as if to resolve the matter once and for all. Is there significance in the fact that he chooses a singer with a higher vocal range for the final appearance of "I stand here on the road"? Well, heaven is upwards, isn't it?

We've combined the choirs of several universities in the region for this occasion, including the Christian college in Moscow. When I meet the guest conductor before the rehearsal, I ask him what he makes of the three statements of *Ich stehe hier am Weg*. "I think by stressing this one line so much, Bach's telling us that prayers will be answered," he says thoughtfully. "You might even interpret *Weg* as being not just a road, but a crossroads. You might have to deliberate about which direction you're going to go in, but there's always a right way. If you're praying hard enough, you know which way to go."

"That makes sense," I reply, "since there's a lot of praying going on in this cantata."

"Yes, there certainly is. And what's more, Bach's never in any doubt about the possibility of salvation. It's something he trusts is going to happen."

I'm lost in thought until the rehearsal begins and I have to come back to the world. I try to think of a composition by Bach where prayers aren't answered, yearning is thwarted, and virtue goes unnoticed, and come up short. Bach never makes it easy, of course – there's the *Fortspinnung* and counterpoint to contend with, but once you've worked through it, you can trust that you'll get your cadence at the right time and in the expected key. It always ends in an orderly, rational manner.

Contrast this with composers whose yearning goes unfulfilled – and there are plenty, since one of the unifying themes in the music and poetry of every culture of the world is not getting what you want. The first piece that springs to mind is Robert Schumann's *Im wunderschönen Monat Mai* ("In the Beautiful Month of May"), whose poetic protagonist sings about his declaration of love. In setting the text to ambiguous harmony, however, Schumann tells us without even needing to use words that the man's passion will not be reciprocated. The very fact of not knowing whether yearning will result in fulfillment is why listening to Schumann is in equal parts ecstatic and painful. And perhaps that's the difference between Schumann's God and Bach's – Schumann's doesn't always reply.

As I persevere through the bassline that accompanies Sean's victorious trumpet solo in the opening chorus, I notice how Bach never drops any of the threads of melody and harmony. Tension always ends in resolution – eventually. Nothing is left open-ended. And with this realization, I feel as if I've understood something important about Bach. The Cello Suites may be firmly in secular territory when it comes to performance venue, but in Bach's language the secular belongs to the sacred. Yearning is heard and answered here too.

IV. SARABANDE

The cello might have been a comparatively new instrument in Bach's time, but it caught on fast. Its repertoire grew and grew, and by the twentieth century almost every major composer had written a sonata or concerto for cello. These days, only singers, pianists, and violinists have more repertoire than we do, and because of this, plenty of instrumentalists with smaller native repertoires will play arrangements and transcriptions of "our" music. Violists, guitarists, trombonists, and saxophonists seem particularly to like Bach's Cello Suites, though I've heard arrangements for marimba and vibraphone too. A lot of composers' work is so idiomatic for a particular instrument that it doesn't lend itself well to transcription, but for some reason Bach's compositions tend to sound good on any instrument. There's something about his language that transcends timbre and tessitura, something universally meaningful.

Cellists like to boast that theirs is the instrument that best imitates the human voice. I don't necessarily agree, since all melodic instruments can sound "singing" in the right time and place. The rhetoric of Bach's music often calls more for a speaking style than a singing one, but there are also occasions when the judicious application of a heartfelt *cantabile* feels like the best plan. There's something very song-like about the Sarabande of the Fourth Suite. In so many other movements in the Cello Suites, Bach uses the angular *style brisé* to conjure up the impression of a multi-voiced texture, but in this Sarabande he creates a long-line melody that dips down into elided chords on other strings rather than disrupt the singing phrase.

Since we're still in E-flat major, this makes the Sarabande rather hard to play in tune, and as I relearn it I start writing little up and down arrows above the staff in my score to remind myself to pitch certain notes a little sharper or flatter to get them in tune within their context. It's particularly tricky to do this while still keeping the principal melodic line going, since everything else must be planned around it. When I make a recording of myself playing and listen back – a chastening but invaluable self-teaching technique – it sounds so choppy that I put down the cello and just sing the melody a few times. Away from the technical constraints of the instrument, singing frees me to articulate the expression I'm aiming for. When I pick up the cello again, I have better perspective on which notes to bring out of the texture. The graceful dotted rhythms practically beg to be "over-dotted," that is, played exaggeratedly. David Ledbetter's fascinating book *Unaccompanied Bach* suggests that the Sarabande strongly resembles the slow movement in one of Bach's violin-harpsichord sonatas from the same Cöthen period, so I listen to this other composition and find myself laughing aloud because it sounds like a mash-up of the Sarabande and *Jesu, Joy of Man's Desiring*. Then I spend half an hour of my practice time singing the Sarabande melody against an improvised *Jesu*-esque accompaniment on the cello, pausing intermittently to get the giggles. I'm afraid this really is how cello professors keep themselves amused.

For this year's Idaho Bach Festival, our guest artist is the baritone Paul Tipton. His solo recital will feature Baroque arias with harpsichord accompaniment, and after an intermission, the cantata *Liebster Immanuel, Herzog der Frommen* ("Beloved Immanuel, Ruler of the Righteous"). The next night we'll have a solos and ensembles concert for university faculty, in which I'll play the Fourth Cello Suite. Then for our closing gala, we'll finish off with the solo cantata *Ich habe genug* ("I Have Enough").

When my flutist colleague Leonard first proposes programming *Liebster Immanuel* in the festival, I don't yet know it. Under normal circumstances, I study the scores of unfamiliar compositions before listening to recordings, but on this occasion I'm having too busy a day. While packing my suitcase for a trip, I stream John Eliot Gardiner's recording of the cantata on my phone, but because I'm only half paying attention and my schoolgirl German isn't good enough to understand the sung text on first hearing, I don't realize what it's about. The next week, when I finally sit down with the score, I get a shock. Listening to the joyful ethos of Bach's musical setting, you wouldn't expect a text like *Lass, o Welt, mich aus Verachtung in betrübter Einsamkeit* to translate to "Leave me, o scornful world, in troubled loneliness!" A less subversive composer might set such dark material in a minor key, with the somber accompaniment of a church organ. Bach, conversely, creates a resolutely major-key ethos with a lively, dancing flute solo.

At first, the aria puzzles me and leaves me feeling curiously unmoved. Given the dramatic text-painting that we can hear in Bach's other compositions – the "Herr, Herr, *HERR!*" of the *St. John Passion*, for example – *Lass, o Welt* just seems strange. "Where's the troubled loneliness in any of this?" I say to Leonard at our first rehearsal.

He's taken aback. "It's completely in keeping with Bach's religious feeling to set it this way," he exclaims. "Bach believed that leaving the world was a positive thing."

Because I've always been afraid of death, my own and those of my loved ones, I find it hard to get my head around this idea. And yet, it makes sense from what I imagine to be Bach's point of view, since by the time he was my age loss and grief had become his constant companions. The text of the other cantata in the festival, *Ich habe genug*, expresses similarly disquieting sentiments such as "I rejoice in my death," but here Bach sets them in minor keys. For some reason, the incomprehensible idea of rejoicing in death seems more acceptable to me in an appropriately gloomy harmonic context.

Bach was evidently proud of *Ich habe genug*, because he performed it several times and made multiple versions and revisions. Anna Magdalena Bach must have regarded it highly too, because she twice copied out part of the second aria, *Schlummert ein, ihr matten Augen*, in her *Notenbuch*. It was first intended as church music at a service for the Feast of the Purification, and tells the story of the *Nunc dimittis*. According to the Gospel of Luke, the Holy Spirit visits a "just and devout" man named Simeon and tells him he won't die until he's seen the Christ Child. So when Mary and Joseph bring the infant Jesus into the temple, the old man takes the child into his arms and says "Sovereign Lord, as you have promised, you may now dismiss your servant in peace."[93] The anonymous poet of *Ich habe genug* develops the idea into an extraordinary lament about yearning for death. "Oh, if only the Lord would rescue me from the chains of my body, oh, if only my farewell were here. With joy I say to you, world, I have enough."

At the heart of *Ich habe genug* is *Schlummert ein*, an aria in the form of a lullaby. While the main key of the cantata is C minor, *Schlummert ein* alone appears in the relative major key of E-flat. Having lived day and night in E-flat major recently while practicing the Fourth Suite for the same occasion, I start to notice an affinity between *Schlummert ein* and the Sarabande. They might not share a metrical or formal structure, but they share more than just a key signature. They open with long, arching melodic lines that depart quickly from the chord of E-flat major and soar upwards to a D-flat – a note that doesn't belong in the key. Whereas most of Bach's opening melodies will at least stick around long enough to establish a sense of the home key, neither the Sarabande nor *Schlummert ein* does this. Something about them is ephemeral, and not quite earthbound. They aren't here to stay.

All the movements of *Ich habe genug* are sung by the same soloist, but there's more than one protagonist. In the opening aria, it's clearly Simeon. In the first recitative, the singer depicts a different, nameless character – maybe the Christian poet? By the time we get to *Schlummert ein*, a third protagonist takes over, singing "Go to sleep, you weary eyes, close softly and blessedly." Whenever I think of this aria, I wonder who the poet is, and who he's addressing. In practice and rehearsal, I keep imagining Anna Magdalena in the lamplight consoling a frail and frightened child. Holding her close, stroking her hair, she assures her that when the moment comes it will be just like falling asleep. Maybe Bach comes home from his long day at the Thomaskirche and watches them, framed by the doorway, his own eyes wet with grief and exhaustion. When I look up the dates, I realize that Bach began work on *Ich habe genug* not long after the death of their three-year-old daughter Christiana Sophia. Small wonder, then, that Anna Magdalena copied out this death-lullaby in her *Notenbuch*. It must have spoken straight to her heart.

By the last night of the Bach Festival, I'm exhausted. The business of running a festival sure isn't for wimps, and the week's logistics, stage management, and audience interaction on top of my usual teaching duties have left me depleted of energy. I'm so tired I can barely keep my eyes open, and I fear that if I go on much longer I'll fall asleep on my feet, like cows and horses do. How on earth am I going to make it through the concert tonight?

Walking out on the stage with the cello in my hand dispels my fear, as it always does. How I love the drama and ritual of performance, the procession out on stage, the synchronized bow, the shuffling of chairs and stands, the last-minute checks that bows are tightened and endpins anchored. And then we start, and the combination of adrenaline and Bach's music feels like a blood transfusion. The life is flowing back into me with every one of my bass notes, with the murmuring of the violins, with the entry of the singer: *Ich habe genug. Ich habe genug. Ich habe genug.*

One of the reasons I love playing continuo basslines so much is the way they seem to walk alongside the singer on our shared musical journey. Tonight, whether it's my exhaustion or the strange magic Bach seems to exert over me, I start to have an eerie feeling that every pacing footstep is bringing us closer and closer to death. I glance up out of the score and around the ensemble at my colleagues. They are all concentrating, counting, nodding, giving each other cues, that tacit language that we've all spent years perfecting in endless rehearsals and concerts. As Paul's achingly beautiful voice rises in the words *Welt, ich bleibe nicht mehr hier, hab ich doch kein Teil an dir, das der Seele könnte taugen*, the sudden thought occurs to me that we're all in this together, that none of us makes it out alive, that we must find meaning where we can. "World, I will stay here no more, I possess no part of you that could matter to my soul." In this split second, there is nothing I would rather be doing than sitting in this semi-circle, harpsichord behind me and singer in front of me, making this music. Nothing else seems to matter.

A few hours later, everyone is gone and the hall is silent. I've taken down the last of the festival banners and posters, and it's time to go home. My family are asleep when I walk in the door, though my dog gets up to greet me. I tiptoe into my daughter's room to check on her. She's sleeping soundly, her little arms cradling the toy moose that is her most cherished possession. I stoop down to kiss her soft warm cheek, and find that I have splashed it with tears.

V. BOURRÉES

In the space between the Sarabande and the first Bourrée, I always feel a sense of coming back from an elevated spiritual plane, and try to leave enough time for a few deep breaths to keep the memory of the Sarabande hanging in the air. I don't want to hang on too long, though, in case a member of the audience takes the opportunity to break the spell by releasing a long-suppressed coughing fit. It's coughs-and-colds season when I perform the Fourth Cello Suite at the Idaho Bach Festival, so I let the Bourrées bring us back to earth sooner rather than later.

Like all the *galanterie* dances, the Bourrées of the Fourth Cello Suite need to hit the ground dancing. They also need quite a bit of interpretive planning. The Bourrées of the Third Cello Suite are similar to each other in length and character, but in a marked departure from precedent, the Bourrées of the Fourth Cello Suite are opposites. The first is very long, with a second "half" much longer than the first. The second Bourrée is tiny by comparison, a mere two-and-a-half lines in Anna Magdalena Bach's manuscript. Texturally, the first Bourrée is mostly linear, with fast exuberant flourishes and punctuating bass notes, but no double or triple-stops, and just one quadruple-stopped chord at the very end. In contrast, the sedate rhythms of the second Bourrée allow for two-part, mostly double-stopped texture. Even the meter is different, with two large beats to a measure for the first Bourrée and four smaller beats to a measure in the second. Because of this, even if the cellist keeps to the same tempo across both Bourrées – a matter of some dispute among performers – the sense of pulse will be dashing in one and stately in the other. The only thing the Bourrées of the Fourth Suite have in common is a key signature. The *galanterie* dances of the first three Cello Suites were in parallel major and minor modes, but those of the second three Suites stick to the same key throughout. I find myself wondering why Bach made the change for the Fourth, Fifth, and Sixth Suites. Is this his way of compelling us to find other, less obvious ways to create contrasting colors in practice and performance?

The Monday after the Bach Festival always feels slightly dreary. Outside, most of the brilliant orange leaves lie liquidizing on the sidewalks, and the sky is dark by the time I leave my office for the day. I find myself envying all the wild animals preparing for their long winter sleep in the forests of Moscow Mountain, since there's no rest for musicians at this time of year. Now that Bach Week is over for another year, the countdown to the Christmas season begins. For my colleagues and me, that means driving all over the icy rural highways of the Pacific Northwest to rehearse and perform Christmas gigs.

Every year, my husband and I go on at least a couple of trips to perform George Frideric Handel's *Messiah*. Some musicians roll their eyes at having to play the *Messiah* for the millionth time, but I'm always up for the chance to play a Baroque bassline. Say what you will about the repertoire cellists love to hate – Johann Pachelbel's *Canon in D* also springs to mind – but between them, Messrs. Handel and Pachelbel paid most of my rent in graduate school. These days, I feel a special thrill when I hear Sean playing the glorious solo on "The Trumpet Shall Sound." When he practices it in our basement, the notes reverberate in every room of the house. Handel's librettist Charles Jennens was completely right about that – trumpets make a *lot* of sound. (Perhaps he was married to a trumpeter too?)

From time to time we'll also get calls from choral societies to play Bach's *Christmas Oratorio*, another magnificent trumpet piece. This year I have an invitation to play continuo for the cantata *Wachet auf*, "Sleepers Wake." One of Bach's best-known sacred cantatas, *Wachet auf* is often performed at Christmas even though Bach designated it for the twenty-seventh Sunday after Trinity in the church year. Inconveniently, this date only occurs during years when Easter has been early, about once every eleven years. People understandably wish to hear *Wachet auf* more often than that, so a little theological flexibility affords music directors the leeway to perform it at Christmastime instead.

The timing is particularly good for me, since *Wachet auf* is mostly in E-flat major and I've been playing the Fourth Cello Suite so much that my E-flat chops are in good order. As a young professional, I used to get a sore left hand from playing in oratorios, since they're long and continuo is…continuous, but playing Bach every day has improved my technique to the point where I can play painlessly in any key for long stretches of time. I find myself wondering if this was part of Bach's pedagogical plan in making each of the Cello Suites successively longer and more difficult. Was he teaching the players of a newish member of the violin family how to build the endurance our profession demands?

You can't be in a bad mood when you're playing *Wachet auf*. The exuberant opening gesture gets thrown around between a group of violins and another of oboes before the choral sopranos make their first entrance – "'Wake up!' calls the voice of the watchmen, high up in the tower!" The lower voices of the choir are quick to respond in increasingly speedy note values, and soon everyone is shouting out the news in jubilant polyphony. Holding everyone together is the cello's bassline, pushing the crowd onwards, rousing anyone who's still asleep with the most joyful wakeup call imaginable.

Wachet auf tells the parable of the five wise and five foolish virgins from the Gospel of Matthew. Interspersed are excerpts from the Song of Songs, with an old Lutheran hymn tune threading the movements together into a unified whole. The choir represents the believers, the tenor soloist takes the part of a narrator, and the bass and soprano soloists sing a dialogue between Jesus and the Soul. If you didn't know all this in advance, you might find certain parts of the text altogether rather sensational. "The bridegroom comes like a roe, like a stag leaping on the hills; he brings you the wedding feast. Wake up, encourage yourself to embrace the bridegroom. There, see, he's coming!" It's a metaphor, of course. He's not a literal bridegroom but a symbol of Christ, with the multiple brides representing Christian believers. This blurring of boundaries between sacred and amorous unions might appear strange, but Bach is just continuing a much older tradition dating back several centuries to the Middle Ages. Many composers of that time were Catholic priests, but this didn't stop them composing love songs to the Virgin Mary as if she were their girlfriend. The passionate sensuality of certain religious texts might raise modern eyebrows, but no blasphemy was intended. The longing for spiritual transcendence didn't, and doesn't, exclude the longing for mortal love.

I was raised without religion, my parents having long ago abandoned the Presbyterian faith of my grandparents. My father settled into benign agnosticism, but my mother felt strong antipathy for religion of all kinds and especially to Christianity. In spite of this, she didn't discard her late father's theological library. When I started studying music seriously, I wanted to understand something of the Christian belief systems that had shaped a millennium's worth of sacred music, so I set about reading through my grandfather's Bibles and Bible commentaries with the detached interest of an unbeliever.

The problem with reading the Bible with this attitude is that you can't really stay detached. So much of Scripture provokes contemplation and troubled, unanswerable questions. The parable of the ten virgins creates particularly conflicting feelings in me because of its unfairness. Summoned to bring lamps in anticipation of the holy bridegroom's arrival, the five wise virgins bring extra lamp oil and the five foolish ones don't. When their lamps run out of oil, the foolish virgins ask the wise virgins to share theirs. The wise virgins refuse and tell them to go out and buy more oil, even though it's the middle of the night. This is the part that bothers me most, since how can the foolish virgins possibly buy more oil when the shops are closed? Why do the wise virgins refuse to help? Why are the foolish virgins punished so harshly for making just one careless mistake that any of us could make, and why are the wise virgins rewarded for their smug, uncharitable refusal?

Most commentaries tell us that the parable of the ten virgins is a lesson to be prepared in case the rapture arrives before we expect it. In secular terms, this is a sentiment that striving musicians can get behind, since it's a point of honor never to show up to a rehearsal unprepared. You don't just have to know your own part, you have to know everyone else's too. You study full scores and multiple recordings, translate foreign texts, obsessively note metronome markings, and practice for hours. You show up early with all your equipment. Anyone who isn't prepared won't be hired next time, and they can't expect much sympathy from the rest of us.

And yet, how many times have I showed up to a rehearsal to discover to my horror that my pencil had no leads in it, or that my endpin stopper didn't work on a tiled floor? On those occasions colleagues gladly loaned me their spare pencils and chair straps, and I did the same for them when they needed it. Why is it considered wise for the better-prepared virgins to refuse to share the lamp oil? Wouldn't a truly virtuous person share what they had, even at the expense of their own success?

I ponder these questions during breaks in rehearsal, or during sections when the conductor is addressing the choir over some point of German diction. Even if I don't like the message of the parable, I can still appreciate the perfection of *Wachet auf*. Sitting here on stackable plastic chairs in the sanctuary of a suburban church, a brightly-lit Christmas tree nearby, I even wish I could believe as Bach did. Whether you believe or not, *Wachet auf* appeals to our longing for joy and fulfillment. How comforting it would be to look forward, as he did, to the certainty of a blissful afterlife. I even feel as if we musicians have a lot in common with the clergy, such as our sense of vocation, our need to proselytize, and a constant shortage of cash, and that's before we even get to the dress-up clothes and dramatic rituals of performance. If only I could summon up religious beliefs, I'd fit right in.

Years ago in music school, I dated a fellow student who was an evangelical Christian. He was concerned for the future of my soul, and urged me to learn to pray. "You should just try it," he told me, "and see if it sticks."

"I'm sorry," I said, "I can't do that. It would be disingenuous. I just don't believe."

The boyfriend bought me a stack of books by an evangelical author who claimed he could prove the existence of God "in a court of law."

"Isn't the whole point of faith that you don't need proof?" I asked.

"Isn't that supposed to be my line?" he replied, exasperated.

We had little in common apart from music, and broke things off amicably when we graduated. We stay sporadically in touch, and a few months after giving birth I call him to tell him about my drugged vision of angels in the delivery room, thinking he'd like the story. He's silent for a moment, then reveals he's become an atheist. I experience a sudden sympathetic pang of loss for him, since religion was once as central to his identity as music. Only music is left now.

∗

Once Christmas is over, I can turn again to practicing and reading as much as I can about the Cello Suites. I've always had a love-hate relationship with practicing, but reading never gets old. Carl Philipp Emanuel Bach once recounted that his father possessed an "unheard-of zeal for studying,"[94] and this inspires a feeling of kinship in me, since I'm never happier than when I'm sitting at my desk surrounded by books and scores. I read right through Allen Winold's two-volume analytical study of Bach's Cello Suites and am startled by his analysis of the second Bourrée of the Fourth Suite. According to Winold, the way the notes move against each other in the two-line texture, eliding and releasing double stops, owes something to the academic discipline of strict counterpoint.[95] To my shame, I haven't actually studied strict counterpoint since college, so I open up an internet browser to review the rules. That's when I get sucked down yet another of the unexpected rabbit holes on my journey through Bach's Cello Suites. The latest member of the entertaining cast of characters is Johann Joseph Fux, best known as the father of counterpoint pedagogy.

A rough and ready definition of counterpoint is the relationship between two or more voices in a musical texture. In a string quartet, for example, four separate lines performed by the four members of the group function both separately, as linear voices, and together, as components in the web of harmony. In the opening chorus of the *Wachet auf* cantata, the four-part choir and multi-part instrumental ensemble use counterpoint to achieve the effect of everyone shouting at once, but in different rhythms and on different pitches. In Bach's *Well-Tempered Clavier*, one person must play multiple lines on a harpsichord using just the ten fingers they were born with. If this sounds hard, it is. As one of my teachers was fond of saying when students complained about the difficulty of some aspect of music-making or other, "If it were easy, everyone would be doing it."

Johann Joseph Fux didn't invent strict counterpoint – the concept had been around for several centuries – but he taught it in memorable fashion in his magnum opus, *Gradus ad Parnassum* (*Steps to Perfection*). In this pedagogical text from 1725, Fux demonstrated how to write contrapuntal exercises in small incremental steps through the first, second, third, fourth, and fifth species. If you thought species were for zoologists and botanists, think again. Fux's exercises start with a given melodic line called a *cantus firmus* or "fixed song," and anything that opposes this line can be classified as one of the five species. A *cantus firmus* is always composed of whole notes, and in first species counterpoint, an added line opposes it note for note. In second species, the added line opposes the *cantus firmus* using half notes; in third species, quarter notes. In fourth species, half notes oppose the *cantus firmus*, but in syncopation, so they sound on the off-beats. In fifth species, the added line gets to use a variety of note values. In Winold's analysis, the second Bourrée of the Fourth Cello Suite owes something to fourth species. This hasn't occurred to me before, so I head to the library in search of Arnold Schoenberg's *Preliminary Exercises on Counterpoint*, the textbook I used as an undergraduate.

Browsing the music theory shelves, it occurs to me that I've never actually read Fux's *Gradus ad Parnassum*. Everyone knows about this book, since it was groundbreaking in music theory and a dog-eared favorite in the bookshelves of Haydn, Mozart, and Beethoven. Bach owned a copy too, though of course *Gradus* postdated the Cello Suites by around five years so we can't count it as a direct influence.

First I have to find a copy I can read. Fux wrote *Gradus ad Parnussum* in Latin, partly because it was still an international language among educated Europeans of the time, and partly because Fux was a monumental show-off. My high school Latin has lapsed, so I pick up the German translation, but that's no good to me either since the eighteenth-century publisher has helpfully typeset it in eyestrain-inducing Gothic script. To my relief, I'm able to lay my hands on the English translation by Alfred Mann, and discover what I've been missing out on.

Gradus ad Parnassum, it transpires, is quite, quite wonderful. I like Fux from the very first pages, where he explains his reason for writing the book: "My object is to help young persons who want to learn. I knew and still know many who have fine talents and are most anxious to study; however, lacking means and a teacher, they cannot realize their ambition, but remain, as it were, forever desperately athirst." This sounds exactly like my college students, most of whom come from rural areas with limited access to music resources, and who long to become well-educated.

"Seeking a solution to this problem," Fux continues, "I began...to work out a method similar to that by which children learn first letters, then syllables, then combinations of syllables, and finally how to read and write. And it has not been in vain. When I used this method in teaching I observed that the pupils made amazing progress within a short time."[96]

But Fux doesn't set this all out in any kind of normal method-book. Instead of simply giving the rules and a few examples, he couches the whole thing as a conversation between an earnest student, Josephus – a thinly-disguised self-portrait – and the master Aloysius. The latter is supposed to represent Fux's hero, the great Counter-Reformation composer Giovanni Pierluigi da Palestrina. That Palestrina had died sixty-six years before Fux's birth was no obstacle – Fux was evidently given to imaginary conversations with dead composers, and their book-length dialogue is the most diverting thing I've read in a long time.

Fux-Josephus, I'm delighted to learn, is a monumental suck-up. "I come to you, venerable master," he appeals ingratiatingly, "in order to be introduced to the rules and principles of music." Who could refuse such a student?

Though flattered, Aloysius hesitates. "But are you not aware that this study is like an immense ocean?"[97] he says. This is still a good question to ask prospective students, because the demands of the music degree can come as a surprise even to those who excelled at the subject in high school. Plucky Josephus is undeterred. He assures Aloysius of his deep love of music and his indifference to wealth – both of which, I might add, are fine qualities in a musician. The lessons commence.

What's striking about *Gradus*, as opposed to many theory textbooks, is how slowly and gently it goes. There are a lot of pauses for Josephus to ask questions, and Fux deliberately makes them the questions of a fairly average, if obsequious, beginner. "You have graciously answered my first question," Josephus says to Aloysius. "Now will you tell me also – if you do not mind – what is meant by this first species of counterpoint, note against note?"

"I shall explain it to you," says Aloysius.[98] And he does.

I'm enchanted by this, since I often talk to dead composers too. Searching the internet for a picture of Fux, I find an oil painting by one Nikolaus Buck. In this 1717 portrait, the composer looks genially at us through heavy-lidded dark eyes, his agreeable features framed by one of the more absurd wigs I've seen. I picture him at the harpsichord with his students, reminding them in kindly fashion that there's no such thing as a stupid question. "*Meine Herren und Damen,*" he might say, "it's perfectly all right to mess up sometimes. I know this because Palestrina told me in a dream that he once wrote a perfect fourth where he wasn't supposed to." The students giggle and roll their eyes. They adore Herr Fux's tall tales and terrible dad jokes.

I have a feeling Bach's teaching might not have had the performative exuberance of Fux's, but that doesn't mean he was a martinet in the classroom. "Are you kidding me?" says Sean when I mention this to him. "He was probably one of those teachers who can perform every skill so brilliantly that he can't tolerate anyone who doesn't immediately understand how to do something. He was probably nice to the smart ones and a grumpy jerk to everyone else." And yet, we have the testimony of one Ernst Ludwig Gerber that his father Heinrich Nicholaus, a Bach pupil, was treated "with particular kindness" by the Capellmeister in his lessons on fugues and inventions.[99] This being the case, we can't make the assumption that he was generally ill-tempered as a taskmaster, even if he was known to be terse with bureaucrats and other authority figures.

Relatively little is known about the particulars of Bach's pedagogy, but we do have an account by Carl Philipp Emanuel stating that his father started students off with the study of four-part harmony.[100] This, by the way, is still a starting point in most present-day freshman music theory classes. Professors set forth the rules on which chord can progress to the next, then show how to accomplish this in each of the four voices – soprano, alto, tenor, bass – while adhering to guidelines on what individual voices are and aren't allowed to do. The method might be different, but the rules aren't so different from those expressed in Fux's *Gradus ad Parnassum*. Our guide in this endeavor is a score with the daunting title of *371 Four-Part Chorales*, a collection of Bach's Lutheran chorale harmonizations. He might not have composed these with the specific aim of showing listless college students how to write harmony exercises, but as a pedagogical model they can show us just about anything we might need to know about the subject. Just as Bach never stopped praying, neither did he ever stop teaching.

VI. GIGUE

Something about Bach's Cello Suites provokes us to look for the shadows of music past and future within their notes. Melodies and harmonies appear both influenced and influencing, referential and self-referential. If we look hard enough, we can find wildly conflicting ideas sitting side by side.

Two readings of the Gigue of the Fourth Cello Suite illustrate this paradox. The British musicologist Wilfrid Mellers describes the long lines of triple eighth notes as "buzzing around a nodal point,"[101] comparing the style to that of a harpsichord piece by François Couperin called *Le moucheron*. "What's that, a fly?" I think, incredulously. A gnat, the dictionary corrects me. I listen to the Couperin piece, and Mellers is right – it's strikingly similar to the Gigue. I start wondering what would happen if I played the Gigue at a quicker tempo, using a light bowstroke to suggest the whirring wings of a gnat. It's not easy, but I inch the tempo upwards with the aid of a metronome, trying to let the weight of the bow do the work of the rapid string crossings. I keep an image of gnats in my head the whole time in the hope that it'll inspire my playing. (There's an idea for my next album – I could call it *The Insects* and include the Gigue, Rimsky-Korsakov's *Flight of the Bumblebee*, Gabriel Fauré's *Papillon*, and Vaughan Williams's *The Wasps*. Some waggish critic will probably beg for insecticide.)

Contrast this lighthearted reading with an alternative by Allen Winold, who hears a resonance with the Lutheran hymn tune *Ein feste Burg ist unser Gott*. In his reimagined analysis of the Gigue, Winold shows that with just a couple of tweaks, you can make the opening melody sound remarkably similar to the way Bach rendered *Ein feste Burg* in a later composition, his Cantata No. 80.[102] The Cello Suites predate this composition by a couple of years, but Bach might have been thinking back to the Gigue of the Fourth Cello Suite when composing the cantata. Or was he anticipating the cantata when he composed the Gigue? It adds yet another unanswered question to our "don't know" file.

Neither Mellers nor Winold is wrong. Bach's Cello Suites might be secular music, but they have a sense of duality that allows for the swatting of a buzzing gnat while simultaneously making an affirmation of faith. Earthbound reality and heavenward anticipation are inextricably combined. "With Bach," writes the endearingly effusive Mellers, "hilarity and ecstasy may be interrelated... Despite its dancing facility, [the Gigue of the Fourth Cello Suite] has a dramatic structure with beginning, middle and end, polarized on the same E-flat major – G minor axis as the prelude. It doesn't deny the prelude's purgatorial experience, though it brings us back to our everyday world... In comically complementing the tragic prelude, the gigue rounds off a cycle of experience."[103]

This thought goes some way to reconcile the conflicted feelings I have getting inside the music of a composer whose beliefs are so alien to my own. The contemporary composer György Kurtág puts it well: "Consciously, I am certainly an atheist, but I do not say it out loud, because if I look at Bach, I cannot be an atheist. Then I have to accept the way he believed. His music never stops praying. And how can I get closer if I look at him from the outside? I do not believe in the Gospels in a literal fashion, but a Bach fugue has the Crucifixion in it... In music, I am always looking for the hammering of the nails... That is a dual vision."[104] Even if we don't think the same way as Bach, performers of his music are just as much characters in a drama as actors performing a play. We are all voices in the tangle of harmonic lines; the way we speak the phrases subtly shades their meaning.

Part Five

DISCORD

Suite No. 5 in C Minor ("Suitte Discordable"), BWV 1011

Seufzer, Tränen, Kummer, Not
Ängstlichs Sehnen, Furcht und Tod
Nagen mein beklemmtes Herz
Ich empfinde Jammer, Schmerz.

"Sighs, tears, sorrow, need
Anxious yearning, fear and death
Gnaw my constrained heart
I feel misery, pain."

Johann Sebastian Bach, *Ich hatte viel Bekümmernis* BWV 21

I. PRELUDE

The Preludes of Bach First, Second, Third, and Fourth Cello Suites have radically different characters, but they all do roughly the same thing: they move in patterns. The chords might be broken into wide-open arpeggios, or circles, or cross shapes, but the harmony always moves ineluctably towards a climactic standstill about two-thirds of the way through. The shock of the crisis changes the melodic style into one that sounds almost improvisatory, but sooner or later the pattern returns. The path towards home is clear, even if we're going to be virtuosos as we follow it.

The Prelude of the Fifth Suite breaks the cycle. Alone among Bach's Six Cello Suites, it takes the form of a French overture. A slow, stately introduction rich with ornamentation concludes on an open-ended cadence, taking us straight into a rapid fugue. As its name suggests, the French overture came from the French court, where it would have preceded an opera or ballet by someone like Jean-Baptiste Lully. Its purpose is to set the scene for the story ahead. Will it be a comedy or a tragedy? When the cellist touches the bow to the strings for the dark opening chord in the Prelude of the Fifth Cello Suite we know right away that we're in for a tale of great anguish and wretchedness.

At the top of Anna Magdalena Bach's manuscript is the subtitle *Suitte [sic] discordable*, followed by a measure showing the pitches C, G, D, and another, higher G, and the word *accord* to indicate that these are the string tunings. The usual cello string tunings are C, G, D, and A. Bach was using the ancient practice of *scordatura*, where strings are deliberately mistuned to create new possibilities for harmony and resonance. In the case of the Fifth Cello Suite, having not one but two strings tuned to G makes for an extra-dark, extra-echoing tone quality in the home key of C minor and the dominant key of G major. It also allows us to reach pitches such as A-flats more easily, which is helpful since A-flat is part of the key signature in C minor.

The usual practice in *scordatura* is to write pitches as they would normally be played on the instrument. Therefore, when Bach writes a note on the top line of the staff in bass clef, an A, the sounding pitch will be a G because of the mistuned A-string. This is just as confusing as it sounds, and I'm not the only person to have struggled with it. Johann Peter Kellner, the earliest copyist of Bach's Cello Suites, attempted to transpose the Fifth Suite to sounding pitch with mixed results. After getting through the Prelude, Allemande, and Courante, Kellner must have realized that he'd bitten off more than he could chew. He left out the Sarabande altogether, probably owing to its complexity, and though he did soldier on through the Gavottes, he only got one line into the Gigue before abandoning it.

I can't judge Kellner too harshly, because the *scordatura* confounded me too when I first learned the Fifth Cello Suite. By this time I was a graduate student in London. No longer a big fish in a small pond, I was feeling a lot of pressure to enter competitions and build my career. Most of the repertoire lists wanted one of the "hard" Bach Preludes – the last three – and I'd chosen the Fifth Cello Suite because I loved its melancholy feeling. Truthfully, there was also the matter of its not being in E-flat major and not requiring a five-string cello, but the task wasn't easy. My perfect pitch – a mixed blessing at the best of times – made it baffling when I produced the sounding pitch of a B-flat from a notated C. I complained about this to Alexander Vassilievich, and he beamed happily at me.

"Yes, Mirandochka. If you have perfect pitch, *scordatura* is like torture."

"You have perfect pitch too, don't you?" I said. "How did you figure out how to do it?"

Alexander Vassilievich looked at me over the tops of his glasses. "Practice," he said. "I practiced *wery* much." Then his lips twitched, and he let out one of his uproarious cackles. "Composers are crazy! They ask us to do terrible things to cello. If you don't like *scordatura* in Bach, wait until you play Zoltán Kodály's sonata. After Kodály, now everybody wants some crazy *scordatura*. *Vhy*? You cannot imagine. It is really not *wery* good for bridge of cello."

I'd already discovered this from my first attempts at tuning the A-string up and down several times a day. "What can you do to protect your bridge from getting warped?" I said. "I just talked to a luthier who told me I can only get it steam-straightened a few times before I have to give up and have a new bridge made, and that's expensive."

"You must get special bridge that you only use for *scordatura*," said Alexander Vassilievich. "Preferably one that you don't like *wery* much."

This wasn't helpful advice for someone who couldn't afford alternative bridges, so I ultimately decided to learn the Fifth Cello Suite using normal string tuning. This was the common practice from the early of the twentieth century onwards, and many published editions accommodate it by notating the Fifth Cello Suite at sounding pitch. It felt a little like cheating, but I rationalized that I was on a tight budget that couldn't accommodate extra visits to pricey London luthiers. Furthermore, when I played the Fifth Cello Suite in competitions it would be alongside other pieces in standard tuning, and if I used *scordatura* I would have to mistune and retune the cello on stage. To this day I have a horror of tuning in front of an audience, since it intensifies my stage fright to the point that I can't tell if I'm sharp or flat. I imagined nightmare scenarios where I broke a string during the competition, or had all the strings unravel at once while the jury members looked at their watches, tapped their fingers on their desks, and muttered "What an idiot, she can't even tune her cello." Nope nope nope, I thought to myself.

Fast forward to the present day, and I decide I'm going to revise my feelings about *scordatura*. Now that I'm older and possibly wiser, I want to be able to play all the notes of the complex multiple-stopped chords that the human hand simply can't reach in standard tuning. There's also a matter of personal pride, since cellists who don't use *scordatura* are now more likely to get criticized for being "Romantic." This insult isn't entirely fair to the Romantics themselves, since almost all the nineteenth-century editors of the Cello Suites used *scordatura* notation for the Fifth Suite. Using standard tuning came later, with Pablo Casals and his followers. Who started it doesn't matter, of course – what matters is Bach's harmony.

There's still the problem of making frequent changes to the tension of the bridge. I really don't want to damage my bridge, particularly since it's already subjected to lots of changes in temperature and humidity on my frequent travels. I take out my old student cello, which these days mostly stands unplayed and collecting dust in the corner of my office. It's not great, but I can keep it tuned to C-G-D-G for as long as I'm working on the Fifth Cello Suite. It may damage the bridge, but at least the damage will be minimized by not having constantly to yank the A-string up and down. Meanwhile, I can play all my other repertoire on my main cello in standard tuning. It's a solution that only works for people privileged enough to own more than one cello, but it'll work for me.

If I thought age and experience would make me better at *scordatura* the second time around, I'm wrong. The problem with having a high-achievement personality is that you don't like doing anything badly. When I'm invited to participate in something I haven't done before, like tennis, my default response is to say "I'd be rubbish at that" and refuse. When I do decide to try something new, like baking, I don't want to start with the fundamentals, I want to skip to the bit where I'm amazing. I try to make a soufflé and get mad when it falls flat, even though everyone told me to start with an easier bake like muffins. Intellectually, I understand that everyone is bad when they first attempt a new skill, but it's still humbling to slam into wrong notes again and again. It's not that I don't know how it's supposed to sound – I know the piece from memory – it's that I keep forgetting the finger patterns. "I'm making the same idiotic mistakes again and again," I complain to Sean over the dinner table. "I've done it wrong so many times that I think I might be teaching myself to be permanently wrong."

"What would you say to a student who was having this problem?" Sean says.

"I'd tell them to stop expecting to be great before they've adequately mastered the new skill," I say. "I'd tell them to create little exercises for themselves. They could start with a scale in the new tuning, or an easy piece."

Sean smiles at this grudging admission. "No kidding," he says meaningfully, and I have to laugh at myself. *Teacher, teach thyself!*

Reading further about *scordatura*, I learn that there are other pieces in the C-G-D-G tuning. Bach didn't suddenly decide to mistune a cello – he was taking his cues from a much older string tuning tradition from seventeenth-century Bologna. Back in the day, C-G-D-G was the standard way to string a cello, and the expected tuning for the earliest solo cello works. The best-known of these are the Seven Ricercare of 1689 by Domenico Gabrielli. A lot of teachers give these pieces to students as a precursor to the

Bach Cello Suites, but I've never taught or played them because on the one occasion I sight-read them I found them a bit boring. I even questioned the conjecture of musicologists that Bach might have used the Ricercare as a model for the Cello Suites – why would the great Capellmeister of Cöthen bother with something so pedestrian?

Pulling the score out of my music cabinet now, I realize that what I have is a heavily edited modern version. I open up an internet browser and go to the ever-obliging International Music Score Library Project to download a facsimile of the composer's manuscript. Gabrielli's three-hundred-year-old calligraphy turns out to be beautiful and surprisingly easy to read. He hasn't written in *scordatura* notation, but of course there was no need for him to do so since C-G-D-G was the normal cello string tuning for him.

I didn't know this the last time I attempted to sight-read the Ricercare, but with my A-string tuned down to a G the notes lie more comfortably under the hand, while the additional resonance from the loosened A-string produces a lovely singing tone. I was wrong for thinking them dull. Then I go off into a daydream about how they must have sounded in the composer's exalted workplace, the gigantic Basilica of San Petronio. Looking for a picture of Gabrielli on the internet, I can't find one that's absolutely certain to be him, but there are a few reproductions of a painting of a man in a dark wig, his face half in shadow. The silver satin doublet and the lace at his wrists and throat suggest a man at the top of his profession. Could this be *Minghino dal violoncello*, "Little Domenico of the cello," as his fans called him? The possible Signor Gabrielli is pictured sitting in front of lutenist, holding a large cello. On his right side rests a second, smaller cello, and to his left – to my delight – is a short-haired terrier. I've always felt that the presence of dogs would greatly improve most rehearsals, and Gabrielli's brazenness in bringing a pet to work makes me like him. Like many musicians, he seems to have had a few problems with rules. On one occasion, an important religious feast day, he didn't bother showing up to play for the service. The outraged church authorities fired him at once, but asked him back five months later because they missed him.[105] I'm glad they appreciated their Minghino for his musicianship, and I hope they let him keep bringing his dog.

Once I've lived with Gabrielli's Ricercare for a couple of days, Bach's Fifth Cello Suite in *scordatura* doesn't seem so daunting any more, and I start working on the Prelude in earnest. I find that I do best when I work from the alternative Bärenreiter edition written in *Klangnotation*, "sounding pitches." As for the mistuned A-string, I slowly get used to it until I can switch back and forth from normal tuning to C-G-D-G without messing up either. Once I'm adept at *scordatura*, I realize how much better it feels and sounds. I'll never go back to playing it in standard tuning now.

Just because the Fifth Cello Suite is easier in *scordatura* doesn't, of course, make it easy in general. Practicing the Prelude is an exercise in stamina, and not just because it's far longer than the Preludes of the first four Cello Suites. The stamina is as much emotional as it is physical because of the unrelieved darkness of the mood. Dissonance follows anguished dissonance, building up into the final outcry that takes us into the fugue.

Bach was one of the greatest writers of fugue ever to have lived, and the fact that he was able to write one for a melodic instrument like the cello is proof of his transcendent compositional skill. The *Well-Tempered Clavier* features forty-eight pairs of Preludes and Fugues for keyboard, but the form is more idiomatic for this instrumentation for the simple reason that you can play more pitches simultaneously on a harpsichord than you can on a cello. In the Prelude of the Fifth Cello Suite, however, Bach manages by some ineffable magic to conjure up the impression of multiple voices going on even within an entirely linear texture.

The word *fugue* has roots in two Latin words whose respective meanings are "to flee" and "to chase." The idea is that voices both chase and are chased on a journey through multiple keys and characters. Remarkably, Bach creates almost two hundred measures' worth of music out of strikingly economical materials. The subject and countersubject alike are based on an opening gesture of just two notes, rising up like a question mark, plus a second, three-note gesture that briskly answers the question. Bach spins out the gesture with his signature virtuosic brilliance over several pages of music, most of it lonely and troubled in mood. I don't know if Bach knew the works of John Dowland – probably not, since they were separated by land, sea, and more than a century – but playing the Prelude of the Fifth Cello Suite always brings to mind the words of *In Darknesse Let Mee Dwell*, Dowland's deeply pessimistic composition for soprano, lute, and viola da gamba. "In darknesse let mee dwell, the ground shall sorrow be / The roofe Dispaire to barr all cheerfull light from mee / The wals of marble blacke that moistned still shall weepe / My musicke hellish jarring sounds to banish friendly sleepe."

Like *In Darknesse*, the Prelude progresses mostly in minor keys until ending unexpectedly on the chord of C major, the parallel major to the home key of C minor. This abrupt "happy ending" isn't as strange as it might seem, since Bach did it repeatedly elsewhere, including in the *Well-Tempered Clavier*. (There's even a name for it, the *Picardy third*, though no one has yet proved that it has anything much to do with the former French province of Picardie.) Is Bach sublimating the sorrow of the journey into a C major conclusion? Is he revealing the face of hope to us?

Whatever he's doing, he only does it once. None of the other movements of the Fifth Cello Suite ends in a major key. If this was a struggle between sorrow and hope, sorrow appears to be winning.

II. ALLEMANDE

Bach's Fifth Cello Suite is the only one of the six for which we have a manuscript in the composer's own writing. The only problem, from a cellist's point of view at least, is that it isn't written for the cello. In the late 1720s or early 1730s, in his new home of Leipzig, Bach made a version of the Fifth Cello Suite for solo lute. The dedicatee on the title page is one "Monsieur Schouster," whom scholars have identified as a local book dealer named Jacob Schuster.[106] This frail treasure is a priceless resource for cellists as well as lutenists, since Bach's autograph manuscript or manuscripts are long gone. What a stroke of luck it is to have a resource in Bach's hand to fill out our understanding of the Fifth Cello Suite.

Thanks to Bärenreiter's *Neue Bach Ausgabe* and the musicologist Andrew Talle, we can now compare it side by side with the other early sources: Source A by Anna Magdalena Bach, Source B by Johann Peter Kellner, Source C by Johann Nikolaus Schober and a second copyist whose name we don't know, Source D by yet another anonymous copyist, plus the first published edition of Louis Norblin. For your average cello nerd, this synoptic edition of the Cello Suites is as absorbing as the *Da Vinci Code*, if twenty times more expensive.

In his revision of the Fifth Cello Suite for lute, Bach changed the key to G minor to bring it into a more idiomatic range for the instrument. Since lutes have more strings than cellos, lutenists can play chords with more notes in them. Bach took advantage of this by adding extra notes to chords, as well as adding some punctuating bass notes that don't feature in the cello version. He apparently also had trouble with his own *scordatura*, as we can see from several messy ink-blots and corrections. I find myself smirking at the thought that even Bach found this stuff hard.

Since Bach was coming back to the Fifth Cello Suite some years after its initial composition, it's no surprise that he wanted to add to it. He cleared up a few mistakes and ambiguities from the cello version, such as a forgotten natural sign in the ascending melodic minor scale at the beginning of the Prelude. He also added some grace notes, turns, and trills that cellists can turn to as primary source material for ornamentation in performance practice. This raises the provoking question of whether cellists should try to play *every* addition and revision in Bach's lute version of the Fifth Cello Suite.

One person who thought we should was the cellist Dimitry Markevitch (1923–2002). An important historian of the cello and enthusiast of the Early Music Revival, Markevitch also had the misfortune to be a Russian cellist at exactly the same time as Mstislav Rostropovich. He was understandably a little miffed about this, and seems to have taken every opportunity to administer a jab or two at his contemporary. In the chapter on Russian cellists in his 1984 book *Cello Story*, Markevitch delivers a two-page encomium to Leopold Rostropovich, father and teacher of Mstislav, before adding the unmistakably passive-aggressive afterthought "Like his father, Mstislav is a gifted pianist as well as a cellist and is becoming increasingly well known as a conductor."[107] At the time Markevitch wrote this grudging praise, the younger Rostropovich had been a superstar for decades. But Markevitch wasn't finished. A few years later, he couldn't resist expressing scorn for Rostropovich's Bach recordings in an Internet Cello Society interview. "When I listened to him play the E-Flat Prelude...I thought I recognized it from somewhere. So I went through my library, which includes 55 editions of the Bach Suites. I went directly to a 1947 edition which was published in Soviet Russia by Kosolupov, Rostropovich's teacher, and I found that Rostropovich was playing in the 1990s like Kosolupov did in 1947. This means that he has not evolved since his student days...his way of playing Bach is old-fashioned."[108]

Petty sniping aside, Markevitch was right. Early music performance traditions had moved on, and Markevitch's interest in old manuscripts and instruments places him firmly on the right side of history. His 1964 edition of the Cello Suites was one of the earliest to incorporate material from Anna Magdalena, Kellner, Schober/Anonymous, and Bach's version for lute of the Fifth Cello Suite. The six-page preface is full of useful information, even if Markevitch's penchant for self-aggrandizement makes him an unreliable narrator. His claims to have "found" the Kellner and Schober copies[109] are a bit of a stretch considering both manuscripts had been the property of the

State Library of Berlin since the early nineteenth century. Still, the edition is both scholarly and practical, and demonstrates how intimately Markevitch understood Bach's music.

Particularly fascinating are Markevitch's two edited versions of the Fifth Cello Suite. In the first, Markevitch uses only the manuscript sources specifically written for the cello, but in an alternative version he incorporates as much as possible from Bach's lute manuscript – bass notes, extra notes, and ornamentation. It is this version that he uses in his 1992 recording of the Cello Suites.

In the practice room I study Bach's lute manuscript, then try out the lute-inspired version from Markevitch's edition. Both are revelatory. The lute manuscript, being set out over a grand staff, gives a clearer idea of voice-leading in the counterpoint. The additional notes in multi-note chords and the punctuating bass notes help to confirm the implied harmonies of the cello version. Markevitch's edition, for its part, brings extra color and rhetoric into the cellist's experience of Bach by taking changes from the lute version into account. Should we, I wonder, accord more authority to Bach's lute version given that it's the only manuscript we have in his writing? Then again, might it be more prudent to assume that Bach only added extra notes to make the Fifth Cello Suite more idiomatic for the lute, an instrument naturally more suited to multi-voiced playing?

After some experimenting, I decide not to keep the additional bass notes from the lute version, since they don't sound as good on the cello as they do on the lute. The ornamentation is another matter, since it isn't necessarily instrument-specific. I'm about to perform the Fourth and Fifth Cello Suites in a few recitals around the Northwest, and it occurs to me that I could play the ornaments from the lute version on the repeats of the dance movements in the Fifth Suite. When there is so much we don't know about how to play Bach, the turns and trills seem like a special bonus gift.

*

With its solemn grandeur, the Allemande of the Fifth Cello Suite feels a lot like an extension of the first part of the Prelude. Both movements feature the same grave dotted rhythms and decorative scalar passages. It's also easy to fall into the trap of playing both of them deathly slow. While relearning the Allemande, it suddenly occurs to me that there are only two half-note beats in the measure. This being the case, why do so many interpreters take it so slowly that any listener would think the beat was four quarter notes, or even eight eighth notes? In my first attempts at the Fifth Cello Suite, the Allemande reminded me of the melancholy viola da gamba music that had so inspired me when I played the Second Cello Suite, and I wanted to give it a feeling of timelessness, even endlessness. I realize now that Bach, by putting it in cut time, was signaling to the self-indulgent performer to get a move on. "*Ach, gnädige Frau*, I beg you to take this Allemande a bit faster. Then we can all go home earlier, *nicht wahr?*"

Another intriguing puzzle presents itself in the twenty-fifth measure. When I last played the Fifth Cello Suite, I practiced it using the Bärenreiter edition, but this time, with the Anna Magdalena Bach facsimile and Kirsten Beisswenger's scholarly performing edition on the stand in front of me, I see something I haven't noticed before. It's a chord so discordant that at first I think it's a mistake. G, D, A-flat – what on earth is this? I've always thought that chord was *B-flat*, D, A-flat – the dominant chord that leads us logically into the next chord, E-flat major. I look over at Anna Magdalena's copy and see that Beisswenger has copied accurately.

How have I never noticed this before? I pull all the modern performing editions I own out of my music cabinet and compare them. Sure enough, the editors have all "corrected" the G to a B-flat. Cross-referencing with the nineteenth-century editions, I realize that only the two earliest, Norblin and Probst, have kept the G. From 1826 onwards, everyone made it a B-flat. And yet if we look at the eighteenth-century manuscripts, every one of them, including the lute version in Bach's hand, contains the "bizarre chord," as musicologists call it. Bach had the opportunity to correct past mistakes when he transcribed the Fifth Cello Suite for the lute, so why didn't he correct the bizarre chord? Could this clashing dissonance, which seems to make no harmonic sense, have been intentional?

I spend an entire day going through every recording of the Fifth Cello Suite I can find. I listen to recordings of the Allemande by one hundred and seventy-six cellists, of whom only twenty-nine play the bizarre chord. Interestingly, it's not necessarily the practitioners of historically informed performance – the cellists using period instruments, Baroque bows, and gut strings – who choose to. Several of the cellists playing the bizarre chord are otherwise "mainstream" players, whereas plenty of hardcore early music specialists play the non-bizarre version.

I'm about to side with the one hundred and forty-seven cellists who opt for non-bizarreness when I come across a blog by Shin-Itchiro Yokoyama, a cellist and editor of the Cello Suites. Reading through his extraordinarily detailed observations, I realize there's more context for the bizarre chord than meets the eye. "This chord is not bizarre," Yokoyama insists. "I will explain it." He does so convincingly from a theoretical perspective, showing that the chord indeed functions in the progression towards E-flat, and gives examples of its use elsewhere in Bach's compositions, including four from the *Well-Tempered Clavier*, two from the *Mass in B Minor*, and one each from the *St. Matthew Passion* and one of the flute sonatas.[110] This is enough to convince me. I'll play the bizarre chord, and I'm sure I'll eventually get used to it.

III. COURANTE

The Courante of the Fifth Cello Suite feels like a close relative of the Prelude. Both open with a double-stopped octave C, followed by a phrase-shape that seems to rise up out of darkness, only to sink back down into it. In character, the Courante is also very similar to the Allemande, like a cousin on the other side of the family. In the process of memorizing the Courante, I catch myself inadvertently launching at the mid-point into the second half of the Allemande instead. Their harmony and style are so similar that I'm muddling them up, even though they're in different meters – two half-note beats to the measure in the Allemande, and three in the Courante. How embarrassing!

And yet, you could quite easily think parts of the Courante were in duple meter if you didn't have the score in front of you, because Bach is writing in *hemiola*. This is a kind of auditory illusion, a play on the 3:2 ratio in rhythm where two measures of triple meter may sound like three measures of duple meter and vice versa. It's the use of *hemiola* that makes this movement the only true French Courante (as opposed to a Corrente) in the Six Cello Suites.

The other thing about *hemiola* is that it sets the expected pulse off kilter. This makes it hard to determine where the musical phrases begin and end. David Ledbetter describes the spun-out phrase structures in the Courante as *enjambement*. I haven't come across this term before – "in-leg-ment"? – so I look it up. *Enjamber*, "to climb over." *Enjambement* is also a poetry term for a sentence that doesn't finish at a line break. A kind of run-on sentence, but for poems, and apparently also for Courantes. I have to smile at that, since every time I submit an article to a scholarly journal, Reviewer 2 – is there some kind of law that Reviewer 2 has to be a complete jerk? – criticizes me for my run-on sentences. Finding a run-on musical equivalent in Bach pleases me immensely.

*

It's October, and Sean and I decide what our family needs is an overnight getaway before the exhausting Christmas gig season starts. We get in the car and drive to the northernmost part of the Idaho Panhandle, not far from the Canadian border. I haven't traveled north of the resort town of Coeur d'Alene before, but Sean has recently returned from a university recruitment trip to Sandpoint and wants to go back. "It's stunning," he says, "and I have a feeling it's going to be even better now that it's fall." Driving north along densely forested mountain highways, the air is cooler and the colors of the foliage more brilliant by the minute. "Wait for it," says Sean with a grin, and a moment later we're out on a causeway across the shining waters of Lake Pend Oreille, maples and aspens blazing color on the mountainsides all around. My daughter and I gasp.

"I thought you'd like it," says Sean.

"It looks just like New Zealand," I tell him. It's true – if I didn't know I was in Idaho, you could convince me I was in Queenstown or Glenorchy in the South Island. Even the light here is like New Zealand – harder and brighter, the kind of light that makes you glad to have sunglasses.

"Oh Mommy, you always think everything good must be from New Zealand," laughs my daughter.

At the town of Sandpoint, we leave our car at a lakeside park and walk around taking photographs. We come across a replica of the Statue of Liberty that doesn't seem to have any particular reason for being there, but we flag down a passing jogger to take a family portrait in front of her.

In the morning we all wake up early. "We don't have to leave right away," I say to Sean. "Why don't we go for a drive to admire these beautiful leaves before they all fall off?" Back in the car, we follow a lakeside road around Lake Pend Oreille, exclaiming alternately over the abundant natural beauty and the enormous gated mansions. From time to time we spot bald eagles wheeling in the sky above us.

That's when we start to see the political billboards. Though the presidential election is coming up next month, we've never actually seen a Trump sign, since no one in genteel Moscow would be seen dead with one in front of their house. A handful of Trump bumper stickers in the economically depressed neighboring town of Lewiston don't count, or so we tell ourselves. Truth be told, we barely pay attention to the political news, since Donald Trump is so absurdly offensive and unqualified a candidate that we can't imagine him winning.

"Sean," I say, "they're everywhere along here. Everywhere."

Sean is uncharacteristically silent.

"Sean," I say again. "You don't think he could win, do you?"

"We're in North Idaho," says Sean. "You know what they say about there being white supremacists up here. I guess we shouldn't be surprised to see Trump signs in the most conservative part of one of the most conservative states?"

"We're not in a white supremacist compound right now," I point out. "We're on a lakeside highway surrounded by millionaires' houses. The people who own these places aren't weirdos stockpiling military-grade weapons, they're respectable pillars of the community."

Sean says nothing. I feel suddenly cold.

"Honey," he says eventually, "why haven't we applied for your American citizenship yet?"

I have no good answer. I've been eligible for citizenship for several years now, and by extension the right to vote. Whenever someone asks me about it, I make excuses: the expense, the paperwork, the inconvenience of multiple three-hour round trips to the courthouse in Spokane. The truth is that I have the privilege to be able to solve all these problems quite easily. I just haven't done it because I'm afraid. Not of losing my New Zealand citizenship – dual citizenship is permitted by both countries – but because to become an American would feel, even if only symbolically, like giving up on the possibility of moving home.

*

Like all Bach's movements for solo cello, the Courante of the Fifth Cello Suite is built on a bassline. Bass notes are my job in an ensemble. We let the violinists think they're the boss, but we bassline players are the ones who subtly but powerfully maneuver the harmony from place to place. The Courante bassline starts with the first five notes of the ascending minor scale, C – D – E-flat – F – G, before plunging back down to C again. It doesn't take much flipping through my mental Rolodex to come up with some other compositions in minor keys with "1-2-3-4-5-1" basslines. One of the first to come to mind is the instrumental *ritornello*, a refrain, from the Prologue of Claudio Monteverdi's *L'Orfeo*.

The opera retells the Greek myth of Orpheus, whose dazzling music convinced the gods to let him retrieve his Eurydice from the underworld. Having broken the very boundaries of life and death, he loses her once more when he turns to look at her on the journey home.

Center stage at the beginning of the opera is neither human nor god but La Musica, the spirit of music herself. It is she who introduces the tragedy, in five stanzas of poetic recitative separated by six iterations of the *ritornello*.

After the introductory *ritornello* she begins her tale with a salute to the gods. "Illustrious heroes, noble bloodline of kings!" (*Ritornello*.) She boasts of her own power to sway human emotion. "I am Music, who in sweet accents can make tranquil every troubled heart. And now with noble anger, and now with love, I can inflame the coldest minds." (*Ritornello*.) She brings up her – and Orpheus's – chosen instrument: "Singing with my golden lyre, I am wont now and then to charm mortal ears." (*Ritornello*.) Suddenly things turn wild: "Desire spurs me to tell you about Orpheus. Of Orpheus, who tamed wild beasts with his singing, who made Hades answer his entreaties." (*Ritornello*.) Then La Musica goes dark. "Now I vary my songs, now happy, now sad. No small bird shall stir among these trees. No wave shall sound on these banks. Every breeze will stop its course." (*Ritornello*.)

It's an extraordinary way to start an opera. By opening with the luminous immortal figure of La Musica, Monteverdi draws you right into the emotion of the story before the action even begins. He doesn't make the mistake of starting with a long monologue; instead, he breaks it up with the *ritornello*, using the ascending bassline to circle back to the "right" key in between stanzas. He grabs our attention, keeps us wanting more. In this context, the *ritornello* works like a picture-frame. It contains, or rather constrains, the big, messy emotions of mortal love.

The upwards-moving bass notes in Monteverdi's *ritornello* and Bach's Courante do the opposite of the descending passacaglia bassline. In *Lamento della ninfa*, Monteverdi's nymph was doomed from the start, but his Orpheus is allowed to get his hopes up before they come crashing down again.

We are wrong to think the Orpheus myth is about the power of music to cross the very frontiers of human mortality. Orpheus's supplications might fleetingly move the gods, but at the moment of his one ruinous mistake they show their true indifference to human suffering.

IV. SARABANDE

The Sarabande of the Fifth Cello Suite is a stark movement. It has no florid polyphony, no harmonizing multi-stopped chords, no distinctive rhythmic patterns. All Bach allows us is a single, broken-up line of clashing intervals. It is the loneliest piece of music I know.

Bach has only one piece remotely similar to the Sarabande, a soprano aria from a cantata of 1713 called *Ich hatte viel Bekümmernis*, "I had much sorrow." The text is darkness itself. "Sighs, tears, sorrow, trouble / Anxious yearning, fear, and death gnaw at my constrained heart / I feel misery, pain." They are the words of a human who has been abandoned by God.

The Sarabande of the Fifth Cello Suite has no words.

*

When I wake my daughter on that dark November morning, she stretches out her little arms to me and says "Is there a girl president now?"

"No, sweetheart," I tell her, and she bursts into tears.

"What happened?" she asks, and I don't know what to say.

*

The music building usually buzzes with activity first thing in the morning. Today it's almost silent. The students are walking through the hallways as usual, but no one is talking. I forget to pick up my lecture notes from my office and have to turn around and get them. Then I have to go back for my textbook. On my last trip into my office I lock the keys inside and have to go to the reception desk for a spare set.

*

"Today's lecture will be about augmented sixth chords," I say to the class. "In harmony, the augmented sixth chord is typically found preceding the dominant." I look around the room at the students and have the sudden thought that Idaho voted overwhelmingly for this new president. Statistically, therefore, it's likely that at least some of these bright-faced young people that I like so much voted for a president who finds it acceptable to treat immigrants as sub-human. That means they, too, might consider immigrants sub-human. I am an immigrant. Perhaps they think I am sub-human.

"There are three types of augmented sixth chord," I continue. "The interval of the augmented sixth is formed by the sixth degree of the minor scale, and the raised fourth degree above it. All three of the types of augmented sixth chord also contain the tonic." Suddenly my lesson plan seems utterly pointless and boring. "Today we'll be studying the Italian, French, and German sixth chords," I say. "The Italian sixth chord only has three tones. The others have four." Do these people think it's also acceptable to make fun of people with disabilities? To oppress and marginalize anyone who doesn't look like them? Is this OK with them?

Familiar white spots start appearing in the center of my field of vision. Migraine. My hands go numb and the whiteboard marker I was holding clatters to the floor. A student stands halfway up in his chair. "Dr. Wilson, are you OK?"

I try to pronounce words but my lips won't form syllables. "I – can't – talk," I manage. The students bustle about, murmuring in alarmed tones, offering to fetch glasses of water and call for help. I wave them away. "Migraine," I explain. "Sorry."

*

Back in my office, I take three caffeinated acetaminophen tablets and wait for my vision and speech to come back. I don't know what to do with myself. I take the rest of the day off and try to run some errands, but everywhere I go I start staring at people in suspicion. The sweet old lady who coos over my daughter in the grocery store, that police officer in the street, the barista who makes my coffee – all of them might have voted for this. Do they believe entire social groups are undeserving of rights and respect? Have they secretly felt like this all along, even as they smiled at me? Do the repulsive views of our new president simply articulate what everyone has been thinking? I can't reconcile this with the America that welcomed me so warmly.

*

Like many professors, I try not to influence students with my own political views. With politicians regularly accusing us of trying to convert their children into atheist liberals, most of us prefer not to look like a walking stereotype. Our syllabuses are required to contain a boilerplate "civility clause," which supposedly protects conservative students from professorial persecution. If only the politicians knew, I think grimly, that I haven't even figured out a way to persecute them into practicing scales.

The president of the university sends an urgent message to the faculty and students, telling us that hate speech is unacceptable in our community, and offering extra counseling services for vulnerable students. That does it. I search the internet for a graphic with the words SAFE SPACE and a rainbow design, print it out, and post it on my office door. They can call it liberal propaganda if they want. It's probably stupid to imagine we can seriously call any space safe anyway.

But the students notice the sign and slowly, one or two a day, start coming in and asking if they can talk to me. They're afraid. "My parents are migrant workers," one of them says quietly. "I'm the only member of my family who has legal status in this country."

"I almost made up my mind to transition this year," says another. "But now I don't think I'll be safe. I'm afraid someone's going to murder me."

"I'm gay," says another. "My parents go to a church where the pastor says gay people are going to hell."

I don't know what to say to any of them because I'm afraid too. As a professor, I'm used to ordering people about, setting them straight, telling them what they need to do to improve themselves, and I've never been lost for words. Now all I can think of to say is "You're not alone." The words sound hollow.

*

Bach's compositional style, writes Wilfrid Mellers, represents "a cross between a melodic horizontal and a harmonic vertical."[111] It's hard not to draw figurative as well as literal crosses all over the score of the Sarabande, a work that tends to stir our most anguished feelings. "The music is a purgation," Mellers writes of it, "the blood of Christ drains, as it were, from his cross-suspended body as the line, pallid in tone, is stretched almost – but not quite – to breaking-point."[112]

Such strong words about strong music might offer consolation to a believer. Where does an atheist go for solace when they can't find it in the suffering of Christ? How do you speak about things that are unspeakable, and to whom?

Mark M. Smith's intriguing reading finds "a purpose for 'Suitte discordable' beyond that of merely indicating a tuning. What was this extra purpose? The answer may be that Bach wanted more than one meaning in this term. For example, from Latin, 'dis' = against or away from, and 'Cor, cordis' = heart (especially concerning the passions and affections)."[113]

Disheartened. That's a good word for it.

V. GAVOTTES

If you've ever wondered what the difference between a Bourrée and a Gavotte is, the answer is not much. Both have two or four beats in a measure, and both have a hint of the shepherds-with-bagpipes ethos about them. The chief difference is that a Gavotte starts in the middle of the measure by way of a pick-up, and the Bourrée doesn't.

There was a time when I cared deeply about the difference between Bourrées and Gavottes. Now, staring out the window at the leafless aspens in my backyard, I can't find it in me to care one way or another. I'm having trouble caring about music in general. A quotation from Leonard Bernstein keeps popping up on my social media feeds: "This will be our reply to violence: to make music more intensely, more beautifully, more devotedly than ever before."[114] I stare at the words, which strike me as pointless. Musicians can say all the noble things they want on Facebook, but the fact is that most people don't listen to classical music. I've made sacrifice after sacrifice, spent huge amounts of other people's money, given up my country, and devoted my life to the pursuit of a kind of music no one cares about. I'm feeling pretty indifferent to it myself, actually.

"What are you thinking about?" says Sean, so I tell him. He looks at me searchingly. "Honey? Do you think it might be time to go talk to someone?"

*

The doctor says I have a major depression and sends me away to get antidepressants, tranquilizers, and talk therapy. The diagnosis surprises me because I thought depression meant feeling sad, and I'm not sad. The only feeling I can summon up right now is boredom. Everything is dreary and tedious, including music. Especially music. My cello sits silent in its case.

*

"I don't even know why I'm here," I tell the therapist. "It's pathetic to be depressed when you're privileged enough that your life is unlikely to change because of who's in the White House. There are people who are actually going to be hurt by this, people who will suffer and die, and they're not feeling sorry for themselves in a therapist's office. I don't deserve to feel depressed."

"Why don't you deserve to?" says the therapist.

"Why is everything you say a question?" I retort.

We sit in silence.

"Why don't you tell me about your mother?" says the therapist.

I pounce. "I knew it! I was wondering when you'd start on that. Therapists always go straight for the mother. Do they teach you that in therapy school?"

"Why do you say that?" says the therapist.

I'm already bored with this stand-off, so I grudgingly decide I might as well cooperate. I tell the therapist about my mother sitting cross-legged on our cork-tiled kitchen floor, teaching me music notes from flash cards before I even mastered the alphabet. I tell her about singing rounds on family car trips, Christmas carols around the grand piano, the birthday cake in the shape of a cello. I tell her about the five a.m. alarm clock, about looking out the bay window of our living room at the neighborhood children playing games down on the beach and not being allowed to join them until I'd done two hours of practice. I tell her about the screaming matches and my father always, always taking my mother's side even when, I later found out, he sympathized with me. I tell her about the punishments, about not being allowed to go to school dances because the loud music might hurt my ears. I tell her about the daily drives across Wellington to lessons and youth orchestra rehearsals and chamber group coachings, the Associated Board exams, the piano and theory and four-part chorale writing and armfuls of compact discs from Wellington City Library and the subscription to New Zealand Symphony Orchestra concerts. I tell her about being taken out of school for extra lessons, about the time our car was totaled and my mother and I spent three hours every day on buses and trains so I wouldn't miss a single lesson or rehearsal.

"Was there a lot of pressure on you to become a musician?" says the therapist.

"You *think?*" I say incredulously.

"What do *you* think?" says the therapist.

I'm getting a bit tired of her interlocutory style, but I'm on a roll. "Once, when I was at high school, the dean sent everyone in my year for individual appointments with the guidance counselor to talk about university applications and majors. When it was my turn, the guidance counselor said 'Well, you'll obviously be going to music school,' and sent me away. I hadn't even opened my mouth. I hadn't said one word. I had no choice, none. No one gave me one single choice. I wasn't allowed to have a choice."

"What would have happened if you'd said, look, no, I want to be something else?"

I stare blankly at the therapist. "That wasn't an option."

"Wasn't it?"

I scowl at her.

"Were you interested in another career path?"

"I could have done a lot of things," I say. "Everyone used to say I was so smart, I could do anything I wanted if I tried hard enough. Just like if you practice enough, you'll somehow magically be given a job playing in a major symphony or a recording contract with Deutsche Grammophon or whatever, and if you don't get those things it's because you didn't try hard enough. But that's the kicker, isn't it? You're never doing enough. Nothing is enough."

"But did you want to do something else?"

"I could have done something that made actual money, so that I could live where I want. I could have done something that actually helps people, like medicine." I shoot the therapist a mean look. "I could have been a psychology major. Looks like it worked out well for you."

"What would your mother's reaction have been if you'd chosen a different path?"

I snort. "She'd have gone ballistic."

"Would she?"

"Wouldn't you want a return on an investment if you'd spent all your energy and most of your money on it? Grown-ups used to say things to me like that I'd been given this huge talent and it would be terrible if I didn't use it They said I was so lucky to have a mother who lived for me and did so much for me."

"Did you not want her to live for you?"

"Of course not. I wanted her to have her own things."

"Do you think that if you hadn't chosen music, your mother would have withdrawn her affection from you?"

The question stops me in my tracks. I think about the day I was seven and came home crying and soaked to the skin after a surprise rain shower on my way home from school. For some reason, I had objected to wearing my raincoat and I thought I would be in trouble over it, but my mother swept me into her arms, took my wet clothes off me, and tucked me up in a soft blanket in front of the fire with a mug of cocoa. I think about the time when I was eleven and crawled into her bed after a nightmare even though I was too big to do that now, and she reached for me half-asleep and curled her long slender body around my back for the rest of the night.

No, my mother would not have withdrawn her affection.

I look down. "It wasn't that I didn't love music myself," I tell the therapist. Because I did love it. Because, even if I don't want to admit it, the choice was mine too.

*

I wonder if Bach ever felt angry at his parents, who died within a year of one another when Bach was ten years old. When I was about that age myself, I used to lie awake at night, weeping with terror that my mother would die in a car crash, get cancer, drown in the sea, or be kidnapped by murderers. What would have happened if I'd actually found myself an orphan the way Bach did? According to Robert Marshall, Bach's calamitous early losses made him distrustful of authority and heightened his tendency toward religious zeal. He bickered with the much older brother who took him in, and with the majority of his bosses. Once, he even called a bassoonist a very rude name that I don't think I need to repeat.[115] (In his defense, who among us has not wished to call a bassoonist a rude name from time to time?)

Sara Botwinick takes a different approach to Bach's childhood bereavements, speculating that "the traumatic loss of mother and father by the age of ten did not in itself preordain irreparable scars to Sebastian's psyche. In order for a catastrophic loss of this sort to have severe long-term consequences, additional factors need to be at work... If following the death of a child's parents he is enabled to bond with a significant other who is capable of nurturing the child while simultaneously alleviating his grief, severe pathological consequences of bereavement can be prevented."[116] What if music was that consoling nurturer? Bach was, after all, from a family who defined themselves by their music-making. When he illicitly copied his brother's manuscripts by moonlight, perhaps Bach was self-medicating with a familiar remedy.

*

I immediately throw away the tranquilizers because they make me feel slow and stupid. The antidepressants don't do much at first, but after three weeks I start to feel as if a dark curtain is lifting. The stage is clear.

*

Johann Mattheson, usually a fountain of useful information about dance forms in music, goes off on a strange, racially-tinged rant when it comes to Gavottes. "Italian composers use a type of gavotte for their violins on which they especially labor," he snipes, "often filling whole pages with their intemperances, and are nothing less, though probably something different than they should be. Yet if an Italian can only elicit admiration for his dexterity, then he makes everything of anything."[117] The irony that Mattheson himself was no stranger to intemperance doesn't seem to have occurred to him.

"I forgive you for your lack of self-awareness, Herr Capellmeister," I say aloud. I've started talking to dead composers again. I've started finding things funny again.

Dexterity and labor are certainly key to the first of the two Gavottes in the Fifth Cello Suite. Chords, both blocked and arpeggiated, keep your fingers racing all around the fingerboard of the cello trying to keep up with the three-person conversation. Then Bach launches into the second Gavotte, changing the texture into a linear, running style in groups of three eighth notes. In this respect, it looks back to the Gigue of the Fourth Cello Suite. Was this Bach's intention? E-flat major and C minor have the same three-flat key signature, and are therefore close relatives. So if the E-flat Gigue hints at *Ein feste Burg*, the mighty fortress of faith, what's the second C minor

Gavotte? A crumbling fortress, closed indefinitely for earthquake-proofing like half the historic buildings in New Zealand?

*

Looking back through the manuscripts, I spot something in the lute version that I hadn't noticed before, a scribbled *Gavotte 2de en Rondeau* across the lines of the staff before the beginning of the second Gavotte. Rondeau, or rondo? I recall studying a poetic song form called rondeau in a Renaissance music history class, though all I can remember about it is that it had an annoyingly complicated formal structure that we had to memorize for the exam. Rondo is an easier concept, a movement with a theme that keeps coming back again and again in various guises.

Back to Mattheson for advice. "What the drinking champions call a round," he pronounces, possibly from personal experience, "must indeed not be confused with that category of our melodies, which one calls, on account of its repetition of the round: a *Rondeau*...and is in music what is indicated by similarly-named rhyme species in poetry." Then he takes a turn I wasn't expecting: "The 136th Psalm is in its way nothing other than a rondeau. Luther calls it a litany. But a litany is a prayer; and the psalm contains a praise of God's kindness. All litanies are prayers *en Rondeau*..."[118]

It's a good analogy. In the New International Version, the twenty-six lines of the psalm text alternate with the refrain "His love endures forever." In the Gavotte, twenty-two measures of melody are interspersed with eight versions of the opening gesture – sixteen, if you play the repeats. If the pointillism of the Sarabande feels spiky and stand-offish, the repetitiveness of the second Gavotte draws us into its captivating round-and-round soundscape. Rituals, social and sacred, are built this kind of entrancement.

VI. GIGUE

When is a Gigue not a Gigue? When it's a Canarie, of course. Compared side by side with some of Bach's other compositions, the Gigue of the Fifth Cello Suite shows a distinct resemblance to the Gigue from the second of Bach's French Suites for keyboard. Both are in C minor; both feature a long-short-long rhythmic pattern composed of a dotted eighth note, a sixteenth note, then an eighth note. Some scholars think the Gigue from the French Suite is better termed a Canarie, a musical-dance form identifiable by its dactylic rhythm. By extension, this arguably makes the Gigue from the Fifth Cello Suite a Canarie too, though some scholars maintain that it's a French Gigue,[119] the sole exemplar of its kind in the Cello Suites.

Bach, serenely indifferent to the bickering and occasional fisticuffs of academic debate, tended to call movements whatever he felt like. Still, I go back to my books on French Baroque dance looking for more information about the Canarie. All sources lead to Thoinot Arbeau, who's always good for a lively description, and when it comes to Canaries he doesn't disappoint. "Some say that this dance comes from the Canary Islands," he tells us. "Others…maintain that it's a ballet composed for a masquerade, where the dancers were dressed as Kings and Queens of Mauritania, or in plumages of diverse colors."[120] The steps of the Canarie appear to have involved much stamping of the heels and toes against the other foot. It sounds irresistible, particularly the part about the feathers, which I assume at first to have come from the tails of canaries that didn't get away fast enough. An atlas sets me straight: the birds were named after the islands, not the other way around. (The islands got their Latin name, Canariae Insulae, from the swarms of dogs that roamed their volcanic terrain in ancient times. Local tribes are said to have practiced a cult of dog-worship, a fact that pleases me immensely.)

*

"Honey," says Sean, "let's adopt another dog to keep Cyril company. He gets so lonely when we're out all day."

"Yes, yes, yes!" shrieks our daughter. "Can it be a girl? Can it, can it?"

At first I try to exercise my veto rights, since I know who's going to end up taking care of a second dog, but they eventually wear me down.

The puppy is so tiny she fits into the palm of my hand, and silky black all over except for two white half-moons on her hind paws. We call her Luna because of the moons, and because (it later transpires) she's a lunatic.

Unlike happy-go-lucky Cyril, she won't settle into her crate that first night. After listening to the heartbreaking wails for an hour, I get out of bed. Overriding Sean's objections, I pick her up, carry her into the living room, and hold her against my chest. We spend all night on the sofa, Luna's tiny soft head nestling between my collarbones. She stops crying right away, and soon all I can hear are her quiet, snuffling dog-snores.

In the morning, Sean says "We'll never get her crate-trained now. What were you thinking?"

"I had to," I tell him. "She was missing her mother."

*

Even though the snow is thick on the ground and still falling, the protest isn't canceled. My daughter wants to know where I'm going.

"I'm going to exercise my right to demonstrate peacefully against the new government's policies on immigration," I tell her.

"I want to come!" she says.

"Are you sure?" I say. "It's cold. You'll need to wear your snowsuit and your snow boots."

"I feel very strongly, Mommy," she tells me. "Immigration is people like you, isn't it?"

We pull the cardboard backing off a giant *Frozen* coloring book to make a sign. Using a thick black marker, my daughter painstakingly writes MY MOMMY IS AN –

"How do you spell 'immigrant,' Mommy?"

I tell her. Then I say "Stop a moment, darling. I want to tell you something very important."

"What is it, Mommy?"

"Darling, you don't have to believe things just because I believe them. You don't have to be like me. You don't have to do the things I do or like the things I like. I want you to be your own person with your own thoughts and your own interests. Whatever makes you happy, whatever you believe in, whoever you love, whoever you want to be, your dad and I will always love and approve of you."

My daughter fixes her enormous different-colored eyes on me for a moment. "I know, Mommy," she says, and turns back to her work.

*

Bundled up against the smiting cold, we trudge along icy sidewalks to Moscow's East City Park. I hadn't expected many people to show up to a protest about immigration policy in Idaho on the coldest day of the year, but there are several thousand here. Dozens of my colleagues from the university, of course, but also people I recognize from local businesses and restaurants, my dentist's office, my hair salon, people of all ages and cultures and walks of life. Strangers see my daughter's sign, grin at me, and say "Welcome!" and "We're so happy you're here." Some of them ask if they can hug me.

On the small outdoors stage, which I've never seen used for anything other than summer concerts and the Renaissance Fair, stand a consortium of faith leaders. A Catholic priest, an imam, a rabbi, and five or six Protestant clergy come forward, arms linked. One by one they take turns with the microphone to speak out against hate and xenophobia, backing up their arguments with lines from the sacred texts of their religions. I'm glad to hear the words of Matthew 25: "Truly, I tell you, whatever you did not do for one of the least of these, you did not do for me." Those who pray, pray. My daughter and I stand and listen, her warm little hand clutching mine.

It's not until the end that I notice another group of people I really needed to see. A voice calls out "Dr. Wilson!" and I turn around and there, pink-faced in ski jackets and knitted hats and scarves, stand a crowd of music students.

I'm unable to speak for a minute. Then all I can manage is "Oh, you guys, *you guys...*"

"We're here for you," one of them tells me, "for you and for all our other professors from other countries."

Tears spilling down my face, I squeeze their mittened hands. "Thank you. Thank you all so much."

On the walk home, the snow starts to fall again. My daughter and I try to distract ourselves from the cold by singing her favorite song about the mother duck and her five little ducklings. Poking up through the snow in people's front gardens are colorful signs in green and orange and purple. In English, Spanish, and Arabic, they read "No matter where you're from, we're glad you're our neighbor."

"Thank you," I say again to no one in particular.

"You're welcome, Mommy," says my daughter, politely.

*

Back in the house, I open up the case of the deliberately mistuned cello to see how it's doing. So much for sparing the bridge – after a few weeks of non-use all the pegs have popped and the strings are hanging loose. The sound-post and bridge appear to have stayed in place, though, and it only takes me ten minutes to get the strings back to C-G-D-G tuning. I play through the Fifth Cello Suite several times, feeling my way around notes that have become as familiar to me as my words. The *scordatura* no longer feels like a foreign language, but a dialect that I've now gotten used to, just as I learned to say "sidewalk" and "math."

Outside the windows the snow is coming down in thick flakes. Next morning there's more than a foot of it on the ground, clean and soft and new.

Part Six

THE RETURN

Suite No. 6 in D Major ("Suitte a cinque cordes"), BWV 1012

I. PRELUDE

Sometimes you get an idea that won't leave you alone. There are all sorts of reasons to try to ignore it, such as impracticality and expense, but it still won't go away, persistently jumping into your consciousness when you're trying to concentrate on something else.

The Prelude of the Sixth Cello Suite is surprisingly like the super-famous Prelude of the First. In many ways, it's the logical conclusion of the techniques set forth in the very first notes of the Cello Suites – the *ondulé* bowstroke, bariolage, and pedal tones, the obsessively repeating bass notes that underpin it all. Unlike the Prelude of the First Cello Suite, which is playable by a talented child or a good adult amateur, the Prelude of the Sixth calls for the kind of gymnastics that only the most skilled players can master.

Structurally, the Prelude takes the form of a *ritornello*, Bach's inheritance from the flamboyant instrumental concertos of the Italian masters. The *ondulé* refrain returns again and again in different keys and guises, interspersed by increasingly difficult "episodes." The second half of the Prelude has an immense outpouring of fireworks that require the utmost command of the instrument. If there's anything tense or inefficient in your technique, you simply won't be up to Bach's demands. If you can do it well, the effect is thrilling.

The Sixth Cello Suite is the only one I've never performed in public, and I'm about to do so for my next recital program as a practice run for my planned marathon performance of all six. The reason I haven't performed it before is its difficulty, or if I'm to be scrupulously truthful, my fear of its difficulty. It's certainly possible to play the Sixth Cello Suite on a modern four-string cello, and the hundreds of existing recordings are testimony to this. The trouble is the extremely wide ambitus of Bach's range of pitches, which take us from the lowest bass notes on the C-string right up to the heights of the A-string. In and of themselves, high notes aren't terribly difficult – the problem is playing them using the *ondulé* and chordal textures Bach demands of us. To play all the notes, you have to contort your hand into huge stretches and liberal use of advanced thumb position technique. On a four-string cello, this puts you at a disadvantage because it makes the instrument less resonant in the high-pitched sections, right at the moment when the drama of the music demands the most glorious resonance you can muster.

I'm determined to get good at this, but a nagging voice in my head keeps saying *What would this be like on a five-string cello?*

It happens every day when I open up my facsimile of Anna Magdalena Bach's manuscript. Right there, on the first line of staff at the top of the Prelude, is the instruction in her haphazard French: *Suitte 6-eme a cinque cordes.* Next to it are the pitches to which the strings are to be tuned: the standard C, G, D, and A, plus an additional high E-string. This is the only clue we have, since there are no further instructions as to the size and manner of playing of the instrument. It's a mystery, and I can't stop thinking about it.

Cellos cost a lot of money and I have approximately zero money, so getting a five-string cello is an impossible dream. Of course, I'm no stranger to impossible dreams – my teenage diaries were full of them. In sparkly pen, dotting every *i* with a heart, I scribbled cringe-making statements like "I honestly believe that just wanting something enough will make it happen." These days I no longer believe that the strength of my desire sets some mystical process into motion by which longed-for objects will materialize, but this doesn't stop me daydreaming about five-string cellos during meetings at work. At Faculty Senate one day, I start imagining how it would feel to play a cello with an E-string on it and what fingerings I would use, and only realize that I've actually put my left arm up into playing position when I come out of my daydream and realize I've inadvertently seconded a motion.

The universe is clearly telling me that I need to get a five-string cello. But how?

My inner teenage girl comes out in full force. I might not have sparkly pens any more, but it turns out I can still write long lists of things I want. I fill up half a notebook with lists of five-string cello options and their pros and cons. And there are a disproportionate number of cons. Every one of the options is impractical, and most are impossible.

The most obvious and least possible is to find a historical five-string cello like the one Anner Bylsma used for his recordings of the Bach Suites, then convince a friendly millionaire to buy it for me. An internet search of rare instrument dealers reveals that there are very few historical five-string cellos. I pluck up my courage to call one of these dealers to ask why. "They've disappeared," he tells me. "Some might have been converted into standard cellos. Since they were smaller anyway, they may have been used as children's instruments."

"Meaning they eventually got trashed?" I ask.

"Yes," he agrees, "eighteenth-century children being very much the same as their twenty-first century counterparts."

What are my chances of getting a historical instrument that I like, anyway? Listening again to Bylsma's recordings, I find myself really missing the big warm bass notes of the standard four-string cello. If even Bylsma can't get a five-string cello to sound as good as a four-string cello, it's possible that very few of the five-string cellos from this experimental era of instrument-building sound great. This could even explain why the standard cello ended up having four strings – perhaps luthiers couldn't figure out how to put five on it while keeping it sounding good. Two top cellists, Steven Isserlis and Jan Vogler, had the chance to play five-string cellos for their respective recordings of Bach, and both ultimately chose not to for sound quality reasons. "Although I spent several interested hours playing a five-string cello before I made this recording," Isserlis observes in the liner notes to his Gramophone Award-winning disc, "I opted instead for the usual four strings for the sixth suite. The sonority of a five-string cello is so much thinner…that I decided that it would sound anti-climactic."[121] Vogler puts it more bluntly, stating that the five-string cello is "too small – and sounds like a trumpet."[122]

As the loving wife of a trumpeter, this isn't enough to put me off, but I'm discouraged that even superstar cellists have trouble making a cello sound good. Of course, not all five-string cellos sound bad, as evidenced by the recordings of Pieter Wispelwey and several others, but it's starting to seem as if the good ones are rare. And the fact remains that I don't have the resources to travel all over the world trying them out, let alone buy one.

My second thought is to commission a new five-string instrument. I've heard of cellists doing this before, and it might be possible if I can get a large enough grant. All inquiries lead back to Dmitry Badiarov, the violinist and luthier whose iconographical and organological detective work led to his reinvention of the violoncello da spalla, a five-string cello played on the shoulder with the aid of a strap.[123] Several artists have recorded Bach's Cello Suites on Badiarov's creation, including Sigiswald Kuijken and Badiarov himself. I spend hours watching violoncello da spalla videos on YouTube, studying the dimensions of the instrument and recommended manner of playing. It looks as if this solution favors violinists, not only because of the shoulder-hold but also the significantly different fingering system.

When I interview Badiarov for *Strings*, I ask him about this and he confirms it. "Almost all the players are violinists, but a cellist doesn't have to play the instrument on the shoulder. You can play it *da gamba*, but you'd probably find it more comfortable to play on slightly bigger ones."[124] I find this both encouraging and discouraging. Badiarov has found a way to make five-string cellos sound wonderful, but I'm not sure this is the way forward for me. If I were an early music specialist with the time to devote to mastering an entirely new instrument, that would be one thing, but I still have to play regular cello in solo and chamber concerts, teach, travel, research, and write. The violoncello da spalla is significantly smaller than a standard cello, and there simply isn't time in my schedule to get good enough at it to play it in public, even if I were to adopt Badiarov's suggestion of playing it between my knees.

My third thought is to buy a cheap student cello and pay a luthier to put a fifth string on it. This mightn't sound like a big deal, but in fact it's major surgery. You can't just grab a thinner string and add it to a cello yourself, because to do so would require a new tailpiece and bridge, a wider fingerboard, and a new peg-box with five holes in it.

This idea is a non-starter, because even a cheap cello is expensive. I figure I could spend five thousand dollars on a student cello that I wouldn't even like in its original state, and thousands more for the luthier's materials and labor, and at the end of it all who knew what the fifth string would do to the sound? The luthier friend I call to discuss it tells me ruefully that "the more strings you put on something, the more it detracts from the sound of all of them."

I realize that none of my ideas are going to work, and I turn back to practicing the Sixth Cello Suite on a standard cello, feeling more dissatisfied than ever.

II. ALLEMANDE

The American system of music theory is in most respects more rational and more codified than the British system I grew up with. It's much easier to learn your note values, for example, when they correspond to fractions. Whole note, half note, quarter note – it's as straightforward as cutting up an apple. You do miss out on some lyrical and amusing names, though, such as the British word for the sixty-fourth note. It's a *hemidemisemiquaver*. You're welcome.

The Allemande of the Sixth Cello Suite has a lot of sixty-fourth notes. The total number of measures is only twenty, but it's actually a fairly long and substantial movement. It used to perplex me that Bach had decided to fill twenty measures of 4/4 time with extremely small subdivisions of the beat. Why not write forty measures but double all the note values so that it would be easier to read?

The answer may have something to do with the tempo. Bach had to use other means for conveying an ideal tempo than metronome markings, because the metronome hadn't yet been invented. Various composers had come up with ways to measure tempo by the beating of one's heart, but this had obvious drawbacks. It was up to intrepid inventors like the music theorist Etienne Loulié to remedy the problem. In 1696, Loulié constructed a device called a *chronomètre* from a six-foot pendulum that swung on a cord.[125] Its size made it cumbersome, particularly since people and rooms were both smaller in the seventeenth century. What's more, the *chronomètre* was silent, which meant musicians needed to look at it to get the beat. This was no small inconvenience when you also had to look at your score and at your colleagues' cues, and so the *chronomètre* never really caught on. It wasn't until the nineteenth century that one Dietrich Nikolaus Winkel at last came up with an early prototype for the metronome. He didn't get to enjoy the glory of his invention, however, because he neglected to file a patent. A shady character named Johann Nepomuk Maelzel took advantage of Winkel's carelessness by swooping in and claiming credit for it, which he retains to this day.

Without a metronome or even a *chronomètre* to play with, Bach had to find other means of conveying tempi. Like so much else in his music, this is left to the judgment of the learned musician. Unlike most other movements in the Cello Suites, however, we do actually have an expressive tempo direction for the Allemande of the Sixth Cello Suite in three eighteenth-century sources. After the Prelude in Johann Peter Kellner's copy are the words *Sequi Allemande adagio*, an interesting trilingual sentence indicating that the following Allemande should be played *adagio*, slowly. In Sources C and D, the direction is *Molto adagio*, very slowly. This raises the question: how slow is slow?

Cellists are an emotional bunch, and there's nothing we love more than wallowing in a good tune. A lot of recordings of the Allemande drag along at a snail's pace, while the cellist marks every nuance with a lengthy rhetorical pause. If you didn't know the time signature was common time, with four quarter-note beats to the measure, you could be forgiven for thinking there were eight eighth-note beats, or even – in some extreme cases – sixteen sixteenth-note beats. But there aren't. Bach was perfectly capable of writing Allemandes in larger note values, as we can see in a remarkably similar Allemande for keyboard in Partita No. 4. His choice to compose the cello Allemande in 4/4 with very small beat subdivisions appears absolutely deliberate. The takeaway is that we should play it at a tempo fast enough to suggest being "in four."

But what of the *molto adagio* direction? As a child of ten, preparing for my Associated Board of the Royal Schools of Music theory exam, I memorized a long list of Italian musical terms. *Largo, lento*, and *adagio* were all defined as "slow," and I assumed this meant they could be used interchangeably. Not until much later did I realize with embarrassment that this wasn't the case. *Adagio*, if we break it into its component parts *ad* and *agio*, literally means "at ease." Being at ease doesn't mean slow; it's a character, not a metronome marking.

Johann Joachim Quantz, author of the delightful *On Playing the Flute* (1756) and a go-to resource for hardcore early music nerds, has this to say on the subject: "To play an Adagio well, you must enter as much as possible into a calm and almost melancholy mood, so that you execute what you have to play in the same state of mind as that in which the composer wrote it. A true Adagio must resemble a flattering petition. For just as anyone who wishes to request something from a person to whom he owes particular respect will scarcely achieve his object with bold and impudent threats, so here you will scarcely engage, soften, and touch your listeners with a bold and bizarre manner of playing. For that which does not come from the heart does not easily reach the heart."[126]

Perhaps this is the key to interpreting the Allemande of the Sixth Cello Suite. A touching and heartfelt request, even beseeching.

*

Meanwhile, I'm beseeching cellist friends all over the world to talk to me about five-string cellos. Even the biggest gear geeks are discouraging. "Five-string cellos don't sound good," says a friend from my competition circuit days. "There's a reason they didn't survive." Another calls the five-string cello a one-hit wonder like the arpeggione, a sort of cello crossed with a viol crossed with a guitar that would have disappeared into the footnotes of history had Franz Schubert not happened to compose an exquisite sonata for it. "You just suck it up and learn to play the Sixth Suite on the four-string cello," says yet another. "There's a reason every competition in the world has it on the program."

This is far from promising, and I almost give up on the five-string idea, especially since I've now practiced the Sixth Cello Suite so obsessively that I'm comfortable performing it on four strings. Of course, I still have to leave out some of the notes from the multi-note chords, but by re-voicing you can still convey Bach's intended harmonies, even if not in the exact order he wanted. Maybe it isn't really that bad on four strings after all.

Then I get a phone call from Rachel Johnston, my inseparable friend from student days in New Zealand and London. I tell her about the five-string cello problem to see if she has any ideas. I tell her that everyone says multi-stringed cellos don't sound any good, and she's dismissive. "That's absolute nonsense. Do these people not listen to rock music?" she asks.

"Do you really need me to answer that?" I reply jokingly.

"But rock musicians are putting five and six strings on cellos all the time," Rachel says, "and they sound great." Since leaving her longtime job in the Australian String Quartet, Rachel has become a well-known folk, pop, and rock cellist, and lives a bohemian existence on the road, touring constantly from festival to festival. Freed from the constraints of classical music etiquette, she dyes her hair brilliant colors and does exactly as she pleases.

"Have you tried one?" I demand, kicking myself for not talking about this with her earlier.

"Yes," she says, "Luis and Clark do one in carbon fiber. You have to custom order it, though."

"How big is it?" I'm already out of my seat and crossing the room to my computer.

"The same size as a normal one," says Rachel.

I'm doubly kicking myself now, because I've been familiar with Luis and Clark instruments for years. When I was studying at the University of Texas, Luis Leguia visited our cello class with an early prototype of his carbon fiber creation. It was a sleek, black instrument, covered in the diamond patterns of the carbon fiber weave, and slightly smaller than a regular full-size cello. For acoustic reasons, it had neither scroll nor corners. Mr. Leguia let us pass it around the classroom so that each of us could try it, and we marveled over the resonance and directness of its tone. Later, when it looked less and less likely that a rich sponsor would materialize to buy me the old Italian cello of my dreams, Sean and I took out a bank loan to buy a four-string Luis and Clark cello, since they cost a tenth of what I'd have to spend on even a semi-decent wood cello. Initially, I thought I might use it mostly for Romantic and modern music and have my wood cello converted into a Baroque instrument, but when I started playing it I found that there was a certain hollowness in the sound that perfectly suited what I was trying to do in Bach. Soon enough I was using it for almost everything, since it was convenient to have an instrument that was impervious to changes in climate and humidity. It hasn't occurred to me that custom-built models were available, though I see now on the website that they've been available all along.

As soon as I'm off the phone with Rachel, I call Luis Leguia's wife Stephanie to ask about their five-string cellos. Have they made a lot of them?

"We've made some," she tells me. "Do you want one with a low F-string or a high E-string?"

"An E-string. Do cello E-strings actually exist? I mean, I know they exist, but can you actually buy them or do you have to have them specially made?"

"They certainly do exist," she says.

It's on the tip of my tongue to give Mrs. Leguia my credit card number and go for it, but financial prudence takes over. We're in debt right now thanks to student loans, my green card paperwork, credit cards racked up during a six-month period of unemployment years ago, and my cello loan. I'm going to have to get a grant for this. I tell Mrs. Leguia that I'll call her back when I get the money, and immediately go to the university website to figure out if I qualify for faculty research funds.

*

"This project reimagines Bach's five-string cello as a twenty-first century solution to an eighteenth-century problem," I type rapidly. Applying for grants is usually a tedious business, but I'm writing this one like a woman possessed. I've got to make the committee care about the five-string cello, or at least understand why I care about it so much. "There is no other cello piece as iconic as Bach's Cello Suites; they define what it means to be a cellist." Too cheesy? No, go big or go home. "The Suites have become so much part of our culture that even people who don't deliberately listen to classical music recognize them from Yo Yo Ma's cameo appearance on *The West Wing*, the Netflix series *Daredevil*, and countless commercials and movie soundtracks." Should I mention that viral YouTube video about the honey badger? No, probably not. "No cellist has yet recorded Bach's Sixth Cello Suite on a five-string cello made from carbon fiber. My project will make an unprecedented contribution to ongoing academic debate about performance practices in Bach's Cello Suites."

I request funds for the five-string cello, a case to store it in, a recording studio booking, the hourly rate for a recording engineer and producer, and the all-in-one fee for a compact disc company to produce, market, and disseminate a recording of Bach's Cello Suites. It's an ambitious request.

"They might want to know why they should buy you a cello you can only play one piece on," Sean points out. "Why don't you ask for money to commission some new repertoire for five-string cello?"

"Genius!" I reply, picking up my phone to sound out a couple of composer friends on how much commissions cost. Another $2,200 in my budget requests brings the total to a pretty huge sum, but I reason that if you ask for a lot and they give you less, at least you get something. I send the file off to my department chair for approval, shut my laptop, and go back to practicing.

III. COURANTE

The Courante of the Sixth Cello Suite opens with a bubbling, optimistic gesture built on the rising arpeggiated D major chord. It's the only Courante in the Cello Suites to start like this, since the first four go in descending melodic motion and the fifth, being the only true French Courante, does something different altogether. The startlingly showy character provokes Allen Winold to compare it to the *Mannheimer Rakete*, or "Mannheim Rocket."[127] This was a signature technique of the large and renowned orchestra at the electoral court in Mannheim in the middle of the eighteenth century. Mannheim musicians were famous for their exceptionally unified group sound, including the ability to heighten musical expression through extremes of dynamic change. The "Mannheim Rocket," which refers a little disappointingly to fireworks rather than to spacecraft, typically featured equal note values and ascending pitches from the tonic triad. In performance, it was usually combined with a rousing crescendo. Practicing the Courante of the Sixth Cello Suite, I decide that a crescendo makes total sense here. In the middle of the first phrase there's a high B that's a little hard to get to, so I add another crescendo and hope that playing it with great confidence will propel the third finger of my left hand up there quickly enough. No matter, it will be much easier with the five-string cello that I'm confident will soon be in my possession.

Like the Courante's fireworks and crescendi, my hopes are up. Also like fireworks and crescendi, they're not particularly good at coming down again. A few weeks after submitting the research grant application, my email inbox pings with a new message from the Dean of the College. I see it right away in the middle of the first paragraph: "...extremely high standards...unprecedentedly large number of applicants...encourage you to consider applying again next year."

I don't even finish reading before I slump back in my desk chair, crushed. My inner teenager is screaming "It's not fair! I *wanted* it!"

*

Later that evening, over Skype, Rachel is sympathetic. "It sucks, doesn't it? Don't you just long to write back and ask 'So am I to understand that if the standards were extremely low and almost no one applied, then I would win?'" she says. She's always quick to come up with a humorous one-liner.

I sniff. "Do you ever want to collect up all the rejection letters you've ever had and wallpaper a room with them as a kind of art installation?"

"Yes," she says, "and I even kept them all, only eventually there got to be so many that they took up too much space and I had to throw them out."

"Music is the worst profession ever," I say bitterly. "It's basically a pyramid scheme. All you ever get to do is practice and beg people for money and then they say no and they don't even care. I don't know if I even want to do this Bach marathon now."

"Oh for goodness' sake, stop sulking," says Rachel. She's the only person who's allowed to talk to me like that.

*

The next person I call is my tenor colleague at the university, Chris Pfund, who recently agreed to become my new co-artistic director for the Idaho Bach Festival. We'd planned to make my Bach Cello Suites marathon concert the centerpiece of the program, and it's only eight months away. "I think I'll still do it," I tell him. "It's disappointing not to have the fancy cello, but maybe I just need to do it anyway." Chris is encouraging, and we start making plans for the other events in the festival, which will include an all-Bach organ recital, a large brass ensemble recital of Renaissance and Baroque compositions, and a closing gala performance of Bach's *Christ lag in Todes Banden*. Chris and our other vocal colleagues will sing the solo parts in front of the choir, and it's my job to get the small instrumental ensemble together. Strings will be easy, since my faculty and Preparatory Division colleagues will help out, and I'll be playing continuo, my favorite activity in the world. Sean's already said he'll play the solo cornetto part. But then there's the matter of finding three trombonists, and I've only signed up two. The third has to have an alto trombone and I'm not sure I know anyone who owns and can play one.

"We'll figure it out. It's going to be great," says Chris insouciantly. "It's going to be amazing." His enthusiasm almost lifts me out of my disgruntlement.

*

Two weeks later I get another email from the Dean's Office. The College of Letters, Arts, and Social Sciences and the new Integrated Research and Innovation Center have somehow cobbled together a smaller research grant for me to custom-order a five-string cello from Luis and Clark. It's not enough for me to make a compact disc of Bach's Cello Suites or commission any new repertoire, but I can still get the cello. I start whooping with joy and dancing gleefully around my office, and only stop when my guitar colleague in the next room taps on my door to ask if everything is all right in there. "I'm getting a five-string cello, I'm getting a five-string cello!" I shriek, and students in the hallway rush over to give me high fives. "Will you let us play it?" they demand.

"Of course!" I tell them.

To celebrate, my family and I go out to dinner at Black Cypress in Pullman. Twirling spaghetti around my fork, all I can talk about is the five-string cello, how it will sound, how it will feel to play, how it will look.

"Mommy, you talk faster than anyone in the world," comments my daughter.

"Here's to five-string cellos," says Sean, raising his glass of cabernet sauvignon.

My daughter holds up her plastic tumbler of milk. "To Mommy!"

IV. SARABANDE

I t will be several months before I can at last lay my hands on the five-string cello. There's a flurry of paperwork, phone calls back and forth with Mrs. Leguia in Boston, and requests from the Integrated Research and Innovation Center for a public presentation about the project. The president of the university happens to mention the cello to a member of the state legislature who has a degree in music education. The politician wants to know more, so the university publicity people and I hastily put together a packet of information to send to his office in Boise. It's gratifying to feel as if I'm contributing to the university's reputation for research, and furthermore, to know that other people are as excited about the five-string cello as I am.

Preparations for my Bach Cello Suites marathon continue with increasing impatience. I'm raring to go and can hardly wait for the grant money to be released so that Luis and Clark can start making the cello. I watch and re-watch YouTube videos of their manufacturing process, imagining when the carbon fiber weave for my cello will be tenderly laid into its red silicon mold to shape the body of the instrument. Mrs. Leguia tells me that they'll use the same mold as for four-string cellos, it's just the bridge, tailpiece, pegbox, and pegs that will be different because they have to accommodate the fifth string. My imagination returns obsessively to the high E-string. What kind of character will it have? Will it sound like the E you can play on the A-string, or brighter? What will the thin wire feel like under my callused fingertips? Will I need to tone down the pressure I apply with the bow so that I don't immediately break it? Should I use a different bow? Maybe I'll use a Baroque bow, whose sloping stick will afford me more delicacy than the robust, concave modern bow. Maybe, maybe…

In the meantime, I practice the Sixth Cello Suite on my four-string cello and realize that it isn't insurmountably difficult like this, at least, not all the movements. Two of them, the Courante and Gigue, don't go very high and are more or less playable. The Allemande and Gavottes are a bit more of a challenge, and the Prelude even more so. The Sarabande is the hardest of all. Because of its repeated multi-stopped chords in uncomfortable hand positions, I keep veering frustratingly out of tune. Some of the chords require contortions that make me fear for the tendons of my wrist, so I borrow various re-voiced versions from the Rostropovich recording. If it's good enough for Mstislav Leopoldovich, it should be good enough for me. Until I get my five-string cello, that is.

If I had to pick a favorite from the thirty-six movements in the Six Cello Suites, I might pick the Sarabande of the Sixth despite its difficulty. Something about its beautifully simple melody suggests transcendence, sublimity. Like the other dance movements in the Sixth Cello Suite, the Sarabande has a second section that is disproportionately longer than the first. This gives Bach the opportunity to develop a cascading musical idea that turns again and again through the life-cycle of related harmony until the final cadence. It's almost unbearably poignant to play.

Since listeners generally associate major keys with lighter feelings and minor keys with gravity and sorrow, the high seriousness of this D major Sarabande may come as a surprise. David Ledbetter aptly describes it as "a major-key lament, in the sense of Handel's 'Lascia ch'io pianga' from *Rinaldo* (1711)"[128] I haven't thought of this comparison before, but he's right. The Sarabande has a lot in common with Handel's exquisite aria, itself a Sarabande, and I look up the score and libretto of the opera to get a context for it. Handel uses the same story as Jean-Baptiste Lully's *Armide*, but his take on it is markedly different. The setting would be interesting enough for its gender expression alone – the knightly hero Rinaldo is sung by a castrato, his future father-in-law Goffredo by a woman in pants – but it's also rather thrilling on a purely musical level. "Lascia ch'io pianga" is the lament of the heroine Almirena after her dramatic kidnap by the Damascene sorceress Armida, who has swooped in by way of fiery chariots and obfuscating black clouds to snatch Almirena away from Rinaldo. Most of us, faced with such disagreeable circumstances, might gnash our teeth and kick down doors, but Almirena's reaction is relentlessly ladylike. "Let me weep over my cruel fate!" she sighs, a trifle helplessly. Luckily for her, some rescuers eventually show up. Luckily for us, moreover, her aria is one of otherworldly beauty.

Bach knew Handel's music well, so it's not inconceivable that "Lascia ch'io pianga" could have been a model for the Sarabande of the Sixth Cello Suite. He might even have known an earlier version of it called "Lascia la spina" from the grandly-named *Triumph of Time and Truth*, an oratorio Handel composed aged only twenty-two. Its text seems more germane to the character of Bach's Sarabande: "Leave the thorn and pick the rose; you go looking for your sorrow! Gray frost by a hidden hand will come when your heart doesn't expect it." The image of a hand reaching for a rose but touching ice sends a shiver through me. There's something more there, the human terror of mortality that I feel when I play the Sarabande of the Sixth Cello Suite. Such music may have an air of timelessness, but whether we will accept it or not our own time is running out.

*

The dogs hear the doorbell before I do. It's midsummer, and I'm practicing in the studio at the back of the house. Suddenly all is commotion, with high-pitched yipping and a clatter of claws on the hardwood floor. My daughter rushes into the studio. "Mommy! Quick, it's here!"

The FedEx driver hefts the huge packing crate over the doorstep and holds out a form, which I sign with shaking hands. My daughter and I set the crate carefully on its back and get to work pulling off the packing tape while the dogs sniff around and try to eat the Styrofoam. Freed from its bonds, the cello gleams in the afternoon sunlight. It seems heavier than my four-string cello, even if it's exactly the same size. Kneeling on the floor, I pluck the strings. C, G, D, A, and there, gossamer-thin and perfect, the E. Its resonance seems to float around the room. My daughter and I are speechless for a minute. Then she says "Oh, Mommy, you have to play something."

I'm shaking as I put the bow to the five strings. I've dreamed of this moment for so long.

V. GAVOTTES

After four movements in a mostly courtly style, the two Gavottes of the Sixth Cello Suite resemble nothing so much as a wild party. We're back in pastoral style, Bach's liberal use of open strings mimicking the drone of the musette. The mood might differ markedly from that in the Gavottes of the Fifth Cello Suite, but Bach uses the same *en rondeau* structure, particularly in the second Gavotte. Between three episodes of the *rondeau* theme – six, if you play the repeats – there are episodes of increasingly high spirits, culminating in the kind of knees-up more suited to a barn dance than to an aristocratic ballroom.

There's some puzzlement among scholars and performers over the key signatures of the Gavottes. In the paired dances of the other Cello Suites, Bach always keeps the key signatures the same between the two. Here, the first Gavotte is in "cut time," with two half-note beats to the measure, which he indicates in the usual manner of a C with a vertical line through it. The second Gavotte has a single "2." These time signatures are sometimes thought to be interchangeable for the purposes of tempo interpretation. If this were the case, however, why would Bach bother writing two different time signatures? Wouldn't he just keep it in cut time?

Flipping open the synoptic Bärenreiter edition, I see another thing I've never noticed before. Unlike Sources A, B, and C, Sources D and E have a time signature of common time for the first Gavotte, that is, four quarter-note beats to the measure. Can it be that Bach at first made a mistake with the time signature, but later, after Anna Magdalena Bach and Johann Peter Kellner had made their copies, inserted some corrections to the lost autograph manuscript that were picked up by the copyist of Source D and by Louis Norblin? This at least would help cellists decide on tempi for the Gavottes. If the first Gavotte were "in four," that would imply a certain emphasis on all four beats that affords the cellist the chance to linger pleasurably over the multi-note chords at a more moderate tempo. In contrast, Bach's time signature of two beats in the measure for the second Gavotte could imply that he doesn't want it to sound too "notey." A faster tempo brings out the best in the second section in particular, giving it a sense of gleeful merriment that you might miss if you played it too slowly. On the *da capo* return to the first Gavotte, all you need to transition back to its more sedate tempo is a little broadening of the two introductory pick-up notes.

*

Now that the five-string cello is in my possession, I've barely put it down. I'm in love. Playing Bach's multi-note chords the way he wrote them is bliss, and makes the Sixth Cello Suite feel like a completely different piece. There have been surprises. Before the five-stringer arrived, I assumed playing it would be a piece of cake. Surely you could just pick it up and play it in exactly the same manner as a four-string cello? This turns out not to be the case. My first few attempts are a mess of bumping wrong strings, and I can't seem to get a consistent tone on phrases that traverse more than two strings. My imaginary five-string cello had a wider bridge and fingerboard than a four-string cello to accommodate the fifth string, so I'm disconcerted to find that they're actually the same. It makes sense, of course – if they were wider it would be impossible for human fingers to reach all the pitches of multi-note chords, even extremely long fingers like mine. This means that the strings are closer together than the strings on a four-string cello, necessitating some marked changes in bow technique. I'm used to knowing exactly what elevation my right arm needs to bow each of the four strings, but when there's a fifth string I find myself launching the bow at what I think is the D-string, only to get the A-string. It's hard to make a good tone on the D- and G-strings, both of which sound muddy when I attempt higher-pitched left-hand positions. The problem is surmountable if I change the fingering patterns to lower positions whenever possible, though I have to think very carefully as I relearn the notes of the Sixth Cello Suite to make sure I accommodate the needs of the instrument.

A bigger issue is the tone quality of the E-string, which sounds louder and brighter than any of the other strings. Many cellos have a slightly raucous tone on the A-string, but on my five-string cello it's positively muted in comparison to the screaming E-string. I try to compensate by bowing quite vigorously on the A-string and easing off the pressure on the E-string, but it sounds stilted and unconvincing. I call Mrs. Leguia to ask if she has any suggestions, and she mails me a *dolce*-gauge E-string and a *forte*-gauge A-string to see if that will even things up. It does, and I can at last proceed with relearning the Sixth Cello Suite on five strings.

I thought it would be easier this way, but it isn't. Does it sound better? Yes, without a doubt, but it takes months of practice to master the idiosyncrasies of this instrument, marvelous though it may be. One of my mistaken assumptions was thinking there would be no need to use thumb position on the five-string cello, the technique where you apply the distal phalanx of the left thumb to the string in order to reach more notes. I realize pretty quickly that you still need to use thumb position in the Prelude if you're going to take the climactic cadenza section at anything approximating an exciting tempo. Another passage at the end of the Gigue also appears to demand it. For some reason I find this annoying, because as far as we know thumb position didn't exist in 1720. What are we to take away from this? That Bach didn't know what he was doing? That the instrument he was writing for must indeed have been so small that you wouldn't need thumb position to reach all the notes?

Perhaps the only person who could have told us more about Bach's intended five-string cello was Carl Friedrich Abel, the son of Bach's Cöthen colleague Christian Ferdinand Abel. The Bach and Abel families were lifelong friends, and Carl Friedrich ended up starting a concert series in London with Bach's son Johann Christian. Like the elder Abel, Carl Friedrich primarily played the viola da gamba. If the instrument was in decline in the father's day, it was definitely almost gone in the son's. As Carl Friedrich's 1787 obituary poignantly remarked, "his favourite [*sic*] instrument was not in general use, and would probably die with him."[129]

Abel did play a few other instruments, including the pentachord, a kind of five-string cello apparently invented by the politician Sir Edward Walpole. The earliest mention of this mysterious instrument is in 1759, nine years after Bach's death, when Abel performed on it at a benefit concert.[130] Oh, to have been a fly on the wall when Walpole showed Abel the pentachord for the first time. In one of my regular flights of imagination, I dream up a conversation between the two bewigged gentlemen in a polite London drawing-room.

Walpole: "I hear you are from Germany, Mr. Abel."

Abel: "Yes, Sir Edward. When I was a boy, I lived in Cöthen, where my father and Mr. Bach's father were colleagues at the court of his most gracious highness Prince Leopold."

Walpole: "Goodness! You two certainly have been friends for a long time. You must have played chamber music together as boys. The elder Bach was a composer of some renown, was he not?"

Abel: "The greatest master music has ever known. He once wrote an extraordinary piece for the five-string cello, an instrument not unlike your own excellent invention, Sir Edward."

Walpole: "Upon my word, what did it look like? Did one play it between one's knees, or under one's chin in the old style?"

That's where my imagination runs out. Why didn't Abel write any of this stuff down?

Looking for clues, I check some of Abel's music out of the university library and start attempting to play it on my viola da gamba, but it's beyond my skill level and I have to switch to the cello. In truth, I'm hoping to find some proof of influence from Bach's Cello Suites, but this turns out to be wishful thinking. Eric Siblin claims to hear the "essential groove" of the First Cello Suite in Abel's solo music for viola da gamba,[131] but try as I might, I can't. Abel's style is more *galant* than Baroque, more like his friend Johann Christian Bach's than Johann Sebastian's. To be fair, there are certainly similarities in compositional technique, such as the liberal use of *style brisé* in arpeggiating chords. We could probably attribute that to both composers' idiomatic understanding of the viola da gamba, rather than to any kind of intertextual relationship. Bach's Cello Suites are clearly influenced by viola da gamba compositions, so if we were to be daringly postmodern we could even assert that old Bach sounds like young Abel more than young Abel sounds like old Bach.

And we're still no closer to knowing what kind of cello Bach had in mind.

Another thought occurs to me. What if Bach wasn't writing the Cello Suites for any instrument at all? Though Bach didn't typically compose music "for the shelf," he did compose *The Art of Fugue* as an exercise in contrapuntal perfection without specifying any particular instrument. Can it be that he was trying for something similar in his Sixth Cello Suite? Was he writing not for the fledgling cellists of his time, but for those of a later age? An age when instrument-building and instrumental technique could finally accommodate the utopian demands of his masterpiece?

*

Returning to the university after the summer, the students are all wild to try out the five-string cello. I pass it around the room in our first studio class of the semester so that everyone can have a turn.

"It's so different from how I thought it would be," exclaims one student. "I thought it would sound more like a four-string cello and that you could play all the standard repertoire on it. I thought it would make something high-pitched like the César Franck Sonata easier to play, but I don't think you could do it. It wouldn't sound right in Romantic music."

"You know what that E-string sounds like?" says another. "A viola da gamba. An incredibly loud viola da gamba." Everyone laughs.

"Dr. Wilson, are you going to play other pieces on it?" asks a third. "It might not work for Franck, but I can imagine it would be just right for the Schubert Arpeggione Sonata, or the Haydn Concerto in D. Especially the high sections."

They're all buzzing with ideas now. "I bet it would be great for Boccherini!"

"And you could pick up a lot of viola da gamba repertoire too because big chords would be easier."

"Not only that – you could play violin pieces on it too. When you're done with Bach's Cello Suites, you could knock out the Violin Sonatas and Partitas, Dr. Wilson!"

"Oh man, I want one of these!"

We're all grinning ear to ear. With the arrival of the cello, a whole new world of possibilities seems to be opening up.

VI. GIGUE

The thirty-sixth and final movement of Bach's Cello Suites represents the journey's end, but Bach doesn't send us off with a solemn amen. Instead, the Gigue of the Sixth Cello Suite sounds something like a *sourcillade*, the eighteenth-century horn-call that alerts the hunt when a stag is in sight.[132] No matter that you've just played thirty-five other difficult movements – you still have to dash all over the cello in a way that suggests action and adventure and the galloping of horses. Bach rounds up all the gestures from the preceding movements in the Sixth Cello Suite –showy Prelude and Courante, yearning Allemande and Sarabande, the exuberant energy of the Gavottes – and brings them gloriously to a concluding downwards arpeggio towards the low D. The cycle is complete, but it feels as if something else is about to begin.

The hall is booked, the cantata scores and parts ordered, the programs formatted. The Idaho Bach Festival committee is working round the clock to check everything off the to-do list. The university publicity team is helping get the word out on social media and Northwest Public Radio. The countdown to the festival is on, and all that remains is for me to consolidate the work of several years so that I can play Bach's Six Cello Suites in one evening.

It's always been a large-scale project, and as the day gets closer and closer, I feel both excited and intimidated by the magnitude of what I've taken on. A Bach marathon is a major milestone in the career of any cellist, and in some ways I've been preparing for it for three decades. There are decisions requiring my immediate attention, however. First, the question people keep asking me: am I going to play from memory? Yes, of course I am. Bach's Six Cello Suites are so ingrained in my memory that they have become part of me. "That's a lot of music to keep in your head," says a fellow cellist.

"Doesn't matter. I'll be playing by heart," I reply, and everyone rolls their eyes.

The next question is whether to play the repeats in the dance movements. All of the dances are in two repeated sections, but some cellists, feeling that the second sections are disproportionately long, only play the first repeat. At first I think I'll play all of them, since so much of their sense of balance and proportion comes with taking repeats. It will be tiring, certainly, but adrenaline tends to take care of that when you're on the stage. Then I do a practice run with a timer on and find that it takes well over three and a half hours from start to finish, before even taking into account the need for an intermission and further short breaks for tuning the instruments. Is it fair to make an audience sit still for so long?

With trepidation, I decide to do something I usually avoid, which is to ask strangers on the internet for their opinions. I don't do this very often, because when you do, you inevitably open yourself up to armchair experts who like to tell you you're an idiot. Sure enough, it happens. I do my best to ignore it, though it means literally sitting on my hands so that I won't fire back "Yes, thank you, please do continue to patronize me and explain my profession to me, *jackass*." Luckily, I also get some thoughtful suggestions from cellists who do know something about the subject. One, who has recently performed a Bach marathon with all the repeats, tells me that he got much more tired than he'd anticipated before he even reached the intermission. As the evening wore on, he started wishing he hadn't committed to the repeats.

"What about the tradition of doing improvised ornaments on the repeats?" I ask, since this is something I enjoy.

Another experienced Bach marathoner chimes in. "I don't do the repeats, but I think it's all right to add ornaments anyway. If you really want to go crazy with ornamentation, you could wait until you make a studio recording in the future, and put ornaments on the repeats then."

That settles it. I do another timed practice run with no repeats, and it comes out at just over two hours. I can work with this.

The next problem is how to put together an efficient Bach practice schedule when your time is at a premium. I've felt many times on this journey that it would be so much easier if practicing Bach was the only thing I had to do, but this has never been an option. I have a full teaching load of lectures, studio students, and ensemble coachings, not to mention rehearsals, concerts, faculty meetings, committee meetings, travel, writing, email, class preparation, and household and family commitments. It's a rare day that I'll have more than two hours to spend practicing for my Bach marathon, and even then I have to be very strict with myself. When even a run-through of the Bach Cello Suites takes longer than the amount of time you have, let alone detailed practice and score study, you need to be careful that you cover all the material to performance standard.

I come up with a plan to practice just two Cello Suites per day, but in pairings that would allow me to review one of the easier First, Second, and Third Cello Suites alongside one of the more difficult Fourth, Fifth, and Sixth Cello Suites. Truthfully, none of them are exactly easy, but I reason that I can budget forty-five minutes a day for one of the earlier three, and the remaining hour and fifteen minutes for one of the later three.

On Mondays I pair the First and Sixth Cello Suites, which enables me to enjoy the many similarities they have, even if their difficulty levels are so disparate. In G major and D major respectively, they're both in a style that suggests joy and transcendence. On Tuesdays, I pair the Second and Fifth Cello Suites. D minor and C minor share a certain darkness of resonance on the cello, and the two Suites share a sense of melancholy. On Wednesdays, I pair the Third and Fourth Cello Suites. Both in major keys – C and E-flat – they have a more jovial aspect. Thursdays, I pair the Second and Sixth Cello Suites because they're in the parallel modes of D minor and D major. Fridays, I pair the Third and Fifth Cello Suites because they're in the parallel modes of C major and C minor. Saturdays, I pair the First and Fourth Cello Suites because they're the ones that are left over, but also because the First is in G major, and G minor is an important secondary key in the Fourth. Sunday is my catch-up day for paying special attention to the movements I find particularly difficult: the Menuets of the Second Cello Suite; the Prelude, Sarabande, and Gigue of the Fourth Cello Suite; the Prelude and Allemande of the Fifth Cello Suite; and the Prelude and Sarabande of the Sixth Cello Suite.

Breaking the task into smaller tasks makes the whole seem more manageable. The only hitch is that I tend to get stuck on Preludes and Allemandes to the neglect of the other movements, mostly because they're the longest and most complicated movements. I solve this problem by practicing the movements in reverse order, starting with the Gigues and moving backwards through the *galanterie* dances; Sarabandes, Courantes, Allemandes, and lastly the Preludes.

Going backwards and forwards like this gives me the chance to reflect anew on these pieces that have been part of my life for so long. When I think of the scrawny little girl struggling to get her fingers around the G major Menuet, I realize how much the meaning of the Cello Suites has changed for me. It's not the fact that I've changed the way I play and interpret them. Who wouldn't change their playing over thirty years? It's more that they've changed *me*. When I had depression, I questioned the power of music to console. Now I see that the Cello Suites are more than a consolation. They're as crammed with memories as the photograph albums in my parents' living room. In their very notes are snapshots of my childhood, my parents, my teachers, all the people I've ever loved, all the places I've ever lived. Everywhere I go, they come with me. They have never strayed far from my thoughts or my fingertips. They're part of me.

Bach's Cello Suites are a true *Gradus ad Parnassum*, not a teach-yourself-cello manual but a companion on the journey of what it means to be a cellist. They accompany our tentative first steps and our highest accomplishments. They console us, provoke us, stir up complicated emotions within us. We'd be wrong to read them as some kind of hallowed and unchanging scripture dictated to Bach by his God; they are living documents, transcending time and place.

The constancy of Bach's companionship was part of what made it bearable to leave New Zealand permanently. I hadn't intended for this to happen. The accepted career trajectory for a New Zealand musician was to get a degree from one of the universities, go to another country for post-graduate study, achieve a level of international success that would grant you professional legitimacy at home, and finally return to New Zealand for a distinguished position in an orchestra or university. This was what my parents had done, and the map I had made for myself. Somewhere along the way, I got lost. Multiple applications for jobs at the University of Otago, the New Zealand Symphony Orchestra, Radio New Zealand, and the Centre for New Zealand Music were unsuccessful. In the meantime, America afforded me a career, an income, a family, and a home, things I'd never imagined I'd be allowed to have.

And so it's with a feeling of ambivalence that I find myself standing in a courtroom in Spokane one gray November day, saying the Pledge of Allegiance for the first time. There are about fifty of us, lined up alphabetically in order of our country of birth. I'm the only New Zealander. To my right is Namibia, and to my left, Norway. Namibia isn't super chatty, but Norway, an elderly woman who turns out to live just down the road from me, is bubbling with excitement. "I've wanted to do this for years," she tells me, "but Norway didn't change its law to allow dual citizenship until recently."

"Do you feel strange about this?" I ask her. "Like you're losing something, even if technically you aren't really?"

"Oh, no," she says. "I'm happy. I'm grateful. You don't have to choose any more. You can have both ways."

Soon it's my turn to walk across the room to the judge, shake his hand, and accept my Certificate of Naturalization. My daughter's high-pitched voice rings out from back of the room, where the families are sitting. "Go Mommy! My Mommy!"

Next to the exit is a table where the new Americans can register to vote. When I've turned in the last form, the volunteers give my daughter and me a little American flag. We wave it, grinning, while my husband takes a photo. "Welcome home, honey," he says as the flash goes off.

Back in Moscow, I put Cyril and Luna on their leashes and go for a long walk down Mountain View Road and out into the countryside. The harvest is almost complete, the dark slopes of Moscow Mountain already dusted with snow. In the fields and woods, small creatures are preparing for their long winter sleep. Far above our heads, geese are flying south in formation. This place that once seemed so isolated and foreign has become as familiar as home. I've lived here longer than any other place but Wellington. Perhaps it really is home now. Well, why not?

Every year for nearly two decades, I've been flying back and forth over the Pacific Ocean. The Air New Zealand aircraft leaves Los Angeles on a hot summer's evening, and takes all night to fly over the dark Pacific, the equator, and the International Date Line. When you arrive in Auckland at dawn, it's winter and you've lost two days, one of which you get back on the return flight. On the long walkway to Immigration, a recording of native birdsong comes out of hidden speakers. You walk through the grand Maori carvings of the entrance-gate, past the sleepy staff in the duty-free stores, and into the line for New Zealand nationals. The border agent scans your passport and says "Welcome home." I feel as if I've been awake for days, but New Zealand is only just waking up. Outside, the sky is pale purple. I never seem to have quite enough time between connecting flights, and I always seem to miss the shuttle that goes between the international and domestic terminals. I end up running there through the rain, which in New Zealand falls sideways. It wasn't until I left New Zealand aged nineteen that I realized rain could come down vertically. That was exactly half a lifetime ago.

It's towards the end of one of these visits home that my parents' phone rings with the horrible news that Judy Hyatt has died. I haven't seen her for a couple of years, because she stopped responding to letters. The last time I saw her, she was very changed since the old days, forgetful and distracted. For a painful moment I wondered if she knew who I was.

She asked me if I'd like to take any of her scores, since she no longer played the cello. I didn't want to, because Judy's music always smelled like her house, of cigarettes and old books. Later I would regret this, but that day I only wanted to sit and talk. I tried to persuade her to tell me some of her old stories and suggested that she write them down.

"Oh no, dear," she demurred, "I couldn't."

"But you did so many amazing things!" I pressed. "What about the time you met Benjamin Britten? What about that time you auditioned for Sir John Barbirolli and he kept grabbing your cello to demonstrate how he thought you should play? What about that time you met Jacques Ibert at a cocktail party and didn't know who he was, and you made him mad by asking him if he played an instrument?"

"My memory's shot, dear," she said, looking out the window. Those once-twinkling dark eyes seemed to have clouded over.

Her funeral is on the morning of my departure, so I pack my bag early. My father and I leave my daughter at home with my mother and drive across Wellington and up the hills into Khandallah. The service is in a tiny church at the end of the street where Judy used to live. It's one of those July days where Wellington's fretful breezes ruffle the harbor and bend the trees this way and that, but it's not really cold. As always, it's a little cooler up in the hills. I seldom go to this part of Wellington, but nothing much has changed.

The solid wood villas built for Victorian doctors and businessmen are still here, still the same. They might get painted different colors from time to time, but there's a sort of permanence about them, as permanent and imperturbable as the protected forest on the hills behind them. The Audis and Lexuses parked in the driveways are bigger than the BMWs of the nineties, but other than that, it's the same Khandallah it's always been.

The parking problem is much worse than it used to be, though, and for a few anxiety-filled minutes I think my father and I are going to be late for my teacher's funeral. But at the last minute we squeeze his little Toyota into the most improbable of parallel parks, and slamming the doors, break into a run across the road.

The church is full of cellists, Judy's old colleagues from the New Zealand Symphony Orchestra, people I've looked up to all my life. Judy's sons and grandchildren speak beautifully and movingly of her life. It was a life well lived, full of music and art and books, of laughter and love. Judy never got to write her memoirs, so it will be up to us to remember her.

Katherine Mansfield once wrote "I think the only way to live as a writer is to draw upon one's real familiar life – to find the treasure in that… Our secret life, the life we return to over and over again, the 'do you remember' life is always the past. And the curious thing is that if we describe this which seems to us so intensely personal, other people take it to themselves and understand it as if it were their own."[133]

And here in this old colonial church, so old that Mansfield herself might once have been in here, I stand and weep.

I don't deal well with death. Does anyone? The vicar clearly doesn't, even though the funerals of old ladies must constitute much of her job. She starts her sermon with a long, pointless story about a frog and a lily pad, and it takes me a few moments of puzzlement to realize that it's supposed to be some kind of allegory. Suddenly I'm angry. This vicar, who clearly never met Judy, doesn't know a thing about her. My teacher was an artist, not a wretched frog.

I've been to so few funerals that I didn't even think to bring a handkerchief. I've read somewhere that if you swivel your eyeballs upwards, you can stop the tears coming out. I look up now to the rafters of the church, carved in the nineteenth century from the wood of the rimu trees that once covered the great hills of Khandallah, and I think *this is real. This is now.*

All these years I've been flying back and forth between my two countries and it hasn't occurred to me until now that one day I may no longer have anyone here to visit. One day I will stand in tears mourning other people I love, one after the other, until everyone who knew me is gone. No one will remember me from strings camp or the New Zealand National Youth Orchestra or the Secondary Schools Chamber Music Competition. No one will remember the majesty and perfect acoustics of the Old Town Hall or the enlightened music collections of the Wellington City Library, both now closed indefinitely as earthquake hazards. No one will remember Judy. No one will remember me. I might remain in the footnotes of a library catalogue as the creator of a few recordings that no one listens to and writing that no one reads. Does it really matter? Why do I find this so unbearable?

How does anyone bear it? Did Katherine Mansfield wonder, alone and hemorrhaging in Fontainebleau, if anyone would remember her? Could Bach bear leaving the *Art of Fugue* unfinished, stopping in mid-phrase, not knowing if anyone would complete it?

The service is over. My father nudges me gently with his elbow to tell me we're supposed to exit the church right after the family, since we're seated in the second row. He's been to lots of funerals, so he knows what to do.

As the mourners are leaving, a recording of the second movement of Schumann's cello concerto comes on the church sound system. Right as we approach the front door, it gets to the section where the principal cello from the orchestra joins the soloist in a heartrending duet. It is a perfect memory of Judy and John Hyatt, who so loved the cello, and music, and each other.

We might get older, we might lose what is dearest to us, we might die, but the music remains. We live with it all our lives. Do we live it, or does it live us? Whether or not we are there, it lives on.

Music is more than a backdrop and soundtrack to our lives. Music transcends time. It gives us back our childhoods. It gives us back our parents and our teachers. It gives us back our homes and our loves and the shadows of the people we used to be and the people we will become.

In the car, my father starts talking about the music he'd like at his funeral. Everyone in my family is weirdly fond of talking about their funerals, as if they don't understand that they won't be there to enjoy them. Does every member of this tribe of garrulous exhibitionists harbor a secret morbid melancholy? Does my father fear this as much as I do, the idea that one day he won't exist, but these rough seas and dark hills will stay here unchanged and impervious?

"I want that bit out of Bach's Christmas Oratorio with the trumpet solo," he tells me, changing lanes so abruptly that the driver behind him has to slam on the brakes.

"I'll try to remember," I say between sobs, "although when the time comes I'll probably be too sedated to think about it."

"I know," says my father. "But you're married to a trumpeter, so all you have to do is tell him about it well in advance, and he'll make sure it happens."

"OK," I tell him. And I will.

Back at the big white house by the sea, my daughter is waking up from a nap. She stretches her little arms out, and I let her pull me down onto the bed with her. "Mommy, I'm so glad we have each other," she says, her face in my neck.

The suitcases are packed, the tickets and passports in the top pocket of my music satchel. The drive along Evans Bay Road to the airport is the worst bit. I hold my daughter's hands and sing to her in the backseat so I don't have to look at the sea-wall and the rocks and the shore, every curve and stone of it as familiar to me as the palm of my hand. The marina with the yachts that used to belong to the fathers of my schoolfriends. The intermediate school where I learned how to bake scones and operate a sewing machine. The Wellywood sign and the orange windsocks and the corner dairy and the golf course and finally the airport terminal.

Every time I leave I ask my parents to drop me at the curb because I can't bear final goodbyes and the fuss my mother always makes at the airport. They always insist on parking and coming into the terminal with me anyway. It's just as well, because there's some bother at the check-in desk over whether my daughter and I are supposed to be traveling on our New Zealand passports or our American ones, and I'm grateful that my father is there to ask the right questions.

The plane rises precipitously away from the tiny airstrip at Rongotai, and the pine-covered bulk of the Miramar peninsula gets smaller and smaller and eventually disappears altogether.

On the night flight out of Auckland, I start to flip through the pile of magazines I bought at the airport bookstore to ward off boredom on the thirteen-hour trip. One of them has a story about Beatrice Tinsley, the New Zealand-American astronomer. I've barely heard of her, but as I read on I find myself filled with a painful, futile yearning to have known her. It's the same feeling I have about Katherine Mansfield, another of those blazing, brilliant New Zealand girls whose outsize talents took them permanently away from these islands. Also like Mansfield, Tinsley was a musician of near-professional quality. She didn't stop playing the violin until cancer paralyzed her body and she no longer had the use of her bow arm. At the very end of her life, knowing she would not recover, she used her violin hand to write a poem about Bach.

Let me be like Bach, creating fugues
Till suddenly the pen will move no more.
Let all my themes within – of ancient light
Of origins and change and human worth –
Let all their melodies still intertwine,
Evolve and merge with growing unity,
Ever without fading
Ever without a final chord…
Till suddenly my mind can hear no more.[134]

I read the poem again and again until the cabin crew dims the lights. By then it's embedded in my memory, and I stare out the window at the fathomless Pacific night, murmuring the lines under my breath. Perhaps Beatrice Tinsley saw the same thing in Bach as she saw in her stars. Her Bach is my Bach.

POSTLUDE

The concert is about to start. Backstage, the four-string and five-string cellos stand side by side in their open cases. On the table beside them is a cake of rosin, a cleaning cloth, a digital tuner, a Kleenex box, and a glass of water. I have never been so terrified in my life.

I check and re-check everything. Endpin out, bow tightened, bow rosined, strings tuned. Is the endpin screw tight enough? Yes. Do I need more rosin? Yes, but now there's rosin dust on the cello. Hastily, I wipe it off.

My hair, stiff with hairspray, is almost certainly going to stay put under the pearl beads I've woven into it. The royal blue satin gown, a remnant from my competition circuit days, rustles satisfyingly around my legs, though my pointy-toed high heels are already starting to pinch. In my imagination, I was going to sweep onstage like a magnificent Virgin Queen, but the face in the mirror looks more like sallow Anne Boleyn waiting to have her head chopped off. Noticing the fire alarm behind me in my reflection, I fight off a sudden impulse to smash the glass and set off the siren so that I don't have to play the concert.

"Dr. Wilson," says the stage manager, "the hall is packed. Like, completely."

"Let me see," I say to her, and tiptoe over to the stage door to peer through the little inlaid fisheye lens. She's right, every seat is filled. I see friends, colleagues, students, children from the music program, their parents, my husband. With a jolt, I realize that the president of the university is here, and his wife, and all his staff. I see the people whose names I don't know but who always show up to concerts, people I've seen around town, people I've never seen before. Seven thousand miles away, in the big white house by the sea, my parents are watching the livestream on my father's laptop. All these eyes, looking at me.

"Is it time?" I ask.

"Five minutes," says the stage manager.

Almost unable to draw breath, I sit down and try to steady my hands. At the beginning of this journey, I was thirty and childless and full of uncertainty. I wanted to accomplish my goal by the time I was forty, and here I am at thirty-eight, two years ahead of schedule. Young for a tenured professor, not so young for a musician or artist. Katherine Mansfield was four years younger than I am now when she died. I'm older than Schubert and Mozart ever lived to be. Soon I'll be older than Chopin and Mendelssohn, and in a few years, I'll outlive Schumann. If I make it past sixty-five, I will be older than my teacher Alexander Ivashkin, older than Bach.

None of them got to finish making the music they wanted to make. It's up to the living to make it for them now, but will there be time?

Tonight's concert hasn't existed before and will never exist again. What Bach's Cello Suites meant to me at ten, twenty, and thirty are radically different things. Bach at forty, fifty, and sixty will be different again. Tomorrow Bach may show me something new that will change everything.

I start to imagine that Bach is here backstage with me. On my other side, Anna Magdalena appears, her skirts swishing lightly against mine. Maybe they're all here in this liminal place, the people who made me who I am: Sebastian and Anna, Sasha and Natasha, Judy and John, Gillian and Roger. One by one, they all show up: my two other favorite Johanns, Mattheson and Fux; the elegant Italians Monteverdi and Gabrielli (the latter with his dog); haughty Jean-Baptiste Lully with his dancer's walk and his absurdly fashionable clothes. Last of all is Katherine Mansfield, resplendent in a kimono, her fingers stained with ink. She looks challengingly at me with flashing dark eyes. "Well?" she says. "What are you waiting for?"

"Dr. Wilson?" whispers the stage manager. "It's seven-thirty."

It's time. I check the endpin and the tension of the bow one more time, and apply a last-minute swipe of rosin over the horsehair. Next to the stage door, I look out once more through the tiny lens at the audience.

That's when it hits me, the answer to the question that has nagged at me for years. *What is music for?* Looking out at the familiar and unfamiliar faces, I almost laugh as I realize it. It's for them, of course.

Music is a gift. A gift for them, and for me, and for everyone.

It's not a free gift. It has cost me dearly. But has it been worth it?

Without looking out again or stopping to consider the question, I know the answer is yes, a thousand times yes. Music is the gift I carry with me everywhere, and when I need it, it carries me, too. Even if God never replies, music has never, ever let me down. It is my home.

"Are you ready?" asks the stage manager.

I can't stop smiling. "Always," I say, hooking my arm around the cello, the bow grasped firmly in my hand.

The door opens and the applause starts before I even begin the long walk. This is it, the sound I live and die for. I step out into the light, and in that moment, even if just for a moment, it's enough.

NOTES

1   Anner Bylsma, *Bach and the Happy Few: About Mrs. Anna Magdalena Bach's Autograph Copy of the 4th, 5th and 6th Cello Suites* (Amsterdam: The Fencing Mail, 2014), 36.

2   Yo Tomita, "The Well-Tempered Clavier, Book 1," accessed April 18, 2020, https://www.qub.ac.uk/~tomita/essay/wtc1.html.

3   Andrew Talle, "Introduction and Report on the Revised Edition," *Johann Sebastian Bach Sechs Suiten* für Violoncello Solo, in *Johann Sebastian Bach Neue Ausgabe Sämtlicher Werke* Band 4:1, ed. Christine Blanken, Christoph Wolff, and Peter Wollny (Kassel: Bärenreiter Verlag, 2016), xxxi.

4   Zoltan Szabó, "Precarious Presumptions and the 'Minority Report': Revisiting the Primary Sources of the Bach Cello Suites," *Bach* 45, no. 2 (2014), 1–33.

5   Johann Sebastian Bach ed. Louis Norblin, *Sonates ou Etudes pour le violoncello solo* (Paris: Janet et Cotelle, 1824), 1.

6   Betty Bang Mather and Dean M. Karns, *Dance Rhythms of the French Baroque: A Handbook for Performance* (Bloomington and Indianapolis: Indiana University Press, 1987), 207–8.

7   Meredith Little and Natalie Jenne, *Dance and the Music of J. S. Bach* 2nd ed. (Bloomington and Indianapolis: Indiana University Press, 2001), 115.

8   Little and Jenne, 114–42.

9   Thoinot Arbeau, *Orchésographie* (Langres: Jehan des Preyz, 1596), 66, translation mine.

10 Pierre Rameau, *Le maître à danser* (Paris: Jean Vilette, 1725), 110–11, translation mine.

11 Rameau, 28.

12 Jane Bellingham, "Sarabande," *The Oxford Companion to Music*, accessed April 18, 2020, https://ida.lib.uidaho.edu:6840/view/10.1093/acref/9780199579037.001.0001/acref-9780199579037-e-5891.

13 Mather and Karns, 26.

14 Natalie Jenne and Meredith Little, *Dance and the Music of J. S. Bach* 2nd ed. (Bloomington and Indianapolis, 2001), 93–94.

15 Tim Janof, "Conversation with Nathaniel Rosen," March 2, 1996, accessed April 6, 2020, http://www.cello.org/Newsletter/Articles/rosen.html.

16 Little and Jenne, 95.

17 Rameau, 85.

18 Little and Jenne, 157.

19 Régine Kunzle, "In Search of L'Académie Royale de Danse," *York Dance Review* 7 (Spring 1978), 10.

20 John Lutterman, "Works in Progress: J. S. Bach's Suites for Solo Cello as Artifacts of Improvisatory Practices" (PhD diss., University of California Davis, 2006).

21 Zoltán Szabó, "Problematic Sources, Problematic Transmission: An Outline of the Edition History of the Solo Cello Suites by J. S. Bach" (PhD diss., University of Sydney, 2016), 55.

22 Dimitry Markevitch, *Cello Story* (Princeton: Summy-Birchard Music, 1984), 62–63.

23 Richard Taruskin, "Six Times Six: A Bach Suite Selection" in *The Danger of Music, and Other Anti-Utopian Essays* (Berkeley, Los Angeles, and London: University of California Press, 2009), 66.

24 Anner Bylsma, *Bach, the Fencing Master: Reading Aloud from the First Three Cello Suites*, 2nd ed. (Amsterdam: Bylsma Fencing Mail, 2001).

25 Christoph Wolff, *J. S. Bach: The Learned Musician* (New York: W. W. Norton, 2000), 411.

26 Cantatas BWV 6, 41, 68, 85, 115, 175, 180, and 183. See Marc Vanscheeuwijck, "Recent re-evaluations of the Baroque cello and what they might mean for performing the music of J. S. Bach," *Early Music* 38, no. 2 (2010), 185.

27 Johann Mattheson, *Das Neu-eröffnete Orchestre* (Hamburg: Benjamin Schiller, 1713), 285, translation mine.

28 Dmitry Badiarov, "The Violoncello, Viola da Spalla and Viola Pomposa in Theory and Practice," *The Galpin Society Journal* 60 (April 2007), 121.

29 See Laurence Dreyfus, *Bach's Continuo Group: Players and Practices in His Vocal Groups* (Cambridge: Harvard University Press, 1987).

30 Lutterman, 304.

31 Michel Corrette, *Methode, Théorique et Pratique pour Apprendre en peu de tems le Violoncelle dans sa Perfection* (Paris, 1741), 7, translation mine.

32 Corrette, 8

33 Leopold Mozart, *Versuch einer gründlichen Violinschule* (Augsburg: Johann Jakob Lotter, 1756), 3, translation mine.

34 Mozart, 3.

35 The German double bass bow is held "underhand," whereas the French bow is held in an overhand hold comparable to the cello bow-hold.

36 Michael Marissen, *The Social and Religious Designs of J. S. Bach's Brandenburg Concertos* (Princeton: Princeton University Press, 1995), 4.

37 Corrette, 9.

38 Hubert Le Blanc, *Défense de la basse de viole contre les entreprises du violon et les pretensions du violoncelle* (Amsterdam: Pierre Mortier, 1740), 22, translation mine.

39 Le Blanc, 30.

40 David Ledbetter, *Unaccompanied Bach: Performing the Solo Works* (New Haven and London: Yale University Press, 2009), 190.

41 Ledbetter, 192.

42 Susan McClary, *Desire and Pleasure in Seventeenth-Century Music* (Berkeley: University of California Press, 2012), 206.

43 McClary, 196.

44 Alexander Silbiger (2001), "Chaconne," Grove Music Online, accessed April 18, 2020, https://ida.lib.uidaho.edu:6758/grovemusic/view/10.1093/gmo/9781561592630.001.0001/omo-9781561592630-e-0000005354.

45 McClary, 196.

46 Helga Thoene, *Johann Sebastian Bach, Ciaccona: Tanz oder Tombeau? Eine analytische Studie* (Oschersleben, Germany: Ziethen, 2003).

47 Michael Markham, "The New Mythologies: Deep Bach, Saint Mahler, and the Death Chaconne," *L.A. Review of Books*, October 26, 2013, https://lareviewofbooks.org/article/the-new-mythologies-deep-bach-saint-mahler-and-the-death-chaconne.

48 Benjamin Shute, *Sei Solo: Symbolum? The Theology of J. S. Bach's Solo Violin Works* (Eugene, OR: Pickwick Publications, 2016), 116–22.

49 Mark M. Smith, "The Drama of Bach's Life in the Court of Cöthen, As Reflected in His Cello Suites," *Stringendo* 22, no. 1 (2000), 33.

50 Horatio Clare, *Something of His Art: Walking to Lübeck with J. S. Bach* (Dorset, UK: Little Toller Books, 2018).

51 Robert L. Marshall, "Toward a Twenty-First-Century Bach Biography," *Musical Quarterly* 84, no. 3 (Autumn 2000), 522.

52 Alexander Silbiger, "Passacaglia," *Grove Music Online* https://ida.lib.uidaho.edu:6758/grovemusic/view/10.1093/gmo/9781561592630.001.0001/omo-978156159263 0-e-0000021024.

53 Silbiger, "Passacaglia."

54 Raymond Monelle, *The Musical Topic: Hunt, Military and Pastoral* (Bloomington and Indianapolis: Indiana University Press, 2006), 212.

55 John Eliot Gardiner, *Bach: Music in the Castle of Heaven* (New York: Alfred A. Knopf, 2013), 459–60.

56 Hans T. David, Arthur Mendel, and Christoph Wolff, *The New Bach Reader: A Life of Johann Sebastian Bach in Letters and Documents* revised ed. (New York and London: W. W. Norton & Company, 1998), 306.

57 David Watkin, "Corelli's Op. 5: 'Violino e violone o cimbalo'? *Early Music* (November 1996), 660.

58 Johann Nikolaus Forkel, *Johann Sebastian Bach: His Life, Art, and Work* trans. Charles Sanford Terry (London: Constable and Company, 1920), 7.

59 Marshall, 506.

60 Christoph Wolff, *Bach: The Learned Musician* (New York and London: W. W. Norton, 2000): 218.

61 Johann Sebastian Bach, *Sechs Suiten für Violoncello Solo*, ed. August Wenzinger (Kassel: Bärenreiter, 1967).

62 Johann Sebastian Bach, *Sechs Suiten für Violoncello Solo*, ed. Hans Eppstein. *Neue Bach-Ausgabe Serie VI: Kammermusik,* Band 2 (Kassel: Bärenreiter, 1988), 1–104.

63 Johann Sebastian Bach, *Sechs Suiten für Violoncello Solo*, ed. Kirsten Beisswenger (Wiesbaden: Breitkopf & Härtel, 2000).

64 Anner Bylsma, *Bach and the Happy Few: About Mrs. Anna Magdalena Bach's Autograph Copy of the 4th, 5th and 6th Cello Suites* (Amsterdam: The Fencing Mail, 2014).

65 Bylsma, *Bach, the Fencing Master*, 117.

66 Bylsma, *Bach, the Fencing Master*, 44.

67 Bylsma, *Bach, the Fencing Master*, 154.

68 Lutterman, 90.

69 Lutterman, 30.

70 Yo Tomita, "Anna Magdalena as Bach's Copyist," *Understanding Bach*, vol. 7 (2007), 60.

71 Zoltán Szabó, "Precarious Presumptions and the 'Minority Report': Revisiting the Primary Sources of the Bach Cello Suites," *Bach* vol. 45, no. 2 (2014), 1–33.

72 Martin Jarvis, *Written By Mrs. Bach* (Sydney: Harper Collins, 2011).

73 Tim Cavanaugh, "Bogus Bach Theory Gets Media Singing," *The National Review* (October 29, 2014), https://www.nationalreview.com/2014/10/bogus-bach-theory-gets-media-singing-tim-cavanaugh/, accessed February 5, 2020.

74 Smith, "The Drama of Bach's Life In the Court of Cöthen," 33.

75 Heinrich Schenker, "The Sarabande of J. S. Bach's Suite No. 3 for Unaccompanied Violoncello, BWV 1009," trans. Hedi Siegel, *The Music Forum* vol. 2 ed. William J. Mitchell and Felix Salzer (New York: Columbia University Press, 1970), 274.

76 Leon Botstein, "Schenker the Regressive: Observations on the Historical Schenker," *The Musical Quarterly* vol. 86, no. 2 (Summer 2002), 239.

77 Schenker, 282.

78 Schenker, 274.

79 Smith, "The Drama of Bach's Life in the Court of Cöthen," 33.

80 Allen Winold, *Bach's Cello Suites: Analyses and Explorations* vol. 1 (Bloomington and Indianapolis: Indiana University Press, 2007), 62.

81 David Yearsley, *Sex, Death, and Minuets: Anna Magdalena Bach and Her Musical Notebooks* (Chicago: University of Chicago Press, 2019), 101.

82 David, Mendel, and Wolff, 293.

83 Johann Mattheson, *Der volkommene Capellmeister*, trans. Ernest C. Harris (Ann Arbor, MI: UMI Research Press, 1981), 454.

84 Ross W. Duffin, *How Equal Temperament Ruined Harmony (And Why You Should Care)* (New York and London: W. W. Norton, 2008).

85 David Ledbetter, *Bach's Well-Tempered Clavier: The 48 Preludes and Fugues* (New Haven and London: Yale University Press, 2002), 38.

86 Steven Maes, *392, Pieter Wispelwey and the Bach Cello Suites* featuring Laurence Dreyfus, John Butt, and Kees Boeke (Mechelen, Belgium: Evil Penguin Productions, 2012).

87 Carl Schachter, "The Prelude from Bach's Suite No. 4 for Violoncello Solo: The Submerged Urlinie" (*Current Musicology* 56, 1994), 70.

88 Benjamin Shute, *Sei Solo: Symbolum? The Theology of J. S. Bach's Solo Violin Works* (Eugene, Oregon: Pickwick Publications, 2016).

89 Gé Bartman, "Christian Symbolism In the First Three Preludes of Johann Sebastian Bach's Six Suites For Cello Solo" (Amsterdam: Bylsma Fencing Mail, 2001).

90 Laurence Dreyfus, *Wagner and the Erotic Impulse* (Cambridge: Harvard University Press), 2010, x.

91 Michael Marissen, *Bach and God* (Oxford: Oxford University Press, 2016), 4.

92 Michael Marissen, *Bach and God* (Oxford: Oxford University Press, 2016), 114.

93 Luke 2:25–29, *New International Version*

94 David, Mendel, and Wolff, 303.

95 Allen Winold, *Bach's Cello Suites: Analyses and Explorations* vol. 1 (Bloomington and Indianapolis: Indiana University Press, 2007), 74.

96 Johann Joseph Fux, *The Study of Counterpoint from Johann Joseph Fux's* Gradus ad Parnassum, trans. Alfred Mann (New York and London: W. W. Norton, 1965), 17–18.

97 Fux, 19.

98 Fux, 27.

99 Stephen Daw, "Bach as teacher and model," *The Cambridge Companion to Bach* ed. John Butt (Cambridge: Cambridge University Press, 1997), 196.

100 Daw, 198.

101 Wilfrid Mellers, *Bach and the Dance of God* (New York: Oxford University Press, 1980), 25.

102 Winold, 124–5.

103 Mellers, 26.

104 Bálint András Varga, ed.: *György Kurtág: Three Interviews and Ligeti Homages* (Rochester: University of Rochester Press, 2009): 45.

105 John G. Suess and Marc Vanscheeuwijck, "Gabrielli, Domenico," *Grove Music Online* (2001): https://ida.lib.uidaho.edu:6758/grovemusic/view/10.1093/gmo/9781561592630.001.0001/omo-9781561592630-e-0000010453.

106 Andrew Talle, "Introduction and Report on the Revised Edition" in *Johann Sebastian Bach Neue Ausgabe Sämtlicher Werke, Revidierte Edition, Band 4, Teilband 1* (Kassel: Bärenreiter, 2016), xxxv

107 Dimitry Markevitch, *Cello Story*, trans. Florence W. Seder (Princeton: Summy-Birchard Music, 1984), 96.

108 Tim Janof, "Conversation with Dimitry Markevitch," February 17, 1999, http://www.cello.org/Newsletter/Articles/markevitch.htm.

109 Johann Sebastian Bach, *Six Suites for Solo Cello* ed. Dimitry Markevitch (Bryn Mawr: Theodore Presser Company, 1964), iii.

110 Shin-Itchiro Yokoyama, "The Bizarre Chord?" Blog post, April 7, 2017. http://bachcellonotes.blogspot.com/2017/04/the-bizarre-chord.html.

111 Wilfrid Mellers, *Bach and the Dance of God* (New York: Oxford University Press, 1981), 38.

112 Mellers, 34.

113 Smith, "The Drama of Bach's Life in the Court of Cöthen," 34.

114 Leonard Bernstein, "An Artist's Response to Violence," November 25, 1963, accessed April 20, 2020, https://leonardbernstein.com/about/humanitarian/an-artists-response-to-violence.

115 Marshall, 503–4.

116 Botwinick, Sara, "From Ohrdruf to Mühlhausen: A Subversive Reading of Bach's Relationship to Authority," *Bach* 35:2 (2004), 2–3.

117 Mattheson, *Der volkommene Capellmeister,* 453.

118 Mattheson, *Der volkommene Capellmeister*, 461.

119 See Ledbetter, *Unaccompanied Bach*, 226, and Little and Jenne, 152.

120 Arbeau, 95, translation mine.

121 Steven Isserlis, liner notes to *Bach: The Cello Suites* (London: Hyperion Records, 2007), 3–4.

122 Laurence Vittes, "Two Different Approaches to Bach's Cello Suites," *Strings*, March 1, 2016, https://stringsmagazine.com/two-different-approaches-to-bachs-solo-cello-suites.

123 Dmitry Badiarov, "The Violoncello, Viola Da Spalla and Viola Pomposa in Theory and Practice," *The Galpin Society Journal* 60 (2007), 121–45.

[124] Miranda Wilson, "Finding My Own Solution to Bach's 300-Year-Old Conundrum," *Strings*, July 17, 2019, https://stringsmagazine.com/finding-my-own-solution-to-bachs-300-year-old-conundrum.

[125] Betty Bang Mather and Dean M. Karns, *Dance Rhythms of the French Baroque: A Handbook for Performance* (Bloomington and Indianapolis: Indiana University Press, 1987), 128–30.

[126] Johann Joachim Quantz, *On Playing the Flute*, trans. Edward R. Reilly (New York: Schirmer Books, 1966): 163.

[127] Allen Winold, *Bach's Cello Suites: Analyses and Explorations* vol. 1 (Bloomington and Indianapolis: Indiana University Press, 2007), 54.

[128] David Ledbetter, *Unaccompanied Bach*, 234.

[129] Walter Knape, Murray R. Charters, and Simon McVeigh, "Abel Family," *Grove Music Online* (2001), https://ida.lib.uidaho.edu:6758/grovemusic/view/10.1093/gmo/9781561592630.001.0001/omo-9781561592630-e-0000000035.

[130] Alyson McLamore, "'By the Will and Order of Providence': The Wesley Family Concerts, 1779–1787," *Royal Musical Association Research Chronicle* 37 (2004), 84.

[131] Eric Siblin, *The Cello Suites: J. S. Bach, Pablo Casals, and the Search for a Baroque Masterpiece* (Toronto: Anansi Press, 2009), 236.

[132] Monelle, 44.

[133] Vincent O'Sullivan and Margaret Scott, *The Collected Letters of Katherine Mansfield* (Oxford: Oxford University Press, 2008), 5–79.

[134] Dennis Overbye, "Overlooked No More: Beatrice Tinsley, Astronomer Who Saw the Course of the Universe." *New York Times* (July 18, 2018), https://www.nytimes.com/2018/07/18/obituaries/overlooked-beatrice-tinsley-astronomer.html.

BIBLIOGRAPHY

Historical Sources

Arbeau, Thoinot. *Orchésographie*. 2nd ed. Langres: Iehan des Preyz, 1596.

Corrette, Michel. *Methode, Théorique et Pratique pour Apprendre en peu de tems le Violoncelle dans sa Perfection*. Paris: undefined publisher, 1741.

Forkel, Johann Nikolaus. *Johann Sebastian Bach: His Life, Art, and Work*. Translated by Charles Sanford Terry. London: Constable and Company, 1920.

Fux, Johann Joseph. *The Study of Counterpoint from Johann Joseph Fux's* Gradus ad Parnassum. Translated and edited by Alfred Mann. New York: W. W. Norton & Company, 1965.

Le Blanc, Hubert. *Défense de la basse de viole contre les enterprises du violon et les prétentions du violoncelle*. Amsterdam: Pierre Mortier, 1740.

Mattheson, Johann. *Das neu-eröffnete Orchestre*. Hamburg: Benjamin Schiller, 1713.

———. *Der vollkommene Capellmeister*. Translated by Ernest C. Harriss. Ann Arbor: UMI Research Press, 1981.

Mozart, Leopold. *Versuch einer gründlichen Violinschule*. Augsburg: Johann Jakob Lotter, 1756.

Quantz, Johann Joachim. *On Playing the Flute*. 2nd ed. Translated by Edward R. Reilly. New York: Schirmer Books, 1985.

Rameau, Pierre. *Le maître à danser*. Paris: Jean Vilette, 1725.

Modern Sources

Badiarov, Dmitry. "The Violoncello, Viola da Spalla and Viola Pomposa in Theory and Practice." *The Galpin Society Journal* 60 (April 2007): 121–145.

Ballinger, Allan J. "The Bach Cello Suites – A Case Study: The Bourrée of Suite No. 4 in E-flat." *Goodwin College Faculty Publications* 27 (2015): 1–20.

Baker, Michael. "A Curious Type of 'Tonal Pun' in Bach's Suites for Unaccompanied Cello." *Indiana Theory Review* 27, no. 1 (Spring 2009): 1–21.

Bartman, Gé. "Christian Symbolism in the First Three Preludes of Johann Sebastian Bach's Six Suites for Cello Solo." Translated by Gerrit Kloosterman. In Anner Bylsma, *Bach the Fencing Master: Reading Aloud from the First Three Cello Suites*. 2nd ed. Amsterdam: Bylsma Fencing Mail, 2001.

Bellingham, Jane. "Sarabande." *The Oxford Companion to Music*. Edited by Alison Latham. Accessed May 1, 2021. http://www.oxfordmusiconline.com.

Bernstein, Leonard. "An Artist's Response to Violence." Accessed April 20, 2020. https://leonardbernstein.com/about/humanitarian/an-artists-response-to-violence.

Blanken, Christine, Christoph Wolff, and Peter Wollny, ed. *Johann Sebastian Bach: Neue Ausgabe Sämtlicher Werke.* Revised edition. Kassel: Bärenreiter, 2016.

Botstein, Leon. "Schenker the Regressive: Observations on the Historical Schenker" *The Musical Quarterly* vol. 86, no. 2 (Summer 2002): 239–247.

Botwinick, Sara. "From Ohrdruf to Mühlhausen: A Subversive Reading of Bach's Relationship to Authority." *Bach* 35, no. 2 (2004): 1–59.

Boyd, Malcolm. *Bach.* 3rd ed. Oxford: Oxford University Press, 2000.

Butt, John. *Bach's Dialogue with Modernity: Perspectives on the Passions.* Cambridge: Cambridge University Press, 2010.

———. *Bach Interpretation: Articulation Marks in Primary Sources of J. S. Bach.* Cambridge: Cambridge University Press, 1990.

———. *The Cambridge Companion to Bach.* Cambridge: Cambridge University Press, 1997.

Bylsma, Anner. *Bach the Fencing Master: Reading Aloud from the First Three Cello Suites.* 2nd ed. Amsterdam: Bylsma Fencing Mail, 2001.

———. *Bach and the Happy Few: About Mrs. Anna Magdalena Bach's Autograph Copy of the 4th, 5th and 6th Cello Suites.* Amsterdam: The Fencing Mail, 2014.

Carrington, Jerome. *Trills in the Bach Cello Suites: A Handbook for Performers.* Norman, OK: University of Oklahoma Press, 2009.

Chafe, Eric. *J. S. Bach's Johannine Theology: The* St. John Passion *and the Cantatas for Spring 1725.* New York: Oxford University Press, 2014.

Clare, Horatio. *Something of His Art: Walking to Lübeck with J. S. Bach.* Dorset, UK: Little Toller Books, 2018.

Cohen, Dalia, and Naphthali Wagner. "Concurrence and Nonconcurrence Between Learned and Natural Schemata: The Case of J. S. Bach's Saraband in C Minor for Cello Solo." *Journal of New Music Research* 29, no. 1 (2000): 23–26.

David, Hans T., Arthur Mendel, and Christoph Wolff. *The New Bach Reader: A Life of Johann Sebastian Bach in Letters and Documents.* Revised ed. New York: W.W. Norton & Company, 1998.

Daw, Stephen. "Bach as teacher and model." In *The Cambridge Companion to Bach*, edited by John Butt. Cambridge: Cambridge University Press, 1997, 195–202.

Dreyfus, Laurence. *Bach and the Patterns of Invention.* Cambridge and London: Cambridge, MA and London: Harvard University Press, 1996.

———. *Bach's Continuo Group: Players and Practices in His Vocal Works.* Cambridge, MA and London: Harvard University Press, 1987.

Duffin, Ross W. *How Equal Temperament Ruined Harmony (And Why You Should Care).* New York and London: W. W. Norton & Company, 2008.

Dürr, Alfred. *Johann Sebastian Bach: St. John Passion. Genesis, Transmission, and Meaning.* Translated by Alfred Clayton. Oxford: Oxford University Press, 2000.

Elie, Paul. *Reinventing Bach.* New York: Farrar, Straus and Giroux, 2012.

Gardiner, John Eliot. *Bach: Music in the Castle of Heaven.* New York: Alfred A. Knopf, 2013.

Geck, Martin. *Johann Sebastian Bach: Life and Work.* Translated by John Hargraves. Orlando, FL: Harcourt Books, 2000.

Hebson, Audrey. "Dance and Its Importance in Bach's Suites for Solo Cello." *Musical Offerings* 1, no. 2 (Fall 2010): 55–64.

Homans, Jennifer. *Apollo's Angels: A History of Ballet*. New York: Random House, 2010.

Horst, Louis. *Pre-Classic Dance Forms*. New York: Kamin Dance Publishers, 1960.

Janof, Tim. "Baroque Dance and the Bach Cello Suites." November 2, 2002. http://www.cello.org/Newsletter/Articles/mansbridge/mansbridge.htm.

———. "Conversation with Anner Bylsma." September 5, 1998. http://www.cello.org/Newsletter/Articles/bylsma.htm.

———. "Conversation with Dimitry Markevitch." February 17, 1999. http://www.cello.org/Newsletter/Articles/markevitch.htm.

———. "Conversation with Nathaniel Rosen." March 2, 1996. http://www.cello.org/Newsletter/Articles/rosen.html.

Kennaway, George. "Editing Bach's Cello Suites." *The Strad* 91 (1980): 561–63.

Knape, Walter, Murray R. Charters, and Simon McVeigh. "Abel Family." *Grove Music Online*, ed. Deane Root. Accessed May 1, 2021. http://www.oxfordmusiconline.com.

Kuijken, Sigiswald. "A Bach Odyssey." *Early Music* 38, no. 2 (May 2010): 263–72.

Kunzle, Régine. "In Search of L'Académie Royale de Danse." *York Dance Review* 7 (Spring 1978): 3–15.

Ledbetter, David. *Bach's Well-Tempered Clavier: The 48 Preludes and Fugues*. New Haven and London: Yale University Press, 2002.

———. *Unaccompanied Bach: Performing the Solo Works*. New Haven and London: Yale University Press, 2009.

Lester, Joel. *Bach's Works for Solo Violin: Style, Structure, Performance*. New York: Oxford University Press, 1999.

Little, Meredith, and Natalie Jenne. *Dance and the Music of J. S. Bach*. 2nd ed. Bloomington and Indianapolis: Indiana University Press, 2001.

Marissen, Michael. *Bach and God*. New York: Oxford University Press, 2016.

———. *The Social and Religious Designs of J. S. Bach's Brandenburg Concertos*. Princeton, NJ: Princeton University Press, 1995.

Markevitch, Dimitry. "Bach's Cello Suites Revisited." *Bach* 30, no. 1 (1999): 65–69.

———. *Cello Story*. Translated by Florence W. Seder. Princeton, NJ: Summy-Birchard Music, 1984.

Markham, Michael. "The New Mythologies: Deep Bach, Saint Mahler, and the Death Chaconne." *LA Review of Books*, October 26, 2013. https://lareviewofbooks.org/article/the-new-mythologies-deep-bach-saint-mahler-and-the-death-chaconne.

Marshall, Robert L. "Toward a Twenty-First Century Bach Biography." *The Musical Quarterly* 84, no. 3 (Autumn 2000): 497–525.

Mather, Betty Bang, and Dean M. Karns. *Dance Rhythms of the French Baroque: A Handbook for Performance*. Bloomington and Indianapolis: Indiana University Press, 1987.

McClary, Susan. *Desire and Pleasure in Seventeenth-Century Music*. Berkeley, Los Angeles, and London: University of California Press, 2012.

McLamore, Alyson. "'By the Will and Order of Providence': The Wesley Family Concerts, 1779–1787." *Royal Musical Association Research Chronicle* 37 (2004): 71–114.

Mellers, Wilfrid. *Bach and the Dance of God.* New York: Oxford University Press, 1980.

Monelle, Raymond. *The Musical Topic: Hunt, Military and Pastoral. Musical Meaning and Interpretation.* Bloomington: Indiana University Press, 2006.

O'Sullivan, Vincent, and Margaret Scott. *The Collected Letters of Katherine Mansfield (1922–1923).* Vol. 5. Oxford: Oxford University Press, 2008.

Overbye, Dennis. "Overlooked No More: Beatrice Tinsley, Astronomer Who Saw the Course of the Universe." *New York Times,* July 18, 2018. https://www.nytimes.com/2018/07/18/obituaries/overlooked-beatrice-tinsley-astronomer.html.

Planer, John T. "Sentimentality in the Performance of Absolute Music: Pablo Casals's Performance of Saraband [*sic*] from Johann Sebastian Bach's Suite No. 2 in D Minor for Unaccompanied Cello, S. 1008." *The Musical Quarterly* 73, no. 3 (1989): 212–48.

Rosand, Ellen. "The Descending Tetrachord: An Emblem of Lament." *The Musical Quarterly* 65, no. 3 (July 1979): 346–59.

Ross, Alex. "Bach's Holy Dread." *The New Yorker* 92, no. 43 (January 2, 2017): 66–73.

Schachter, Carl. "The Prelude from Bach's Suite No. 4 for Violoncello Solo: The Submerged Urlinie." *Current Musicology* 56 (1994): 54–71.

Schenker, Heinrich. "The Sarabande of J. S. Bach's Suite No. 3 for Unaccompanied Violoncello." Translated by Hedi Siegel. In *The Music Forum* 2, edited by William J. Mitchell and Felix Salzer, 274–82. New York: Columbia University Press, 1970.

Shute, Benjamin. *Sei Solo: Symbolum? The Theology of J. S. Bach's Solo Violin Works.* Eugene, OR: Pickwick Publications, 2016.

Siblin, Eric. *The Cello Suites: J. S. Bach, Pablo Casals, and the Search for a Baroque Masterpiece.* Toronto: House of Anansi Press, 2009.

Silbiger, Alexander. "Chaconne." *Grove Music Online.* Edited by Deane Root. Accessed May 1, 2021. http://www.oxfordmusiconline.com.

Silbiger, Alexander. "Passacaglia," *Grove Music Online.* Edited by Deane Root. Accessed May 1, 2021. http://www.oxfordmusiconline.com.

Smit, Lambert. "Towards a More Consistent and More Historical View of Bach's Violoncello." *Chelys* 32 (2004): 45–58.

Smith, Mark M. "The Cello Bow Held the Viol-Way; Once Common, but Now Almost Forgotten." *Chelys* 24 (1995): 47–61.

———. "A Deceptive Edition of the Bach 'Cello Suites." *Bach* 9, no. 1 (January 1978): 26–29.

———. "The Drama of Bach's Life in the Court of Cöthen, As Reflected in his Cello Suites." *Stringendo* 22, no. 1 (2000): 32–35.

———. "Johann Sebastian Bach's Violoncello Piccolo: A Violoncello Small Enough to be Held on the Arm." *Flinders University of South Australia Music Studio* (1980): 1–16.

Solow, Jeffrey. "My Turn: Performing Bach's Solo Cello Suites." *American String Teacher* 56, no. 2 (May 2006): 92.

Suess, John G., and Marc Vanscheeuwijck. "Gabrielli, Domenico." *Grove Music Online.* Edited by Deane Root. Accessed May 1, 2021. http://www.oxfordmusiconline.com.

Szabó, Zoltán. "Precarious Presumptions and the 'Minority Report': Revisiting the Primary Sources of the Bach Cello Suites." *Bach* 45, no. 2 (2014): 1–33.

———. "Remaining Silhouettes of Lost Bach Manuscripts? Re-Evaluating J. P. Kellner's Copy of J. S. Bach's Solo String Compositions." *Understanding Bach* 10 (2015): 71–83.

———. "The Road Towards the First Complete Edition: Dissemination of Bach's Cello Suites in the Nineteenth Century. *String Praxis* 2, no. 1 (August 2013): 1–14.

Talle, Andrew. "Introduction and Report on the Revised Edition." In *Johann Sebastian Bach: Neue Ausgabe Sämtlicher Werke*, edited by Christine Blanken, Christoph Wolff, and Peter Wollny. Kassel, Germany: Bärenreiter, 2016.

Tanenbaum, Faun. "The Sarabande of J. S. Bach's Suite No. 2 for Unaccompanied Violoncello, BWV 1008: Analysis and Interpretation." *Theory and Practice* 5, no. 1 (July 1980): 40–56.

Taruskin, Richard. *The Danger of Music, and Other Anti-Utopian Essays*. Berkeley, Los Angeles, and London: University of California Press, 2009.

Tatlow, Ruth. "A Missed Opportunity: Reflections on *Written By Mrs. Bach*." *Understanding Bach* 10 (2015): 141–57.

Thoene, Helga. *Johann Sebastian Bach, Ciaccona: Tanz oder Tombeau? Eine analytische Studie*. Oschersleben, Germany: Ziethen, 2003.

Tomita, Yo. "Anna Magdalena Bach as Bach's Copyist." *Understanding Bach* 2 (2007): 59–76.

———. "The Well-Tempered Clavier, Book 1." https://www.qub.ac.uk/~tomita/essay/wtc1.html.

Vanscheeuwijck, Marc. "Recent Re-Evaluations of the Baroque Cello and What They Might Mean for Performing the Music of J. S. Bach." *Early Music* 38, no. 2 (2010): 181–92.

Varga, András Bálint, ed. *György Kurtág: Three Interviews and Ligeti Homages*. Rochester, NY: University of Rochester Press, 2009.

Vittes, Laurence. "Two Different Approaches to Bach's Cello Suites." *Strings*, March 1, 2016. https://stringsmagazine.com/two-different-approaches-to-bachs-solo-cello-suites.

Vogt, Hans. *Johann Sebastian Bach's Chamber Music: Background, Analyses, Individual Works*. Edited by Reinhard G. Pauly. Translated by Kenn Johnson. Portland, OR: Amadeus Press, 1988.

Watkin, David. "Corelli's Op. 5 Sonatas: Violino e Violone o Cimbalo?" *Early Music* (November 1996): 645–64.

Wilson, Miranda. "Finding My Own Solution to Bach's 300-Year-Old Conundrum." *Strings*, July 17, 2019. https://stringsmagazine.com/finding-my-own-solution-to-bachs-300-year-old-conundrum.

Winold, Allen. *Bach's Cello Suites: Analyses and Explorations*. Bloomington and Indianapolis: Indiana University Press, 2007.

Wolff, Christoph. *Bach: Essays on His Life and Music*. Cambridge, MA and London: Harvard University Press, 1991.

———. *Johann Sebastian Bach: The Learned Musician*. New York and London: W. W. Norton & Company, 2000.

Yearsley, David. *Bach and the Meanings of Counterpoint.* Cambridge: Cambridge University Press, 2002.

———. *Sex, Death, and Minuets: Anna Magdalena Bach and Her Musical Notebooks.* Chicago: University of Chicago Press, 2019.

Yokoyama, Shin-Itchiro. "The Bizarre Chord?" Blog post, April 7, 2017. http://bachcellonotes.blogspot.com/2017/04/the-bizarre-chord.html.

Young, Percy M. *The Bachs: 1500–1850.* London: J. M. Dent & Sons, 1970.

Scores

Bach, Johann Sebastian. *Sonaten: Violoncello.* Edited by Hugo Becker. Leipzig: Peters, 1911.

Bach, Johann Sebastian. *Sechs Suiten für Violoncello Solo BWV 1007–1012 mit Faksimile.* Edited by Kirsten Beisswenger. Wiesbaden: Breitkopf und Härtel, 2000.

Bach, Johann Sebastian. *Sechs Suiten für Violoncello.* Edited by Alfred Dörffel. Leipzig: Breitkopf und Härtel, 1879.

Bach, Johann Sebastian. *Six Solos ou Etudes pour le Violoncelle.* Edited by Justus Johann Friedrich Dotzauer. Leipzig: Breitkopf und Härtel, 1826.

Bach, Johann Sebastian. *Sechs Suiten für Violoncello Solo BWV 1007–1012.* Edited by Hans Eppstein. *Neue Bach Ausgabe.* Kassel: Bärenreiter, 1988.

Bach, Johann Sebastian. *Six Sonates ou Suites pour Violoncelle Seul.* Arranged by Friedrich Grützmacher. Leipzig: Peters, 1866.

Bach, Johann Sebastian. *Sonaten: Violoncello.* Edited by Friedrich Grützmacher. Leipzig: Peters, 1867.

Bach, Johann Sebastian. *Sechs Suiten für Violoncell.* Edited by Julius Klengel. Leipzig: Breitkopf und Härtel, 1900.

Bach, Johann Sebastian. *Sechs Suiten für Violoncello Solo.* Edited by Robert Hausmann. Leipzig: Steingräber Verlag, 1898.

Bach, Johann Sebastian. *Six Sonates ou Etudes pour le Violoncelle Solo Composées PAR J. SEBASTIEN BACH, Oeuvre Posthume.* Edited by Louis Norblin. Paris: Janet et Cotelle, 1824.

Bach, Johann Sebastian. *Six Suites for Solo Cello.* Edited by Dimitry Markevitch. Bryn Mawr, PA: Theodore Presser Company, 1964.

Bach, Johann Sebastian. *Sechs Suiten für Violoncello Solo BWV 1007–1012.* Edited by Andrew Talle. *Neue Bach Ausgabe.* Kassel: Bärenreiter, 2016.

Bach, Johann Sebastian. *Sechs Suiten für Violoncello Solo BWV 1007–1012.* Edited by August Wenzinger. Kassel: Bärenreiter, 1950.

Dissertations

Chambers, Mark. "The Mistuned Cello: Precursors to J. S. Bach's Suite V in C Minor for Unaccompanied Violoncello." DMA diss., Florida State University, 1996.

Cho, Yoonju. "A Study of Baroque Tempo Practices and Their Applications to the Violoncello Suite No. 2 by Johann Sebastian Bach." DMA diss., University of Washington, 1998.

Chung, Lisa. "The Development of the Left Thumb Use in Cello Playing from its Beginning Until 1900." DMA diss., University of Auckland, 2014.

Dube, Michelle Claire. "Prelude of Suite V for Cello Solo by J. S. Bach: Options for Performance." DMA diss., University of Arizona, 1993.

Kaplan, Harriet. "An Examination of Johann Sebastian Bach's Fifth and Sixth Suites for Solo Cello, BWV 1011 and 1012." DMA diss., University of Cincinnati, 1994.

Kinney, Gordon James. "The Musical Literature for Unaccompanied Violoncello." PhD diss., Florida State University, 1962.

Knobel, Bradley James. "Bach Cello Suites with Piano Accompaniment and Nineteenth-Century Bach Discovery: A Stemmatic Study of Sources." D.M. diss., Florida State University, 2006.

Kramer, Laura Elizabeth. "Articulation in Johann Sebastian Bach's Six Suites for Violoncello Solo (BWV 1007–1012): History, Analysis, and Performance." DMA diss., Cornell University, 1998.

Kutz, Eric. "Towards a Formal Paradigm for the Bach Cello Suite Preludes." DMA diss., Juilliard School, 2002.

Lutterman, John Kenneth. "Works in Progress: J. S. Bach's Suites for Solo Cello as Artifacts of Improvisatory Practices." PhD diss., University of California Davis, 2006.

Marckx, Leslie Hirt. "French Baroque Influences on Johann Sebastian Bach's "Six Suites for Violoncello Solo" with an Emphasis on French Court Dance and Suite V." DMA diss., University of Washington, 1998.

Markovska, Nadya. "Bach's Suites for Solo Cello (BWV 1007–1012) and the Textual Geographies of Modernity." PhD diss., University of Southampton, 2016.

Prindle, Daniel E. "The Form of the Preludes to Bach's Unaccompanied Cello Suites." MM diss., University of Massachusetts Amherst, 2011.

Qureshi, Rifat Javed. "The Influence of Baroque Dance in the Performance of Johann Sebastian Bach's 'Six Suites a Violoncello Senza Basso." DMA diss., Rice University, 1994.

Snustad, Nancy. "The Allemandes in the Six Suites for Solo Cello by J. S. Bach: An Analysis and Comparison." DMA diss., Indiana University, 1994.

Szabó, Zoltán. "Problematic Sources, Problematic Transmission: An Outline of the Edition History of the Solo Cello Suites by J. S. Bach." PhD diss., University of Sydney, 2016.

Youngerman, Irit. "J. S. Bach's Suite in C Major for Violoncello Solo: An Analysis through Application of a Historical Approach." MM diss., University of Cincinnati, 2002.